*Justice of punishment*

# DUKE UNIVERSITY PUBLICATIONS

DANTE'S CONCEPTION OF JUSTICE

# Dante's Conception of Justice

By
ALLAN H GILBERT
*Professor of English in Duke University*

Most sacred virtue she of all the rest,
Resembling God in his imperial might;
Whose sovereign power is herein most exprest,
That both to good and bad he dealeth right,
And all his works with JUSTICE hath bedight.
—The Faerie Queene.

DUKE UNIVERSITY PRESS
DURHAM, NORTH CAROLINA
1925

COPYRIGHT 1925
DUKE UNIVERSITY

THE PRESSES OF
THE SEEMAN PRINTERY INCORPORATED
DURHAM, N. C.

# PREFACE

When Dante in his Ninth Epistle spoke of himself as "a man preaching justice," and in the Paradiso represented Beatrice as saying to him that he made frequent mention of the living justice, he indicated one of the most important subjects on which he meditated and wrote, and thus encouraged his readers to enquire how he regarded it. As the result of such an enquiry, I present in this volume some of the materials Dante would probably have employed in the treatise on justice he planned to include in the unfinished Convivio, and with them as a basis attempt to explain his concrete and imaginative presentation of justice in the Divine Comedy.

As the basis of my discussion I have taken the commentary of St. Thomas Aquinas on the fifth book of the Ethics of Aristotle, which is wholly concerned with justice. This commentary and the text which it explains form the chief systematic work on justice familiar to Dante. I was influenced to undertake its study partly by Professor Francesco Flamini's book entitled Il Significato e il Fine della Divina Commedia, and, so far as the commentary on the fifth book of the Ethics is concerned, I believe that my first two chapters justify his high estimate of the importance to Dantists of Aquinas' commentaries on Aristotle. In particular they show the reasons for Dante's strong wish to remove all temptation to avarice from the ruler described in the De Monarchia.

Justice lies at the heart of the Commedia. The poem cannot be morally or even æsthetically acceptable unless the punishments and rewards of which it treats are accepted as justly assigned. Its structure and purpose cannot be grasped without an understanding of its author's conception of justice, nor can its allegory appear rational or artistic. The interpretation of the Purgatorio has especially suffered from the lack of any principle of justice as a guide. In the present work the penalties of purgatory are treated as parts of a connected allegory and distinguished in significance from those of hell. The chapter on the Paradiso is intended to show how that part of the poem fits into Dante's allegorical scheme as a presentation of the divine justice at work among living men. Interpreters of the Paradiso have too commonly been content with the literal meaning alone.

In the body of the work all quotations from languages other than English are given in translation; the originals may be found in the Appendix. It is hoped that students familiar with the original tongues will pardon any inconvenience resulting from this arrangement, in the interest of a wider circle of readers.

Longfellow's translation of the Divine Comedy, and Miss Aurelia Henry's translation of the De

Monarchia have been used, with the permission of the publishers, the Houghton Mifflin Company, and Dr. William W. Jackson's translation of the Convivio, with the consent of the Oxford University Press. Messrs. Burns, Oates, and Washbourne have allowed the use of the translation of the Summa Theologica by the English Dominican Fathers. For the translations from the commentaries of St. Thomas I am myself responsible. With the permission of the Oxford University Press, the quotations from Dante have been taken from the fourth edition of Le Opere di Dante Alighieri. Quotations from Aquinas follow, with slight exceptions, the text of the Parma edition, 1852-66.

My thanks are due to the officials of several libraries, especially those of St. Louis University and the University of Pennsylvania. Without the Fiske Dante Collection in the library of Cornell University the work could hardly have been done; Mr. E. R. B. Willis, the reference librarian there, has aided me with bibliographical information. Professor Arthur M. Gates has read and criticized my translations from Aquinas. In preparing my manuscript for the printer and reading the proofs I have been assisted by Professor Paull F. Baum, to whom I am indebted for many suggestions.

# TABLE OF CONTENTS

PREFACE .................................................................................. v

CHAPTER I: THE MATERIALS FOR DANTE'S TREATISE ON JUSTICE: ST. THOMAS' COMMENTARY ON ETHICS 5.1-9 .................................................. 3

CHAPTER II: THE MATERIALS FOR DANTE'S TREATISE ON JUSTICE, CONTINUED: ST. THOMAS' COMMENTARY ON ETHICS 5.10-15 .................................... 33

CHAPTER III: THE COMMEDIA AS A POEM OF JUSTICE .................. 67

CHAPTER IV: THE INFERNO: JUSTICE IN THE LIFE OF THE WICKED ........................................................................ 73

CHAPTER V: THE PURGATORIO: JUSTICE IN HUMAN SUFFERING .................................................................. 112

CHAPTER VI: THE PARADISO: THE JUSTICE OF VARIATION IN HUMAN TALENTS ................................................. 142

APPENDIX: THE ORIGINALS OF QUOTATIONS GIVEN IN ENGLISH IN THE BODY OF THE WORK

INDEX .................................................................................. 233

# DANTE'S CONCEPTION OF JUSTICE

# CHAPTER I

THE MATERIALS FOR DANTE'S TREATISE ON JUSTICE:
ST. THOMAS' COMMENTARY ON ETHICS 5.1-9

The fourteenth tractate of the Convivio, the last but one of the work as planned, Dante, as he twice says in the treatise[1], intended to devote to the subject of justice. In the first passage he alludes to the greatest work on justice accessible to him, the fifth book of the Ethics of Aristotle, which doubtless would have been the chief source of the proposed tractate on justice. Being unable to read Greek, he necessarily followed one of the mediæval Latin versions, probably making habitual use of that now commonly included with the works of St. Thomas rather than of the "old" version mentioned in the Convivio.[2] In addition, Dante apparently read St. Thomas' commentary on the Ethics, to which he twice alludes.[3] Hence it is not strange that on proceeding through these two works one finds many passages related to Dante's utterances on justice.

In his commentary St. Thomas sometimes modifies or supplements the views of Aristotle, though usually he holds himself to his task of making plain what the Philosopher means, and nowhere directly

---
[1] Convivio 1.12.87; 4.27.101. See Appendix, p. 183.
[2] 2.15.68. See Moore, Studies in Dante, Oxford, 1896, 1.312.
[3] Convivio 2.15.126; 4.8.4. For details see Appendix, pp. 183-4.

disagrees with him or represents his ideas as inadequate. To the explanation of justice in the commentary must be added the passages on justice in the Summa Theologica. In this work St. Thomas is not restrained by the necessity of explaining the text of Aristotle, and can freely present matters as they appear to him, yet here also he leans heavily on his master.

When the passages in which Dante alludes to justice are brought into relation with the discussions of Aristotle and Aquinas, the result indicates the nature of at least much of the material Dante would have presented in the discussion of justice in the Convivio. The following analysis observes the order of the fifth book of the Ethics and of Aquinas' commentary, omitting reference to matter not immediately connected with Dante.

### Chapter 1, Lectio 1[4]

After an introductory paragraph, Aristotle gives the common definition of justice—the moral state *(habitus)* by which men are doers of just things, and by which just things are done, and men will just things. The opposite is true of injustice. Aristotle is here assuming what he has laid down in the second book of the Ethics, namely that virtue is a moral state.

Dante depends on this in his characterization of justice in Convivio 4.17.62-4 as that "which disposes

---

[4] Chapters are those of the fifth book of the Ethics; Lectiones are the divisions of the commentary; the two do not always correspond.

# CHARITY AND JUSTICE

us to love and practise uprightness in all things." But the Philosopher's thought that man should will just things is raised higher by Dante, who will have men love what is just. Love is for him the motive force of justice:

> Charity or right love clarifies and brightens the mental attitude toward Justice. In whomever, therefore, right love can be present to the highest degree, in him can Justice find the most effective place. . . . Charity, scorning all else, seeks God and man, and therefore the good of man. And since to live in peace is chief of man's blessings, as we said before, and since this is most fully and easily accomplished by Justice, charity will make Justice thrive greatly; with her strength will the other grow strong.
> —De Monarchia 1.11.93-110.

The close relation between justice and charity here indicated is not actually pointed out by Aquinas in his commentary, though he gives sufficient basis for it. For that one must go to the Summa Theologica, because the virtue of *caritas,* or charity, in the sense of I Corinthians 13, being unknown to Aristotle, is not discussed in the commentary on the Ethics. As a theological virtue, charity is directed toward God; yet the charitable man is also concerned for his neighbor:

> It is clear that it is specifically the same act whereby we love God, and whereby we love our neighbor. Consequently the habit of charity extends not only to the love of God, but also to the love of our neighbor.
> —Summa Theol. II.ii.25.1.

As will appear, justice likewise is concerned with the relation of man to his neighbor. Aquinas, like

Dante, makes peace the result of both charity and justice:

> Peace is the work of justice indirectly, in so far as justice removes the obstacles to peace: but it is the work of charity directly, since charity, according to its very nature, causes peace. For love is a unitive force.
> —Summa Theol. II.ii.29.3.

To this may be added that charity, like justice, is said by St. Thomas to reside in the will.[5] Hence it is fitting that justice, the moral virtue described by Aristotle, and charity, the theological virtue, should go hand in hand.

In his comment on this part of the Ethics, Aquinas lays emphasis on the relation of the will to justice, saying of Aristotle: "He conveniently makes justice intelligible by reference to the will." Elsewhere he writes: "Justice is a habit whereby a man renders to each one his due by a constant and perpetual will."[6] Further he decides that the will alone is the subject of justice:

> We are not said to be just through knowing something aright. Hence the subject of justice is not the intellect or reason which is a cognitive power. But since we are said to be just through doing something aright, and because the proximate principle of action is the appetitive power, justice must needs be in some appetitive power as its subject. Now the appetite is twofold; namely, the will which is in the reason, and the sensitive appetite. . . . The act of rendering his due to each man cannot proceed from the sensitive appetite, because sensitive apprehension does not go so far as to be able to consider the relation of one thing to another; but

---

[5] Summa Theol. II.ii.24.1.
[6] Summa Theol. II.ii.58.1.

this is proper to the reason. Therefore justice cannot be in the irascible or concupiscible as its object, but only in the will.

—Summa Theol. II.ii.58.4.

This is taken over by Dante, who writes:

And here we must know that every good quality that is peculiar to anything is lovely in that thing. . . . And, moreover, the more distinctive any quality is the more lovely it is; so that, although every virtue is lovely in a man, that is loveliest in him which is most distinctively human, and such is justice, which exists only in the rational or intellectual part of a man, that is, in his will.

—Convivio 1.12.61-74.

Continuing Dante gives a list of the "inhuman" sins opposed to justice.[7]

Dante's suggestion that the intellect is the truly human part of man probably depends on such passages as Aristotle's Politics 1.1, on which St. Thomas comments:

The word *human* indicates what is useful and what is harmful. It follows from this that it signifies the just and the unjust. For justice and injustice consist in a man's receiving equable or inequable treatment in helpful or injurious things. And this word is applicable only to men, for the reason that in contrast to all other animals they alone have understanding of good and evil, and also of injustice, and other similar matters which can be designated in speech.

Aristotle also discusses the subject in Politics 7.14, and St. Thomas remarks in his extended comment on the passage:

Certainly the ultimate end of human life cannot consist in the act of the irrational part of the mind, for it necessarily

[7] See p. 53, below.

consists in something peculiar to man, in which he is distinguished from others, and this last end of man is peculiar to him; therefore it would consist in some perfection pertaining to the rational part of the mind.

## Chapter 2, Lectio 1 (continued)

Following the method of learning about justice from its contrary, Aristotle gives the three ways in which a man may come to be called unjust: (1) by breaking the law; (2) by being avaricious; (3) by desiring to have less than his proper share of what is evil. Since the last two have to do with equality, the just may be called the legal and the equal. The unjust man who is avaricious is not avaricious in respect to all that is good, but only in respect to the goods of fortune. These are always good in general, but not always good for every man. A man ought to desire only what is good for him in particular.

This passage, with its reference to fortune, is quite in harmony with what the Middle Ages was familiar with in Boethius' Consolation of Philosophy, book 2. Aristotle also touches on the idea in Politics 7.13:

> The good man makes good use of poverty and sickness and other injuries of fortune; but what is able to bring happiness is of a contrary sort. Moreover, it is determined in discourses on morals that there is a sort of man who is good, and to whom on account of his virtue things are good which are simply good. For we hold that fortune exists as mistress.

In his comment, lectio 10, St. Thomas speaks of the goods of fortune as external goods.

Dante fully presents his idea of Fortune in the Inferno 7.77-96, referring to her as the mistress of "mundane splendors" and of "empty treasures." Aquinas explains in his comment that the goods of fortune are not always good for all men, because they are not equally adapted to all. Yet man desires these in prayer to God as though they were suitable for him, and thus is made avaricious and unjust; but he ought to pray that he might choose what is good for himself, that he may labor as he should according to virtue.

Something of this may have entered into Convivio 4.12,13, where Dante speaks of men who think to obtain satisfaction in riches, but are led to avarice. The desires engendered by the accumulation of wealth cannot be consummated without wrong to some one. Indeed both canon and civil law are directed against the injustice of cupidity more than against any other wrong. The man of right desires does not love riches, though willing to make use of them when they "are adapted to serve some necessary purpose."

Aristotle then continues to show that the man who desires to escape his proper share of toil may be called avaricious, since privation of evil is in a sense a good. But, as St. Thomas says, this injustice is more correctly called inequality, since inequality appears in attempting to have both more of good and less of evil. The latter part of his commentary runs thus:

This illegality according to which anyone is called illegal, which is also a state of inequality, in so far as a man does not have an equal share as determined by law, contains universally all injustice, and is a characteristic common to injustice of every kind.

## Chapter 3, Lectio 2

Aristotle then discusses the legally just, and points out that the laws of any state are designed for the purpose of bringing felicity to those who make them, whether the makers of the law be all the citizens, or the best citizens, or those who are powerful in any way. Hence in one sense we call just whatever tends to bring about and preserve happiness in the state. This topic is developed in Politics 3.6, where we are told that in a properly ordered state the government is conducted not in the interest of the ruler or rulers alone, but in the interest of all the citizens. Further, the end of the state is, as Aristotle puts it in Politics 3.9, "to live happily and well," or, as St. Thomas writes in his commentary on the passage, "the end for which a well-ordered state is set up is to live or work according to perfect virtue."

In the Summa Theologica II.i.90.2 St. Thomas deals with the end of law. He quotes from this part of Ethics 5, and says that "since one man is a part of the perfect community, the law must needs regard properly the relationship to universal happiness," and that a precept which is not referred to the good of the community is not properly to be considered as a law.

These passages are quite in the spirit of the De Monarchia:

> Whoever contemplates the good of the state contemplates the end of Right, as may be explained thus. Right is a real and personal relation [or proportion] of man to man, which maintained preserves society, and infringed upon destroys it. . . . If our definition truly comprehends what Right is and wherefore, and if the end of all society is the common good of the individuals associated, then the end of all Right must be the common good, and no Right is possible which does not contemplate the common good. Tully justly notes in the first book of the Rhetoric that "The laws should always be interpreted for the good of the state." For if the laws are not directed for the benefit of those under the laws, they are laws merely in name, they cannot be laws in reality.
>
> —De Monarchia 2.5.1-21.

The same thought appears elsewhere in the De Monarchia;[8] and indeed the whole work is founded on the author's interest in the good of man.

Aristotle next proceeds to speak of justice defined as "complete virtue, not indeed complete without reservation, but in respect to a neighbor." Hence justice is often thought the most desirable of virtues, —"neither Hesperus nor Lucifer is so admirable."

St. Thomas' comment on this section is little more than a paraphrase; however, where Aristotle speaks only of justice, he speaks of legal justice. He uses the term to indicate justice as established by laws directed toward their proper end. Aristotle's figure of speech he extends as follows:

> Neither Hesperus, that most brilliant evening star, nor Lucifer, that most brilliant morning star, shines as does justice.

[8] See p. 45, below.

Dante refers to the passage thus:

> Truly, then may be applied to her the words of the Philosopher: Neither Hesperus nor Lucifer is so wonderfully fair.
>
> De Monarchia 1.11.32-4.

In this instance Dante is apparently quoting directly from Aristotle, and not from the commentary of Aquinas, though in the Summa Theologica II.ii.58.12 Aquinas quotes the clause without expansion.

Dante refers as follows to legal justice:

> For, as says the Philosopher in the fifth book of the Ethics, legal justice disposes the Sciences for our learning, and in order that they may not be forsaken, commands that they should be learnt and taught.
>
> —Convivio 2.15.127-32.

Since this is not a direct quotation from Aristotle, Moore, in his Studies in Dante 1.104, suggests that Dante may have "mixed up some commentary or paraphrase with the text itself." Perhaps he did have in mind book 5, lectiones 2 and 3, of the commentary of Aquinas, which are concerned with legal justice. In the part of the Convivio from which the quotation is taken he is giving the resemblances between the heavens and the various branches of knowledge. The task was sometimes difficult, and what now seem impossible parallels are given. Having learned from the commentary that Aquinas made legal justice include all virtue, in relation to man's conduct in society, Dante felt justified in assuming that legal justice would inculcate the pursuit of studies which he thought contributory to human

## AVARICE AS INJUSTICE

happiness. If some definite passage is to be selected as Dante's source, it probably is the following sentence:

> Whatever enactments are established by law with respect to training which is for the common good are productive of all virtue.
> —Ethics 5.5.

St. Thomas comments on it:

> It is manifest that those things which are laid down by law have power to produce all virtue, according to the education through law in which man is appropriately trained for the common good.
> —Commentary 5.3.

Dante's dependence on Aquinas is revealed by his attribution to Aristotle of the expression "legal justice," for though prominent in the commentary, it is not used in the text of this part of the Ethics.

### Chapter 4, Lectio 3

Aristotle next deals with the justice which is a part of virtue, not the whole of it, and similarly with the injustice which is a part of vice. He explains that a man may act unjustly, but not avariciously, as by throwing away his shield in battle because of cowardice. But a man may act avariciously, and yet not in accord with all vices, but in accord with a particular vice only, and we speak of him as unjust. Hence there is a particular kind of injustice which is a part of that general injustice which is against the law. By the use of the word *avare* (with almost the same meaning as *unjustly*) the Latin text puts much emphasis on covetousness; "facit avare" ("he acts avariciously") should be understood to mean that a man disturbs equality by grasping more than his share.

This emphasis on avarice as the distinguishing feature of particular injustice is very clear in St. Thomas:

Thus other vices can be present in a man without the avarice which is specially called injustice. . . . But on the contrary it happens that some one sins by taking through avarice the property of another, and yet does not sin according to one of the other vices nor according to all of them, and yet sins according to a special vice. This is evident because for such an action he is censured as unjust.

Aristotle then proceeds to show that various sins may be referred to various vices, but if a man has put something into his own pocket ("lucratus est") he is called only unjust. There are two kinds of injustice, one concerned with all unvirtuous action, the other concerned with honor, wealth, safety, and the like, which arises because of the pleasure which comes from gain.

St. Thomas enforces these ideas in his commentary:

He who commits adultery that he may gain at the expense of some other man is not properly to be called lustful, since he does not direct his efforts toward the end of lust. But he seems rather to be unjust, since for the sake of lucre he has acted against justice. . . . If a man has enriched himself beyond measure, by taking the property of others, this is not attributed to any other vice, but to injustice alone. . . . And Aristotle says that particular justice is concerned with those things which men are expected to share with others, such as honor and wealth and the things pertain-

# AVARICE IS OPPOSED TO JUSTICE

ing to the health or damage of the body, and with other things of the sort. There is a particular justice not only concerning external things, but also because of the pleasure which follows from gain, for the sake of which a man may sometimes get more from others than he ought to.

In the Summa Theologica II.ii.118.3 St. Thomas speaks even more plainly:

> The sin of covetousness consists in a man's exceeding the measure in the things he possesses. But this measure is appointed by justice. Therefore covetousness is directly opposed to justice. Covetousness denotes immoderation with regard to riches in two ways. First, immediately in respect of the acquisition and keeping of riches. In this way a man obtains money beyond his due, by stealing or retaining another's property. This is opposed to justice, and in this sense covetousness is mentioned (Ezech. xxii.27): 'Her princes in the midst of her are like wolves ravening the prey to shed blood . . . and to run after gains through covetousness.' It belongs properly to justice to appoint the measure in the acquisition and keeping of riches from the point of view of legal due, so that a man should neither take nor retain another's property. Covetousness as opposed to justice has no opposite vice: since it consists in having more than one ought according to justice.

Elsewhere in his commentary[9] St. Thomas makes the tyrant one who secures to himself too much of the good things, and too few of the undesirable things. The just ruler, on the contrary, observes the proper proportion of justice in taking things for himself.

This connection of avarice and injustice, so much clearer in the Latin text and the commentary of Aquinas than in the Greek, must be grasped by

[9] See p. 35, below.

everyone who wishes to understand the De Monarchia, for part of the treatise is hardly intelligible to a reader who does not appreciate how serious the vice of greed seemed to Dante. The Thomistic conception of avarice and injustice is the key to Dante's belief that an emperor is essential to the happiness of society, because he alone can be raised above covetousness or injustice, and hence be a righteous ruler. Dante puts his belief as follows:

In regard to the will, it must first be noted that the worst enemy of Justice is cupidity, as Aristotle signifies in the fifth book to Nicomachus. When cupidity is removed altogether, nothing remains inimical to Justice; hence, fearful of the influence of cupidity which easily distorts men's minds, the Philosopher grew to believe that whatever can be determined by law should in no wise be relegated to a judge. Cupidity is impossible when there is nothing to be desired, for passions cease to exist with the destruction of their objects. Since his jurisdiction is bounded only by the ocean, there is nothing for a Monarch to desire. This is not true of the other princes, whose realms terminate in those of others. . . . Avarice, scorning man's competency, seeks things beyond him; but charity, scorning all else, seeks God and man, and therefore the good of man.
—De Monarchia 1.11.69-105.

Now, as was shown above, a Monarch can have no occasion for cupidity, or rather less occasion than any other men, even other princes, and cupidity is the sole corrupter of judgment and hindrance to Justice; so the Monarch is capable of the highest degree of judgment and Justice, and is therefore perfectly qualified, or especially well qualified,to rule.
—De Monarchia 1.13.47-55.

He writes in the same strain in Convivio 4.4.22-44:

Wherefore, inasmuch as the mind of man does not rest content with a limited possession of land, but always desires to acquire more land, as we perceive by experience, disagreement and wars must needs arise between kingdom and kingdom. Such things are the scourges of townships, and through townships of neighbourhoods, and through neighbourhoods of families, and through families of individuals, and thus happiness is hindered. Wherefore, in order to do away with these wars and their causes, it is necessary that the whole earth, and all that is given to the race of man to possess, should be a monarchy, that is to say, a single princedom; and should have a single prince, who, possessing everything, and having nothing left to desire, should keep kings confined within the borders of their kingdoms, so that peace should reign between them, and townships should rest in peace, and while they so rest neighbourhoods should love each other, and in this mutual love families should satisfy all their wants; and when these are satisfied, a man should live happily, which is the end for which he is born.

The example Dante had ever in mind was the unjust city of Florence. In his Sixth Epistle (150-60) he attacks the blind cupidity of his countrymen:

Neither, because ye are blind, do ye perceive the cupidity that rules you, flattering you with its venomous whisper, restraining you with its vain threats, imprisoning you within the law of sin, and, moreover, forbidding you to obey the most sacred laws, which imitate the image of natural justice; the observance of which laws, if it is glad, if it is free, is not only proved not to be servitude, nay, rather, to him who observes closely it is manifest that it is the highest liberty itself.

These and similar passages are plain in the light of Dante's study of Aristotle and Aquinas, and show that his conception of justice is theirs. He is not dealing with cupidity—excessive desire for external goods—in itself, but is following his teachers in considering it as almost identical with injustice. Hence when Dante in the De Monarchia plans to put the ruler above avarice, he believes that he is also putting him above injustice.

## Chapter 5, Lectio 3 (continued)

Aristotle then points out that particular justice is a part of universal justice. The law prescribes action in accord with virtue in the widest sense. Laws which tend to produce all virtue are those which have been instituted for the training of men for the common benefit. The Philosopher promises later to consider whether the discipline which makes a good man is the same as that which makes a good citizen, for the good man and the good citizen perchance are not always identical.

In his comment St. Thomas says that there are some laws which do not pertain directly to the exercise of any virtue, but merely to the disposition of external goods. He also refers to Aristotle's discussion of the relation of the good man to the good citizen:

It is manifest that those things which are laid down by law have power to produce all virtue, according to the education through law in which man is appropriately trained for the common good. Nevertheless there is another education according to which man is trained for the act of virtue according to what benefits him as an individual, that is, for his own good, so far as man through this is made good in himself. Hence one can doubt whether training of this sort is connected with politics, or with some other science. And he says that this is to be determined later, to wit, in his work on politics. For in the third book of the Politics he shows that it is not the same thing to be a good man merely, and

# THE GOOD CITIZEN

to be a good citizen, under any sort of government. For there are certain forms of government, not on good principles, in which a man can be a good citizen, though not a good man. But under the best form of government no one is a good citizen who is not a good man.

In De Monarchia 1.12.63-71 Dante writes:

Since a Monarch loves men greatly, a point already touched upon, he desires all men to [become] good, which cannot be among players at crooked politics. Whence the Philosopher in his Politics says, "Under bad government the good man is a bad citizen; but under upright government 'good man' and 'good citizen' have the same meaning."

This is not a direct quotation from the Politics, where Aristotle does not say that in the perfect state the good man and the good citizen are one, and where he concludes that, in states as they are, the virtue of the good man and of the good citizen need not be the same. He does show, however, that the training of the good man and the good ruler are one:

We say that the excellent prince is good and prudent, but the politic prince is necessarily prudent. And nevertheless they thereupon say that the education of the prince is certainly different, just as the sons of kings seem to be taught horsemanship and warfare. But we may recall the saying of Euripides: No vanities for me, but things of which the state has need. This is the right principle for the education of a prince. So the education of the good prince and the good man are the same.
—Politics 3.4.

Yet he thinks that the citizens of the perfect state need not be good men, if they are good citizens:

Since it is impossible for all the citizens to be alike, the virtue of the good citizen and the good man will not be the same. For it is necessary that virtue characteristic of the excellent citizen should be present in all the citizens, for thus the state must needs be best. But it is impossible that the characteristic virtue of the good man should be present in all the citizens, unless it is necessary that all the citizens of an excellent state be good men.

—Politics 3.4.

Still further Aristotle concludes that the virtue of the good citizen is that of the good man only in the instance of the statesman or ruler, real or potential. Aristotle does not suggest that a bad man may be a good citizen, though he allows us to infer that the best man is not always the best citizen. Evidently, then, the last sentence of the quotation just above from St. Thomas is not taken from Aristotle, but is the commentator's own addition. Hence, considering the similarity in thought and language of Dante's apparent quotation from Aristotle to the passage from St. Thomas, we may feel sure that Dante's source was not the Politics itself, but the commentary of Aquinas on the Ethics. It is especially valuable to have this sign of Dante's familiarity with the commentary on the fifth book because he refers directly only to that on some of the other books. By evidence somewhat similar to that just given, Moore, in his Studies in Dante 1.105, has established the poet's knowledge of the comment on the tenth book.

### Chapter 5 (continued), Lectio 4

Aristotle points out that there is a kind of particular justice having to do with the distribution of honor or wealth among those who share in the state. This is called distributive justice.

On this section St. Thomas comments:

> Under an aristocratic form of government, in which certain men rule because of virtue, dignity is determined by virtue; that is, the more virtue a man has, the more dignity he should have.

This reminds one of the just distribution of rewards to the blessed in the Paradiso;[10] their gains are in harmony with their merit. In the distribution of riches on earth, however, conditions are quite different:

> I say that their imperfection may be noted firstly in the lack of discrimination shown in their advent, in which no distributive justice is conspicuous, but almost always unalloyed injustice, and this injustice is the peculiar effect of imperfection.
> —Convivio 4.11.51-6.

## Chapter 6, Lectio 5

The just is the equal. In every operation there may be more or less or a state of equality. The equal is a mean, and hence the just is a mean. It must be the mean and equal in respect both to some objects and to certain people. According as it is a mean, it is so with respect to a greater and a less quantity of things, and as it is equal, it is so with respect to two people. As it is just, it is so with respect to both things and people. Hence there must be justice with respect to four terms. Conflicts arise because equals do not have equal things, or those who are

[10] P. 153, below.

not equal have equal things, or receive them in distribution. Distribution ought to be in proportion to worthiness; but worth is not always the same, depending here on freedom, there on wealth, elsewhere on noble blood, and in the aristocratic state on excellence.

Aquinas comments at some length on this, especially on the section in which Aristotle says that there are four terms, two people and two things, concerned in the proportionality of justice. He says, for example:

> It is clear, therefore, that the joining of a twofold portion of property with a person who has a double measure of worth, and of a half share of property with a person having a half share of worth, is in accord with distributive justice. Such justice is a mean. For the mean is proportional between excess and defect, because proportionality is equality of proportion.

This passage more than any other in the Ethics suggests Dante's definition of right *(jus)* in De Monarchia 2.5.3-6, for which no exact source has yet been found:

> Right *(jus)* is a real and personal [proportion] of man to man, which maintained preserves society, and infringed upon destroys it.

But in truth it is hardly possible to find a single source for such a definition. It is probably Dante's own composition from Aristotelian and Thomistic material. The word "proportion" could come from this part of the Ethics. The word "real" relates to

# THE DEFINITION OF JUSTICE

property, and hence would signify the material things with which justice is concerned. The word "personal" indicates the relation in worthiness of the two men concerned. Hence Dante's definition indicates the just proportion of material things to be assigned to two or more men of the same or varying degrees of desert. The notion that justice, or proper proportional distribution, is necessary to the good of the state, underlies, as we well know, Aristotle's whole treatment of the subject; for example, we read in the Politics 1.2: "Justice is the order of a civil community. And indeed justice is the determination of what is just." It seems, then, that Dante's definition is an attempt to gather together all he had learned concerning Aristotelian justice.

Continuing, Aristotle declares that the just is proportional. Proportionality is equality of proportion. He then proceeds to give examples of proportion, of the sort which, he says, the mathematicians call geometrical.

## Chapter 7, Lectio 5 (continued)

He concludes that the just presents this proportion, and that the unjust is out of proportion.

We may imagine that this section, with its representation of proportional quantities by means of letters,[11] would have been attractive to Dante, and that its method would have figured in the fourteenth book of the Convivio, as it does in the De Monarchia.

[11] See Appendix, p. 191.

## Chapter 7 (continued), Lectio 6

Aristotle speaks of the function of the judge. When men are in doubt about the mean in a transaction, they go to the judge, as to one who is just, for the judge is supposed to be the embodiment of justice. His function is to make things equal.

In his comment St. Thomas writes:

> When men doubt concerning this mean, they take refuge with the judge, for this is the same as taking refuge with what is just, for the judge ought to be as it were the idea of justice endowed with life, that his mind may be wholly possessed by justice. Those who take refuge with the judge seem to seek a middle ground between the parties which dispute. Thence judges are called middlers, or mediators, and if they attain the mean, it is because they win men over to what is just.

The suggestion of Aquinas that the judge should be "justice endowed with life" reminds one of Justinian's statement that he was inspired by the "living justice."[12] Yet he is perhaps rather the lawgiver whose intention "is fixed on true good, which is the common good regulated according to divine justice," of whom Aquinas speaks in the Summa Theologica II.i.92.1. Aquinas' amplification of Aristotle to the effect that "when men doubt concerning this mean, they take refuge with the judge" may have suggested to Dante the words:

> For when human judgment fails, either because it is wrapped in the darkness of ignorance or because it has not the aid of a judge, then, lest judgment should remain forsaken, recourse must be had to Him who so loved her, etc.
>
> —De Monarchia 2.10.2-7.

[12] Paradiso 6.88.

## OLD MEN AS JUDGES

The suggestion that the judge should be the embodiment of justice is in harmony with Dante's belief that judges should be of the age at which justice is most prominent in the characters of men:

> It is also meet at this age to be just in order that a man's judgments and his authority should be a light and a law to others. And because this unique virtue, namely, Justice, was perceived by philosophers of old to show itself in perfection at this age, they committed the government of the state to those who were of this age.
> —Convivio 4.27.88-95.

If any source need be assigned for this, it might be such a passage as Politics 7.9; part of the comment of St. Thomas on this runs as follows:

> The prudence and virtue which are especially necessary to counsel and judgment flourish in a higher degree than elsewhere in men advanced in age; and therefore functions relating to counsel and judgment should be assigned to men when they have reached advanced age.

### Chapter 7 (continued), Lectio 7

In the Ethics it is next, as St. Thomas says in the heading of this lectio, "made manifest by an example drawn from a line in what way the judge himself reduces all things to equality."

At the conclusion of his comment St. Thomas remarks:

> From the foregoing it is evident that the justice now being dealt with is the mean between loss and profit; this justice is none other than the preservation of equality before a transaction and after, even against the will of one of the parties, as is evident in the case of a man who on the order of the judge restores to another what he had in excess of his due.

The judge is not mentioned at this point by Aristotle. His function as the forcible maintainer of justice is that which Dante assigned in the De Monarchia to the ruler who is to sustain justice over the entire earth and prevent the unjust aggressions of princes. We may suppose that Aristotle's illustration of the line would have appeared in Dante's treatment of justice in the Convivio.

## Chapter 8, Lectio 8

Aristotle proceeds to discuss what he believes the partly erroneous opinion of the Pythagoreans, who held that the just was the "contrapassum" or counterpassion, that is, that each man should suffer according to what he had done. This was also the saying of Rhadamanthus, who declared: "If he suffers what he has inflicted, justice is exactly vindicated." But often the principle does not hold, for if a man strikes a prince he ought not to be struck merely, but to be severely punished. Then there is a great difference between the punishment proper to voluntary and involuntary actions.

St. Thomas comments:

It is manifest that a greater injury is done when one strikes a prince than when one strikes some private person, for thus not alone the person himself, but the whole state suffers. In punishments it is expected not merely that the equality of justice should be restored through the reparation to the victim of what has been taken from him, but also that the guilty person should bear a penalty for the evil he has done. Hence some are punished by law for crimes which have not resulted in injury or damage to any one, and the thief is compelled not alone to restore what he has taken, that the

## THE COUNTERPASSION

equality of justice may be restored, but is further punished because of the crime he has committed.

In the Summa Theologica II.ii.61.4 St. Thomas discusses in much the same way "whether the just is absolutely the same as counterpassion" and concludes that the counterpassion holds in commutative justice, but not in distributive justice.

This statement of the justice of the infliction of penalties is helpful in understanding the sufferings of the Inferno. Dante undoubtedly would have agreed with Aristotle and Aquinas in rejecting the counterpassion as the full equivalent of justice, yet it is always the starting point, and sometimes perhaps the fulfilment of justice. Bertram dal Bornio uses the very word to express the justice of his suffering:

> Thus is observed in me the counterpoise.
> —Inferno 28.142.

It is in the thought of Beatrice when she says in purgatory:

> So that the sin and dole be of one measure.
> —Purgatorio 30.108.

It is also found in the explanation for the necessity of the Incarnation:

> The human creature . . .
>     to his dignity no more returns,
> Unless he fill up where transgression empties
> With righteous pains for criminal delights.[13]

[13] Paradiso 7.82-4. See also 7.97-100; 13.42.

Aristotle passes on to say that in commutative transactions there must often be not a simple giving of one thing for another, but that a proportional equality must be found. "Through reciprocal action the state retains proportion." Among the various citizens the builder of a house must equate his product with many articles of less value produced by others. Without this just diversity the state cannot exist.

St. Thomas comments:

> Men keep up reciprocity when one man returns something to another for what he receives. If there is no such restoration, there will be no equality of things exchanged, and thus men will not be able to keep up their reciprocal relation, because nothing prevents the work of one artificer from being better than that of another, as a house is more valuable than a sandal. Hence it is necessary that the values of these things be fairly adjusted, according to the proportion which has been mentioned, in order that there may be just exchange.

This thought appears in Dante's conversation with the spirit of Charles Martel, in which it is laid down, following Aristotle, "the master," that man is happiest as a citizen, and that there cannot be citizens without diverse functions.[14]

In this section Aristotle says also that a man should hasten to requite services done for him, because this requital holds society together, and that he should himself be forward to do favors.

Elsewhere St. Thomas develops his idea of the proportion gratitude should recognize between the

---

[14] Paradiso 8.116 ff.

amount of the benefit and the amount given in requital:

> Gratitude regards the favor received according to the intention of the benefactor; who seems to be deserving of praise, chiefly for having conferred the favor gratis without being bound to do so. Wherefore the beneficiary is under a moral obligation to bestow something gratis in return. Now he does not seem to bestow something gratis unless he exceeds the quantity of the favor received: because so long as he repays less or an equivalent, he would seem to do nothing gratis, but only to return what he has received. Therefore gratitude always inclines, as far as possible, to pay back something more.
> —Summa Theol. II.ii.106.6.

Dante shows his interest in gratitude in relation to justice when in Convivio 1.12.80 he places ingratitude among the inhuman sins of injustice against the imputation of which men may defend themselves.

## Chapter 8 (continued), Lectio 9

As a result of the necessity for carrying on exchanges between those whose products were different, money was devised, as a medium of exchange. But in truth the measure in exchange is need, for if men did not have common needs there could be no commutation. Hence the use of money was agreed upon.

St. Thomas comments:

> Money is made in accord with a compact, that is, an agreement among men, for the sake of the interchange of what is needful, that is, of necessary things. For it is agreed among men that he who offers money shall receive what he lacks. That is why money is called *numisma,* for *nomos* means law,

since money is not a measure according to nature, but according to *nomos,* or law, for nature can remove the value from coins and render them useless.

The belief that it was unnatural to receive interest, general in the Middle Ages, and employed by Dante in his representation of the usurers in the Inferno,[15] could find support in this passage, and still more in Politics 1.9, and the commentary of Aquinas on it, in particular the following:

> Since man is constituted from things which are in accord with nature, other existing things furnish him food. Hence there is in all men a natural pecuniative instinct, that is, an instinct to acquire food, or money for food, from natural things, as fruits and animals. But that man should acquire wealth not from natural things, but from money only, is not according to nature.

### Chapter 9, Lectio 10

Aristotle makes just activity a mean between doing what is unjust and suffering it. Justice is a middle state, but not in the same way as the other virtues, because it is the mean, and injustice pertains to both the extremes, and not, as is usual with vices, to but one.

St. Thomas develops this by explaining that justice is not a mean between two vices, as is liberality between illiberality and prodigality. He continues:

> It can be called an effective middle state, inasmuch as it is able to bring the mean into being, for any act is a just act which is the mean between doing injustice and suffering injustice. Of these two, one, the doing of injustice, pertains to malice, that is, to injustice; this is one of the extremes,

---

[15] See p. 92, below.

since it gets for itself more good things and fewer bad things. But to suffer injustice is not connected with any state of malice, but is rather an affliction.

Dante overlooks this distinction and classes justice with the virtues that mediate between vices in the usual way:

And each of these virtues has two enemies, that is, vices, one on the side of excess, the other on the side of defect. And the virtues are the mean states between these.
—Convivio 4.17.65-8.

Aristotle goes on to say that justice is a habit according to which the just man is said to be able to act according to the choice of what is just, and is capable of distributing between himself and some one else, and likewise between two other men, so that neither has too much or too little, but each his proper proportion. In a similar way injustice leads toward the unjust; it is a superabundance of the good, or too little of what is bad.

In his commentary Aquinas points out that in making justice a matter of deliberate choice Aristotle is following his general idea of the virtues as given in the second book of the Ethics, namely, that, as Aquinas puts it, "moral virtue is a settled habit of choice."

Dante refers to it thus, using some of the same words:

And they [virtues] all spring from one principle, that is, from our habit of right choice. It may therefore be said generally that they are 'a habit of choice residing in the mean.'
—Convivio 4.17.68-72.

As is suitable in this section, Aquinas applies Aristotle's words to the judge:

> Any one can do what is just through choice in two ways, both in making exchanges and in distributing things. In one way the decision is between oneself and another. In the other it is between two other persons, as when a judge or umpire makes a decision. The just man will do what is just. He distributes equably according to proportion.

Dante, who thought of his monarch as the wholly just man, naturally took up this idea and applied it to the ruler, pointing out that the just man could exercise justice with respect to two or more other men only as he possessed magisterial power:

> In its operation, man's justice may meet opposition through want of power; for since Justice is a virtue involving other persons, how can one act according to its dictates without the power of allotting to each man what belongs to him?
>
> —De Monarchia 1.11.46-51.

# CHAPTER II

THE MATERIALS FOR DANTE'S TREATISE, CONTINUED: ST. THOMAS' COMMENTARY ON ETHICS 5.10-15

## Chapter 10, Lectio 11

Here Aristotle deals with the problem of the unjust man. Since he who does something unjust is not necessarily an unjust man, what sort of unjust actions must a man perform in order to be called unjust in some particular? For one who does something unjust as the result of passion is not therefore to be called unjust. Aristotle says that he is dealing at once with justice in the strict sense of the word, and with political justice. The latter implies an association for an existence satisfactory to free and equal persons. The just is present where law exists. But the presence of law also implies injustice, for punishment is the judgment of what is just and unjust. Yet the doing of some injustice does not imply injustice in everything.

St. Thomas comments:

The justice here dealt with is justice in the simplest form, which is political justice. Political justice consists in a certain community of life, which is so arranged that there may be because of this community a sufficiency of those things which pertain to human life. And such is the community of the state, in which should be found all those things which suffice for human life.

This political justice is that of which Dante wrote in the De Monarchia, for he wished such a condition of justice that the human race might actualize its highest end in speculation through a bringing together of all the lesser things needed for the best life—that is, all the things "which pertain to human life":

> I speak of things to be done, which are controlled by political sagacity, and things to be made, which are controlled by art, because they are all handmaids of speculation, that supreme end for which the Primal Good brought into being the human race.
> —De Monarchia 1.3.85-90.

And as for the belief of Aristotle that there can be true justice only among the free, Dante gives a chapter to showing the value of freedom, thus, for example:

> With this in mind we may understand that this freedom, or basic principle of our freedom, is, as I said, the greatest gift bestowed by God upon human nature, for through it we attain to joy here as men, and to blessedness there as gods. If this is so, who will not admit that mankind is best ordered when able to use this principle most effectively? But the race is most free under a monarch.
> —De Monarchia 1.12.38-48.

The reign of the monarch will be the era of freedom and justice.

Aquinas then develops the idea that liability to the penalties of the law is a sign that political justice rules over those subject to the law.

This might be extended to the sufferers in Dante's Inferno, who as free men are subject to the penalties of justice.

Aristotle then points out that we do not wish that an individual should rule, because he may become a tyrant, but prefer that reason or law *(ratio)* should rule. The prince is the guardian of what is just and equable. Hence he will not attribute to himself more than he merits, but will work for his neighbor. For this reason justice is called the good of others. Such a ruler ought to receive honor and glory; one who wishes more is a tyrant.

Aquinas comments:

In the well-ordered government of the multitude we do not permit men to hold the first place, with free action for the human will and human passions, but we insist that man shall be under law, which is the precept of reason, or under a man who acts according to reason, because if a prince follows human passions he may so act for himself that he may receive a greater share of good things, and a lesser share of bad things, and become a tyrant; but tyranny is contrary to the reason underlying the office of the prince. For the prince is set up that he may guard justice, and consequently equality; but he would reject equality when he usurped to himself too many good things, and too few evil things. Since the prince, if he is just, assigns to himself no more good things than he does to other men, except according to the proper proportion of distributive justice, it comes about that the prince does not work for his own benefit, but for that of others. For this reason it was said above that legal justice, according to which the prince governs the multitude, is the good of others. Since, therefore, the prince labors for the multitude, he should receive reward from the multitude, that is, glory and honor, which are the greatest of the good things that can be given by man. Hence if there are any princes to whom these things are not sufficient for reward, but they seek lucre, they are unjust, and tyrants. And in addition to the reward presented by men, good princes may expect a reward from God.

In De Regimine Judaeorum 6 Aquinas writes that "the princes of the nations are set up by God, not that they may seek personal profit, but that they may bring about the common good of the people," and in the commentary on Politics 5, lectio 8, he writes to the same effect.

These opinions explain Dante's idea, the heart of the De Monarchia, of the removal from the monarch of all temptation to cupidity, the great enemy of justice and source of injustice:

> It must first be noted that the worst enemy of Justice is cupidity, as Aristotle signifies in the fifth book to Nicomachus. When cupidity is removed altogether, nothing remains inimical to Justice; hence, fearful of the influence of cupidity which easily distorts men's minds, the Philosopher grew to believe that whatever can be determined by law should in no wise be relegated to a judge.
> —De Monarchia 1.11.70-8.

In the following paragraph charity, or love, the friend of justice, and cupidity, its enemy, are further contrasted. Similarly in Paradiso 15.1-3 the love "that righteously inspires" is contrasted with cupidity.

Some of the spirits Dante met in paradise were eager for the reward St. Thomas allows to good rulers:

> This little planet doth adorn itself
> With the good spirits that have active been,
> That fame and honour might come after them.
> —Paradiso 6.112-14.

In the light of the words of Aquinas on honor and

glory as the reward of a good ruler, these rulers were justified in their ambition, even if they might have risen higher than to desire only the greatest of human rewards. But they have not failed to obtain also the heavenly reward of which St. Thomas speaks.

Those who without thought of earthly reward fulfilled the ideal of a prince are placed in a still higher heaven, where Dante sees their spirits form the words: "Love justice, ye that be judges of the earth."[1] And in contrast to them we learn of many rulers who because of their evil deeds, often the result of avarice, were rightly called unjust men and tyrants.

The monarch who carries out the true ideal of the ruler is the one for whom Dante wishes in De Monarchia. The emperor will be free from the cupidity which leads men to assign too much to themselves, and hence will not be a tyrant. Justice is the good of others, and Dante's monarch, since justice resides in him, will be full of love for others:

In whomever, therefore, right love can be present to the highest degree, in him can Justice find the most effective place. Such is the Monarch, in whose person Justice is or may be most effective. . . . The more a cause is a cause, the more it loves its effect, for such love pursues its cause for its own sake. As we have said, other princes are causes merely by virtue of the Monarch; then among mortals he is the most universal cause of man's well-being, and the good of man is loved by him above all others.

—De Monarchia 1.11.95-140.

[1] Paradiso 18.91-3.

In the next chapter he recurs to this thought. Indeed the prince of Aquinas is the princely servant of Dante:

> It is also evident that although consul or king may be lord of others with respect to means of governing, they are servants with respect to the end of governing; and without doubt the Monarch must be held the chief servant of all. Now it becomes clear that a [Monarchy] is conditioned in the making of laws by [its] previously determined end.
>
> —De Monarchia 1.12.83-91.

This last sentence is in accord with what we have just read in Aquinas of the "ratio," or nature and end of the prince.

### Chapter 10 (continued), Lectio 12

Aristotle next discusses the two divisions of political justice, natural justice and legal justice. Natural justice has everywhere the same weight—whether apparent or not. Legal justice exists only as some law has been especially decreed. Some think all justice is legal, for what is natural is always the same. For example, fire burns in Persia as in Greece, but what is just is not the same. But the example is not conclusive, for with the gods what is natural is not changed, but among us it may be. Yet there is a justice which is natural and one that is not.

The suggestion that justice is different among different nations is developed by Dante:

> Nations, kingdoms, and cities have individual conditions

which must be governed by different laws. For law is the directive principle of life.
—De Monarchia 1.14.38-41.

He gives as examples the Garamantes of the far south, and the Scythians of the frozen north.

The term "legal justice" as St. Thomas employs it in his comment seems not to mean the same thing as the "legal justice" of Lectio 2. Here it means what is enacted by law, without respect to the justice of the enactment; there it meant what was in accord with the end of law—to bring men felicity. Part of the comment follows:

> Isidore says in his book of Etymologies that *justice (jus)* is so called because *just*. But there seems to be some contradiction here, because the political is the same as the civil; and so that which by the Philosopher is set down as divided, among the jurists seems to be considered as dividing, for they make civil law part of positive law. But it must be observed that one thing is taken as political or civil by the philosophers, and another by the jurists. For the Philosopher names political or civil justice from the practice of the citizens; but the jurists give political or civil justice its name because it has been set up by some state. And hence this is conveniently called by the Philosopher legal, that is, established by law, which they call positive. Yet political justice is conveniently divided into these two, for citizens use that justice which nature imparted to the human mind, and also that which is established by law.

We may suppose that something of this sort would have appeared in Dante's treatment of justice. He evidently knew something of the jurists, for he quotes from the Infortiatum,[2] and from the Vecchio Digesto takes the words: "Written law is the art of

[3] Convivio 4.15.175-8.

well-doing and of equity."[3] On this he elsewhere comments:

> That account in the Digests does not teach what the essence of Right is; it simply describes Right in terms of practice.
> —De Monarchia 2.5.6-9.

He is comparing it with his own definition, which as we have seen is derived from Aristotle and Aquinas. He seems to agree with Aquinas that the jurists, when compared with the Philosopher, are superficial.

The word *jus,* which appears in the quotation from Aquinas, is frequently employed in the De Monarchia, as in book 2, chapter 5, with a broad and perhaps somewhat variable meaning. It is often rendered by the word *right,* though *natural justice* seems frequently to be a more satisfactory rendering.

On statutory and natural justice St. Thomas comments:

> The justice laid down by some state or prince is of authority only among those who are under the jurisdiction of that state or prince. In another way Aristotle makes this justice plain, according to its cause, when he says that natural justice does not consist in seeming or not seeming, that it does not spring from some human opinion, but from nature. It is just as in speculative matters, where some things are naturally known, as indemonstrable principles and the like, and where certain matters with the ideas related to them are worked out by human industry. So in practical life there are some principles naturally known as indemonstrable principles, with their related ideas, as that evil should be shunned, and the like. Others are thought out by human industry; these are called the legally just.

[3] Convivio 4.9.87.

Dante applies these ideas as follows:

> In the art of empire there are certain matters which are purely technical, as, for instance, the laws of marriage, of slavery, of military service, of succession to rank. In all these matters we are entirely subject to the Emperor without any doubt or question. There are other laws which are, as it were, the satellites of Nature, such as that which constitutes a man of ripe age for administration; and in these we are not entirely subject to the Emperor. There are many other matters which appear to have some relationship with the art of empire; and here it is, and always was, a mistake for any one to believe that the imperial decision in this department is authoritative. Such a matter is the season of youth, regarding which no consent to any imperial authority is required by virtue of the office of Emperor; therefore let that which is God's be rendered to God.
>
> —Convivio 4.9.150-67.

The subject of natural justice, which Aquinas here treats with the brevity proper to a commentator faithful to his author, was of interest to him as a Christian theologian. His discussion may be summarized as follows:

All the things subject to Divine Providence are ruled and measured by eternal law, and hence participate to some extent in the eternal law. Man, as a rational creature, participates in eternal law more excellently than do the rest. The participation of the rational creature in the eternal law is called the natural law. By the natural law we discern what is good and what is evil. The irrational creature does not share in the law intellectually and rationally; hence its participation is not properly called law.

Another division of eternal law is divine law, which is given to men by revelation from God. "By natural law the eternal law is participated proportionally to the capacity of human nature. But to his supernatural last end man needs to be directed in a yet higher way. Hence the additional law given by God, whereby man shares more perfectly in the eternal law."[4]

The third division of law is human law, which is a dictate of reason for the direction of human acts. "Human law has the nature of law in so far as it partakes of right reason; and it is clear that, in this respect, it is derived from the eternal law. But in so far as it deviates from reason, it is called an unjust law; and has the nature not of law but of violence."[5]

The first precept of the natural law is that "good is to be done and ensued, and evil is to be avoided." All the other precepts of the law of nature are derived from this. All the things to which man has a natural inclination are apprehended by reason as good, and consequently to be gone after, while evil is to be avoided. Man has certain natural inclinations in common with all substances, others, of a higher sort, in common with all animals, and finally those proper to man's rational nature—as "to know the truth about God and to live in society."[6] "To the natural law belongs everything to which man is inclined according to his nature. . . . The rational soul is the proper form of man."[7] Hence man is naturally inclined to work in accord with reason, that

[4] Summa Theol. II.i.91.4, ad 1.
[5] Summa Theol. II.i.93.3, ad 2.
[6] Summa Theol. II.i.94.2.
[7] Summa Theol. II.i.94.3.

is, in accord with virtue. Thus all acts of virtue are in accord with nature.

Human law, as has been said, is derived from natural law:

> Every human law has just so much of the nature of law, as it is derived from the law of nature. But if in any point it deflects from the law of nature, it is no longer a law but a perversion of law.
> But it must be noted that something may be derived from the natural law in two ways: first, as a conclusion from premises, secondly, by way of determination of certain generalities. Some things are therefore derived from the general principles of the natural law, by way of conclusions; e.g., that one must not kill may be derived as a conclusion from the principle that one should do harm to no man: while some are derived therefrom by way of determination; e.g., the law of nature has it that the evil-doer should be punished, but that he be punished in this or that way is a determination of the law of nature.
> Accordingly both modes of derivation are found in the human law. But those things which are derived in the first way, are contained in human law not as emanating therefrom exclusively, but have some force from the natural law also. But those things which are derived in the second way, have no other force than that of human law.
>
> —Summa Theol. II.i.95.2.

The whole idea of the De Monarchia might be called the working out of natural law. It is a natural desire of men to live in freedom and exercise their mental powers to the utmost, for this is the end of man, or represents his "form." Therefore laws in harmony with this desire are the only good laws, and would in their full number represent the totality of good law—hence justice. One of the functions of natural law is to lead men to live together in communities. The ideal of Dante is this and even more. He desires that the opportunity for the perfect life should be furnished to men—a state in which human law and natural law would fully coincide, or in which human law would show clearly its participation in eternal law. Then justice, the virtue "which is most human,"[8] would everywhere prevail.

Dante clearly states his belief that the natural is the just, or, as the translator has it, the right:

> What nature has ordained comes to pass by Right [or natural justice], for nature in her providence is not inferior to man in his; if she were, the effect would exceed the cause in goodness, which cannot be. . . . Nature, then, in her ordinances does not fail of this provision, but clearly ordains things with reference to their capacities, and this reference is the foundation of Right on which things are based by nature. From this it follows that natural order in things cannot come to pass without Right, since the foundation of Right is inseparably bound to the foundation of order. The preservation of this order is therefore necessarily Right.
>
> —De Monarchia 2.7.1-22.

> Let us set up, then, this indisputable truth, that whatever is repugnant to the intention of nature is contrary to the will of God. If this were not true, its contrary would not be false, that whatever is repugnant to the intention of nature is not contrary to the will of God. And if this is not false, its consequences are not false. For in necessary consequences a false consequent is impossible without a false antecedent. . . . That God wills an end for nature is manifest; otherwise the heavens would move to no purpose, which it is not possible to claim.
>
> —De Monarchia 3.2.9-32.

It easily follows that, as Aquinas says, human

[8] Convivio 1.12.71.

## THE DIVINE WILL IS JUSTICE

laws are good only as they are derived from natural law, which, as we have seen, is the part of eternal law especially adapted to the rational creature, and if human laws are not derived from natural law, they are not laws at all. Essentially this is said by Dante:

> From these things it is plain that inasmuch as Right [or justice] is good, it dwells primarily in the mind of God; and as according to the words, "What was made was in Him life," everything in the mind of God is God, and as God especially wills what is characteristic of Himself, it follows that God wills Right according as it is in Him. And since with God the will and the thing willed are the same, it follows further that the divine will is Right itself. And the further consequence of this is, that Right is nothing other than likeness to the divine will. Hence whatever is not consonant with divine will is not right, and whatever is consonant with divine will is right. So to ask whether something is done with Right, although the words differ, is the same as to ask whether it is done according to the will of God. Let this therefore base our argument, that whatever God wills in human society must be accepted as right, true, and pure. —De Monarchia 2.2.39-61.

He applies this principle to all human institutions, asking if they represent the truly just, and if they are working out their natures according to the eternal law:

> If the end of all society is the common good of the individuals associated, then the end of all Right [or justice] must be the common good, and no Right is possible which does not contemplate the common good. Tully justly notes in the first book of the Rhetoric that "the laws should always be interpreted for the good of the state." For if the laws are not directed for the benefit of those under the laws, they are laws merely in name, they cannot be laws in reality. Law ought to bind men together for general advantage.
> —De Monarchia 2.5.11-23.

Hence all the actions of the Romans which were directed to the end of the good of the state were just:

Whoever has in view the end of Right [or justice] proceeds according to Right; the Roman people in subjecting the world to itself had in view the end of Right, as we plainly proved in the chapter above; therefore the Roman people in subjecting the world to itself acted with Right, and consequently appropriated with Right the dignity of Empire.

That this conclusion may be reached by all manifest premises, it must be reached by the one that affirms that whoever purposes the end of Right proceeds according to Right. For clearness in this matter, notice that everything exists because of some end, otherwise it would be useless, which we have said before is not possible. And just as every object exists for its proper end, so every end has its proper object whereof it is the end.

—De Monarchia 2.6.7-25.

Dante is here using the principle that according to natural law all things justly desire their proper end. Hence it was according to natural law for the Romans to work for the Empire. Their specific actions were just only as they were in harmony with the end toward which they properly worked. So far as these specific actions are, as it were, derived from the end, as human law is derived from natural law, they are just. As Dante says,

It is impossible to attain a good condition of one's members without health; and so it is impossible to seek the end of Right [or justice] without right as a means, for each thing has toward its end the relation of consequent to antecedent.

—De Monarchia 2.6.36-41.

Thus in truth the end justifies the means. Dante is not dealing with the appearances of things, but with their reality; and is at the antipodes of saying that evil deeds can be done for a good end:

If anything calling itself the end of Right be reached other than by means of Right, it would be the end of Right, that is, the common good, only as the offering made from ill-gotten gains is an alms. Since in this proposition we are considering the existent, not the apparent ends of Right, the objection is invalid.
—De Monarchia 2.6.61-7.

The same principle of the legality of a human institution or action only as it is in harmony with right —with nature and God—appears in various other passages. Constantine's donation was not valid because it was contrary to the nature of the Emperor that he should divide the Empire, contrary to fundamental justice that the Empire should be divided, and contrary to the nature of the Church to receive such a gift:

No one is free to do through an office assigned him anything contrary to the office, for thereby the same thing, in virtue of being the same, would be contrary to itself, which is impossible. But to divide the Empire would be contrary to the office assigned the Emperor, for as is easily seen from the first book of the treatise, his office is to hold the human race subject to one will in all things. Therefore, division of his Empire is not allowed an Emperor.

—De Monarchia 3.10.30-40.

Continuing, Dante shows that it is contrary to the end of the Church to hold property for herself; she can act only as the dispenser of it to the poor.

Indeed, one of the features of the De Monarchia is the struggle in Dante's mind between his conception of the emperor and the empire as they should be according to their natures, and as he really might hope that they would be on earth. He says, for example, that the monarch is one in whom "justice is or may be most effective"[9] and that "the monarch can have no occasion for cupidity, or rather less occasion than any other men."[10] In the qualifications he recalls himself from the ideal emperor to the earthly possibility.

The relation of political to natural justice, according to the ideas of Aquinas, also appears in Dante's Sixth Epistle.[11]

Returning from Dante's development of the Aristotelian idea to the tenth chapter of the fifth book of the Ethics, we read that in contingent things it is evident what is natural and what is established by agreement. The laws of men vary from place to place, and there are various forms of government, but one alone is universally best. The acts of men are many, but laws are universal, and the just or the unjust is so by nature. When justice or injustice is put into operation, the act is called a "justificatio" or an "injustificatio."

Aquinas comments:

The reasons for mutable things are immutable; hence whatever is natural to us as pertaining to the very reason of man is in no way changed; for instance, actions and arrangements of motion are seldom changed. And likewise things which pertain to the very reason of justice can in no way be changed. For example, there must be no theft, because theft

[9] De Monarchia 1.11.99.
[10] De Monarchia 1.13.48-50.
[11] P. 17, above.

is unjust. The things which follow from the reasons may be changed as belonging to a less important group.

All laws are established as fits the end of the state; yet according to nature one form of government alone is everywhere the best.

This last would justify Dante's conviction that it was possible to prove that monarchy was the only form of government which could exhibit justice in its purity, an opinion in which he has the support of Aquinas.[12]

## Chapter 10 (continued), Lectio 13

Aristotle now takes up the question of the just and unjust actions according to which a man is called just or unjust. A man is just, or the reverse, when he voluntarily does what is just, or the contrary. When he acts involuntarily, he does neither what is just nor what is unjust, except accidentally. The voluntary character of the action is the important thing. When a man voluntarily does the unjust thing, he is censured, and his action is unjust. Hence an action may be unjust, but still will not be called an "injustificatio" unless it is voluntary, and voluntary in the full sense of the word, including complete knowledge of the persons and circumstances involved. Moreover, if a person performs a just or an unjust action from fear or the like, his action cannot be called a "justificatio" or an "injustificatio." Some voluntary actions are the result of

---

[12] Summa Theol. II.i.105.1. The same thought appears in De Regimine Principium 1.2, and in the commentary on Politics 3, lectio 13, and Politics 4, lectio 1.

previous planning, some are not. There are three ways in which injuries may be done: in ignorance, or contrary to reasonable expectation, or deliberately. The last only are called "injustificationes." Men in anger may perform "injustificationes," but their actions are not because of malice, and they are not called unjust men. The unjust person is not the one who acts in wrath, but the one who provokes the wrath. In actions where anger is involved, the angry man thinks that he is unjustly treated, but the man who makes an evil plan has no such belief; he knows who is injured. If he from choice does an injury, he does what is unjust. Hence a man who deliberately performs a just or an unjust action is just or unjust. Involuntary acts of injustice are venial, unless committed as the result of some passion neither human nor venial.

The idea that men are just or unjust only through the exercise of their wills is, as we have seen, common in Dante. It often appears in the De Monarchia (e.g., 1.11), and is close to the theme of the Divine Comedy. In the Epistle to Can Grande we read that by meriting or demeriting "through liberty of choice" men are exposed to the rewards and punisments of justice. The Commedia is concerned with men whose virtue or vice has been with open eyes and free judgments.

Aristotle next shows that unless man is altogether free he cannot be said to act justly or unjustly at all. The freedom of the will receives its clearest expression in Dante in the lines where Marco Lombardo

## INJUSTICE DEPENDS ON THE WILL

shows that man is free to be virtuous or malicious as he wills:

> Ye who are living every cause refer
>   Still upward to the heavens, as if all things
>   They of necessity moved with themselves.
> If this were so, in you would be destroyed
>   Free will, nor any justice would there be
>   In having joy for good, or grief for evil.
> The heavens your movements do initiate,
>   I say not all; but granting that I say it,
>   Light has been given you for good and evil,
> And free volition; which, if some fatigue
>   In the first battles with the heavens it suffers,
>   Afterwards conquers all, if well 'tis nurtured.
>      —Purgatorio 16.67-78.

Only the deliberate purpose of a wrong act gives it full evil quality, and hence renders the doer liable to full punishment. On the other hand, the capacity for deliberate purpose, just or unjust, is the form into which the love or the cupidity of the whole life hardens:

> A will benign, in which reveals itself
>   Ever the love that righteously inspires,
>   As in the iniquitous, cupidity.
>      —Paradiso 15.1-3.

The same opposition between charity, the source of justice, and cupidity, the source of injustice, appears in the De Monarchia 1.11.91-7.

### Chapter 11, Lectio 14

Aristotle decides that no one willingly suffers injustice, for no one wishes to be treated unjustly, an opinion in which he is followed by Aquinas in the Summa Theologica II.ii.59.3. The incontinent man, however, led by incontinence, may do what he knows to be other than good for him, and as a result may be treated with injustice.

St. Thomas in his comment explains as follows about the incontinent man:

The incontinent man does things injurious to himself because of the will. Through himself he has desire for good, but through concupiscence is dragged toward the evil. This which has been said Aristotle proves in this way: since desire is for what appears to be good, no one wishes what he does not think to be good. But the incontinent man when not under the influence of passion does not think what he does to be good, and therefore does not absolutely wish it. But nevertheless he does that which he thinks he should not do, because of concupiscence, which is in the sensitive appetite, while will is in the reason.

The relation of this to Dante's belief that justice resides in the will and the reason is obvious.[13] The incontinent sinner, hurried away by passion, is not so fully determined to do evil as is the man who sins under the influence of reason. Hence, as is explained, with a reference to Aristotle, in the Inferno 11, the incontinent sinners occupy the higher and less dismal circles of hell, while those who sin with dispassionate volition are assigned to lower circles.

In the Latin translation of this chapter, Aristotle is made to say: "No man wishes anything which he does not estimate as *studiosum.*" The word *studiosum* is equivalent to the 'good' *(bonum)* of St. Thomas. From this it follows that evil men do not wish to be treated unjustly. Such an idea perhaps

[13] See p. 6, above.

offers more basis than anything else in the Ethics for Dante's assertion that evil men love justice:

> Justice is so lovely, that, as the Philosopher says in the fifth book of the Ethics, her enemies such as thieves and robbers love her, and therefore we see that her opposite, namely, injustice, is most of all hateful, as, for example, treachery, ingratitude, falsehood, theft, rapine and deceit and the like. All of these are such inhuman sins that long custom allows a man to speak of himself in order to exonerate himself from the reproach of these.
> —Convivio 1.12.74-84.

However, the passage can hardly be considered Dante's source, even with the addition of part of Aristotle's preceding paragraph: "No one voluntarily suffers injustice." These two, together with Aristotle's praise of the loveliness of justice in Ethics 5.3, might be developed into what Dante says, but there is no such direct statement as Dante seems to quote.

Justice is especially the virtue that holds society together, and the "thieves and robbers" of whom Dante speaks are among the chief enemies of justice because they disturb the proportionate distribution of good things. As St. Thomas says, in the Summa Theologica II.ii.66.6, "If men were to rob one another habitually, human society would be undone." Similarly, the vices of injustice which Dante mentions are especially opposed to Aristotelian justice. This is plain with respect to "theft, rapine, deceit and the like," which deal with property. Falsehood is perhaps also to be classed with them as relating to property. St. Thomas, however, explains that truth is necessary because without it human society could not exist;[14] hence it is obviously related to justice. Ingratitude is also especially opposed to justice, as Aristotle points out when he says that we ought to requite good, since this is necessary to society. Gratitude involves requital with some regard to the amount of benefit received, and hence has something to do with the proportion of justice.[15] Treachery is especially unjust not merely as involving ingratitude, but as a throwing off of all human obligations. These sins are "inhuman" because they are opposed to justice in that they destroy the social life of man. For justice is a virtue in which peculiarly human traits appear, and which enables man to live in accord with his nature as a "civil animal."[16] Without justice, and the human society dependent on it, men would live like animals. If justice is peculiar to man, injustice is also peculiar to him, as Dante indicates when he writes:

> But because fraud is man's peculiar vice,
> More it displeases God.
> —Inferno 11.25-6.

## Chapter 12, Lectio 15

Is the unjust man he who gives more than is proper, or he who receives more? Aristotle asks. Is a man unjust if, while receiving nothing for himself, he deliberately and wilfully distributes to another more than is just? Is he not unjust to himself? For

---
[14] See p. 108, below.
[15] See p. 28, above.
[16] Quoted from Aristotle in Convivio 4.27.29.

the modest man is inclined to moderation. Or the case may not be so simple, for the distributor may receive some other good, such as glory. But if no one willingly can receive injustice, the distributor receives injury, but not injustice. It is evident that the distributor does the injustice, and not the recipient; for the man who possesses an unjust share is not the man who does the injustice, but he who wills the injustice; and the originator of the action is the distributor. A man who in ignorance gives a wrong decision is not legally unjust, though he violates "the prime justice." But if a man knowingly judges unjustly, he acts avariciously, for he obtains a reward, whether of property, pleasure, revenge, or some other benefit.

St. Thomas explains the prime justice *(primum justum)* of Aristotle as the natural justice which a man cannot be ignorant of, because it is impressed on his mind by nature.

The mention of avarice in this chapter of Aristotle again reminds us of the De Monarchia 1.11, and its association of greed and injustice. The association is especially apparent because here Aristotle connects cupidity with the judge. Dante endeavored to get rid of the possibility of cupidity on the part of his monarch by giving him everything, so that he would have nothing to desire. So far as the bounds of the monarch's dominion are concerned, he has nothing more to desire, unless he sighs for more worlds to rule, but in other respects Dante does not specify how the monarch is to be kept from perverting justice, for the sake, perhaps, of some of the various rewards mentioned by Aristotle.

### Chapter 13, Lectio 15 (continued)

Aristotle next says, according to the text now received, that it is not easy to be just. But the text used by St. Thomas runs as follows:

Men think that it lies in their own power to do what is unjust, and therefore that it is easy to be unjust, but that is not true. For to commit adultery with the wife of one's neighbor, and to strike one's companion, and to give a bribe are easy in themselves. But to do these things as expressions of habit does not lie in one's power.

On this Aquinas comments:

Aristotle says that many think that the possibility of doing an unjust act is always ready at hand; whence they suppose that it is easy for any one to be habitually unjust. But this is not true. For it is easy, and continually in the power of every one, to do things that are unjust, for example to commit adultery with the wife of one's neighbor, and to strike one's companion, and to take money from the hand of another, or to give a bribe with the purpose of bringing about homicide, or anything of this sort. But that men should do this sort of thing as a result of habit, to wit, promptly and pleasurably, is not easy, nor always in a man's power, but he comes to the ability to do it only through long habit.

The sinners in Dante's Inferno are those who have learned to do unjust actions "promptly and pleasurably." Dante, as we may infer from the similarity of the wording, had these passages in Aristotle and Aquinas in mind when he wrote:

There are also activities upon which our reason reflects in the very exertion of the will, as, for instance, the giving offence or pleasure, standing firm or fleeing in battle, keeping chaste, or wantoning. These are wholly subject to our will; and therefore from them we are called good or bad, because they are wholly our own. Wherefore so far as our will can prevail, so far does our own activity extend.

—Convivio 4.9.65-75.

The hardened sinner is he to whom evil deeds have become wholly his own, or natural and habitual.

Aristotle continues by saying that men think it easy to distinguish between the just and the unjust, as it is easy to know what the laws say. But the laws are just only through accident. It is more difficult to understand what is just than to understand the laws of health. A knowledge of medicines is not hard to get, but to know how to prescribe them is really to be a physician. Men also think that the just man may act unjustly no less than justly, since it is easier for him than for others to do unjust actions, such as committing adultery, and throwing away his shield though he is brave. But a brave man does not fear, or a just man act unjustly, except by accident. To do just things because of one's moral bent is like practising medicine in the proper way.

St. Thomas comments:

To do injustice of one's own accord is to commit the aforesaid evil acts through force of habit, that is, to be eager and ready to do them.

A mind so set on evil, as Dante shows in his representation of the lost souls, would be wholly alienated from the love of God and man, and hence fit only for hell.[17]

## Chapter 14, Lectio 16

Aquinas heads this section: "He debates whether equity is the same as natural and legal justice." Aristotle says that equity seems not to be quite the same as justice, and yet not to be of another genus. We praise things as equitable as though the more equitable things were the better. But it often appears improper that something worthy of praise should be praised as equitable but not as just. For either the just is not good *(studiosum)*, or the equitable is something other than the just, or both are the same. They have nothing contrary to each other, for the equitable, though better than some just things, is just, and not something of a different and better genus than the just. The just and the equitable are good things of the same sort, but the equitable is the better.

In his comment St. Thomas attempts to give the composition of the Greek word "epiichia," meaning equity.

The word used in Greek is *epiiches,* meaning what is suitable or fitting, from *epi,* meaning *above,* and *icos,* meaning *obedient;* through *epiichia,* then, one obeys in a more excellent way, while one observes the intention of the legislator, where the words of the law are contradictory.

The word ἐπιεικής meaning *equitable*, is really derived from ἐπί as St. Thomas says, and from εἰκός, meaning *equitable* rather than *obedient*. There is,

[17] See p. 74, below.

## EQUITY IS BETTER THAN LEGALITY 59

however, no reason to suppose that Aristotle thought of the word as a compound one, and St. Thomas' explanation must be considered a product of mediæval fancy.

From Dante's fondness for such attempts at derivation, we may infer that he would have employed this one in his treatise on justice.

In his further comment Aquinas explains that the equitable is better than the legally just, but is contained in natural justice. Hence it cannot be called something other than the just.

Dante's opinion on the relation of the legally just and the equitable can be gathered from his treatment of Rhipeus. Though a pagan, this Trojan is placed in paradise because he

> Set all his love below on righteousness.
> —Paradiso 20.121.

As his conclusion from the presence of this man in heaven, Dante gives the warning:

> And you, O mortals! hold yourselves restrained
> In judging.
> —Paradiso 20.133-4.

The poet is here speaking of a more exalted equity than Aristotle considered, yet is emphasizing the possibility of exceptions, for the sake of justice, even to the most just laws.

Aristotle continues by saying that there is some doubt whether the equitable is just, yet not in accord with law, but capable of making legal justice truly righteous. The reason for this is that law is of universal application; however, about some things correct general laws cannot be made. Yet when it is necessary to make them, though they cannot be in every instance right, the law covers the majority of cases, without ignoring the possibility of error. And law is not the less just, for the sin is not in the law, or in the lawgiver, but in the nature of the particular case, for the matter of things to be dealt with is of this sort. Hence, where the law speaks universally, but there is a particular case which does not fall under the universal statement, and the simple interpretation of the law would work wrong, it is necessary that what is wrong should be made right. If the maker of the law were present, he would approve of this, or if he had known of it he would have adapted the law.

St. Thomas comments that in respect to contingent things it is not possible to say that anything is universally true: "And such are human actions, concerning which laws are made." Hence laws cannot have absolute application. He also points out that the correction of legal justice necessary in special cases should be in harmony with natural justice.

Dante refers to this section as follows:

Municipal laws do fail at times and have need of regulation, as the Philosopher shows in his commendation of equity in the fifth book to Nicomachus. Nations, kingdoms, and cities have individual conditions which must be governed by different laws. For law is the directive principle of life. The Scythians . . . need other laws than the Garamantes.

—De Monarchia 1.14.35-47.

But Dante develops the topic in a way not suggested by Aristotle and Aquinas. When they say that the universally pronounced law must be modified in a variety of special cases, they make no indication that they refer to more than a single country. Dante's thought is that while the general principles of law for the human race "in general matters pertaining to all peoples" are the same throughout the world, the laws of various countries must be adapted to local conditions. In fact Dante does not quite represent Aristotle by saying that municipal laws sometimes fail, for the Philosopher's assertion is that all laws are liable to failure.

Dante sets equity above written law, because, like Aristotle, he makes it equivalent to natural law:

And inasmuch as in all these voluntary activities, there is a certain equity to be preserved, and a certain breach of equity to be avoided; and this equity may be destroyed for two reasons, either through not knowing what it is, or through not wishing to follow it, written law was invented in order both to demonstrate and to prescribe it. Hence Augustine says that "If men had known it (namely, equity), and had upheld it when known, there would have been no need of written Law." Therefore in the beginning of the Old Digest it is set down that "Written Law is the art of well-doing and of equity."

—Convivio 4.9.75-84.

In his Sixth Epistle Dante asserts that the best statute laws are in harmony with natural law, and hence with the principles of righteousness. Any sin, such as cupidity, forbids men to obey the laws, which "imitate the image of natural justice." On the other hand, the observance of good laws, being in harmony with nature, is complete liberty.

Aristotle continues to explain that this failure of the universal application of laws is the reason why equity must be sought, for the indeterminate cannot be measured by a fixed rule, but a flexible standard like the leaden rule of the Lesbian masons must be employed. It is manifest that the equitable man is not he who is accurately just "for the worse," because he allows no exceptions in strict enforcement of law, but the man content with a lesser portion even than the law supports him in taking. His habit of mind is equity, which is a sort of justice, and not some other state.

In his comment St. Thomas writes:

Aristotle decides what is characteristic of such a virtuous man, and says that such a man is not accurately just (that is, diligently following up justice for the worse, to wit, to the inflicting of punishment, like those who are strict in punishing), but they diminish the penalties although the law aids them in punishing. For the penalties are not devised by the legislator for their own sake, but as a sort of medicine for sins. Hence the reasonable man does not apportion more of punishment than suffices for the restraint of the sins.

The conception of punishment as a medicine is one to which St. Thomas elsewhere recurs:

Punishment may be considered as a medicine, not only healing the past sin, but also preserving from future sin, or conducing to some good. . . . No one is punished in spiritual goods without any fault on his own part, neither in this nor in the future life, because in the latter punishment is not medicinal, but a result of spiritual condemnation.

—Summa Theol. II.ii.108.4.

# MEDICINAL PUNISHMENT

The same comparison appears in his comment on Ethics 2, lectio 3, and elsewhere.[18]

The suggestion that the punishments of the damned are not medicinal is helpful in the understanding of Dante's Inferno, in contrast with his presentation of purgatory, where the punishments are remedial, and show the mercy of the Lawmaker.

## Chapter 15, Lectio 17

This section is headed: "No one is able to act unjustly to himself; not even he who kills himself seems to act unjustly to himself, since he is injured according to his own will." The suicide does, however, act unjustly to the state, and hence disgrace attaches to him.

In his comment Aquinas alludes to the custom of denying burial to the body of the suicide, a touch which suggests the statement of Peter of Vinea, in the Inferno 13, that the suicides would not at the day of judgment reassume their bodies as would the remainder of the dead. Aquinas also develops a suggestion of Aristotle to the effect that one part of the mind, such as the irascible faculty, may, in causing suicide, act unjustly against the rational part of the mind. But even this hardly explains Dante's puzzling treatment of Peter of Vinea, the suicide unjust to himself.[19]

[18] Summa Theol. II.i.87.3, reply 2; II.i.87.7; II.ii.43.7, reply 1; II.ii.66.6, reply 2.
[19] P. 88, below.

## Divine Justice

Dependent on Aristotle for his conception of justice as Aquinas was, he did not find the Philosopher wholly satisfactory. Human justice might have been exhausted by the Greek, but he had not considered the justice of God. Hence St. Thomas is obliged to deal with this for himself, as has already appeared in his discussion of divine law.[20] What he says is, however, built on what he had learned from Aristotle about human justice.

He makes use of Aristotle's larger conception of justice as equivalent to all virtue:

> It belongs to general justice to do good in relation to the community or in relation to God, and to avoid the opposite evil.
>
> —Summa Theol. II.ii.79.1.

This justice enjoins the practice of all virtues:

> The community for which the Divine law is ordained, is that of men in relation to God, either in this life or in the life to come. And therefore the Divine law proposes precepts about all those matters whereby men are well ordered in their relations to God. Now man is united to God by his reason or mind, in which is God's image. Wherefore the Divine law proposes precepts about all those matters whereby human reason is well ordered. But this is effected by the acts of all the virtues: since the intellectual virtues set in good order the acts of the reason in themselves: while the moral virtues set in good order the acts of the reason in reference to the interior passions and exterior actions. It is therefore evident that the Divine law fittingly proposes precepts about the acts of all the virtues.
>
> —Summa Theol. II.i.100.2.

---

[20] P. 41, above.

## JUSTICE TOWARD GOD

In the strict Aristotelian sense we cannot, however, render justice to God:

> Since justice implies equality, and since we cannot offer to God an equal return, it follows that we cannot make Him a perfectly just repayment. For this reason the Divine law is not called *jus* but *fas*, because, to wit, God is satisfied if we accomplish what we can. Nevertheless justice tends to make man repay God as much as he can, by subjecting his mind to Him entirely.
> —Summa Theol. II.ii.57.1.

Yet we must keep the divine laws, which fully carry out the intention of the divine lawgiver. As human laws are for the good of the state, so the eternal laws lead directly toward the general and final good, which is God.

For infringement of the divine commands, penalties may be inflicted by divine justice—sometimes as absolute punishment, and sometimes as medicine against sin, whether past, present, or future.

In the Divine Comedy Dante is concerned less with justice among men—the theme of De Monarchia—than with the relation of man to God. Hence he considers offenses against other men less in their specific character as acts of injustice to others than in their general character as offenses against the divine order. Thus every man is examined not in his relation to what is contingent, but *sub specie eternitatis*. The sinners and the saints of Dante represent universals in the great conflict between good and evil, and every sufferer or blessed one exemplifies the relation of mankind to the end of the whole creation.

The parallels between Dante's references to justice and the views of Aristotle and Aquinas make it evident that his conception of justice is prevailingly Thomistic. It is not necessary to suppose that he would have used the fifth book of the Ethics and the commentary on it as the only sources for the proposed treatise on justice in the fourteenth tractate of the Convivio. Yet it seems likely that he would have relied on them for much of his material, and that he would seldom have dissented from their principles. The treatise would have been prevailingly an adaptation of Aristotle and Aquinas to the unlearned readers for whom the Convivio was designed.

Dante was evidently so familiar with Aristotelian conceptions of justice as presented by Aquinas that he could use them with freedom. They were, in fact, so well assimilated that he may be supposed to have employed them in his thinking without immediate consciousness of their origin. Hence they could become the materials not merely of a prose treatise, but of poetry itself, where the mind of the author is revealed in full artistic liberty. If we would enter into Dante's conception of justice, we must follow the road prepared by St. Thomas. With our admiration of the Divina Commedia we may properly mingle gratitude to the mediaeval scholar whose patient analysis of Aristotle furnished fuel to the fire of Dante's genius.

# CHAPTER III

### THE COMMEDIA AS A POEM OF JUSTICE

The theme of justice is as important in the poetry as in the prose writings of Dante. According to the Tenth Epistle, 172-5, indeed, justice is the subject of the Commedia, for Dante wrote to Can Grande:

> If the work is taken allegorically, the subject is man, as by meriting or demeriting through his freedom of choice he is subject to justice, which has the function of rewarding or punishing him.

Though the authenticity of this letter has been disputed, at the present time it is generally admitted. If it is not the work of Dante, it must have been written by some one who well understood the Commedia, for it sets forth an idea that pervades the poem. Dante's vision is morally and intellectually acceptable only when the justice of the punishments he describes is accepted. If their justice be denied, the poem is chaos or burlesque. Its effectiveness and value as a whole depend on the truth and fitness of the treatment accorded to men by the divine government. Unless the reader feels that the punishments of the wicked and the rewards of the good are rationally ordered, the purpose of Dante is unfulfilled.

In whatever way Dante's personal experience appears in the poem, God's justice is still its theme. If, as by Flamini, the work is made the story of Dante's conversion, the justice of God is still that which convinces him of the folly of a wicked life and assures him of the wisdom of righteousness. Not by a single biting personal stroke is the poet brought from sin to the right way, but by a presentation of all of human life through a great variety of examples. If the personal aspect of the poem is little emphasized, and Dante becomes an observer, who is to remember and write for the help of others, the panorama is still that of man under divine government. However much or little the vision may mean to Dante as an individual, it is still universally applicable.

Though varying estimates of the autobiographical qualities of the Divine Comedy cannot wholly alter the character of the poem as a vision of God's justice in dealing with man, there are places where these estimates are of importance in interpretation. One such place is the introductory canto, where the poet writes that in his dream he found himself in a dark forest, from which he escaped only by passing on his miraculous journey through the realms of the dead. An explanation presented by some excellent commentators is that the dark forest represents vicious habits of the poet's own life; as he attempts to escape he is driven back by three beasts, signifying his own evil tendencies, fraud, violence, and incontinence, or lust, pride, and avarice.

# AVARICE IN SOCIETY

This explanation is not so cogent as to exclude others. Indeed, in view of the various interpretations permitted to an allegory by Dante, others might subsist at the same time as this one. Virgil explains to Dante that he cannot escape the wolf of avarice except by another path than the direct way up the happy mountain, for the beast utterly impedes the passage. Moreover, the evil nature of the wolf is never satisfied, but after it has eaten its hunger is greater than before. This ever-gnawing hunger is in the Convivio 4.12 instanced by Dante as one of the evils attendant on wealth: the rich man cannot obtain enough; as he grows richer he demands riches the more. Similarly in the Purgatorio 20.12 the wolf of avarice is "infinitely hollow" with hunger. Deliverance will come through the mysterious hound, the *veltro,* which is the opposite of the wolf in freedom from avarice, and devotion to wisdom, love, and virtue. The *veltro* is obviously also a political deliverer, who will save Italy—the Italy consecrated by the blood of Camilla, Euryalus, Turnus, and Nisus, who fell as Aeneas carried out his divinely appointed duty of establishing Rome. The spirit of this passage carries one back to the De Monarchia with its theme of the divine hand in Roman history, and its conviction that the world will be well ruled only by a divinely sanctioned Roman emperor, who will be just because free from avarice. Under his rule injustice will be put to flight; the meagre wolf will be driven back to hell by the hound.

Considered in this way, the wolf is not Dante's personal vice of avarice, but the avarice that filled Italy and all the world with injustice, bringing about war and confusion. The unrighteousness that possessed Florence and drove Dante forth as an exile is only one manifestation of this. But such an interpretation of the wolf in his conflict with the hound reflects back on the significance of the wolf in his first encounter with Dante, when, with the other animals, he forced the poet again into the dark forest. May the wolf there receive a political interpretation in place of, or in addition to, a personal one? Since Dante is not the only one he hinders,[1] he apparently represents the evil force that keeps all men from the short road to the delectable mountain, and forces them back into the dark forest. Mankind would live on a happy mountain if it could attain its end, to actualize "continually the entire capacity of the possible intellect," as Dante puts it in the De Monarchia 1.4.3. From attaining this end the human race is hindered because government and all society exhibit the injustice that springs especially from avarice, and are characterized by fraud and violence. Mankind is obliged to turn back from its high end to the dark forest of an evil world. In the dark valley man wanders bewildered, full of fear, and the more discouraged that his way to the light is barred by the apparently irresistible animals. He is as helpless as the youth mentioned in the Convivio 4.24.124, who, having entered the "forest of wandering" of

---

[1] Inferno 1.95.

this life, cannot find the right road. Into this dark forest Dante himself—for here the personal application is evident—went "ruining" down, having lost all "hope of the height."

But though the world seemed a hopeless place to Dante, a way of escape presented itself. Virgil appeared to tell him that notwithstanding the power of injustice on earth, he could by passing through hell and purgatory arrive at the city of the great emperor who rules the whole creation. Since the power of God is over all, injustice on earth is not superior to the divine justice. Yet Dante's deliverance from fear is not the result of a sudden illumination, but of the opportunity to see with his own eyes the truth about the world. Even in the dark forest he can find good, though so mingled with evil that to treat of the good he found there, he must treat of the hideous and repulsive as well. The divine justice appears in its dealings with evil. In order to see this, to gain full experience, as Virgil explains to Mahomet,[2] and not because sin leads him, Dante passes through hell.

The poet's full experience comes from the sight of a great number of punishments inflicted and rewards bestowed by divine justice in accord with the merits of those who suffer or are blessed. Throughout the poem, though most often in the Inferno, Dante reminds his readers that he is giving examples of the justice of God. If the sight of these punishments and rewards is to give proper experience, they must

[2] Inferno 28.48.

be wholly just; that is, they must accord with the system of justice in which Dante believed, and must exemplify its workings. A punishment or a reward cannot exhibit merely a clever outward appropriateness; it must exemplify also the principles of Aristotelian and Thomistic justice.

In addition, it must be susceptible of allegorical interpretation, that it may exhibit the workings of divine justice not merely among the dead, but in the world of living men. If God's justice is not active in the world here and now, Dante and Job have no immediate escape from the dark forest of the evils of this life. The faith that sustained the Italian poet to write his song of triumph among the sufferings of exile is not a faith in a distant millenium, but faith in an ever-present executor of the destiny that in the freedom of his will man has determined for himself. He looked first of all for the punishments of hell or the rewards of heaven in the characters of men about him, as they are stamped by inexorable justice. There he saw that injustice in government and society is not a cause for despair, but that the life and activity even of evil men, when clearly seen, is a vindication of eternal righteousness. Holding this truth, the outwardly defeated Dante gives utterance to his living convictions in a song which, like that of Milton amid the ruin of his political hopes, aims to "justify the ways of God to men."

# CHAPTER IV

### THE INFERNO: JUSTICE IN THE LIFE OF THE WICKED

Approaching the portal of hell, Dante reads as part of the inscription over it:

> Justice incited my sublime Creator.

And with justice are joined power, wisdom, and love, the virtues essential to the understanding and execution of justice. So it is impressed on the poet, as he enters the house of woe and pain, that here all the divine attributes are to be manifested.

Those whom Dante is to see are dolorous because they have given up "the good of the intellect,"[1] that is, "the truth, which is our final perfection, as the Philosopher says in the sixth book of the Ethics, when he affirms that Truth is the good of the intellect."[2] By so doing they have yielded up humanity, and forfeited their right to the blessedness that comes to man when he attains his proper end. This abandonment of the proper state of humanity, and turning to evil, is opposed to justice in the broadest sense, as complete virtue with respect to one's neighbors. In so far as sin consists in an inordinate turning toward a communicable good, an inordinateness opposed to the proportion of justice is introduced.

---
[1] Inferno 3.18.
[2] Convivio 2.14.40-4.

This can be reduced to the order of justice only through punishment, "since it is just that he who has been too indulgent to his will, should suffer something against his will, for thus will equality be restored."[3] But since the damned in the Inferno have turned fully toward evil, their punishment is unending. Aquinas explains this as follows:

> Now it is just that he who has sinned against God in his own eternity should be punished in God's eternity. A man is said to have sinned in his own eternity, not only as regards continual sinning throughout his whole life, but also because, from the very fact that he fixes his end in sin, he has the will to sin everlastingly. Wherefore Gregory says (Moral. xxxiv) that the wicked would wish to live without end, that they might abide in their sins for ever.
>
> —Summa Theol. II.i.87.3.

Herein lies the allegory of the Inferno. Dante is representing evil men as they actually live on earth. By a figure he permits us to see the reality of evil in the lives of ourselves and other men as we go about our business and pleasure. Hence every punishment is an allegory of the evil and unrepentant life the sufferer actually lived; as no sinner manifests any desire to escape from hell, so men in this world live in satisfaction with their unrighteous lives. This part of the poem teaches that divine justice operates among living men by making each evil life its own punishment, lived without hope in genuine, though perhaps concealed, misery. Dante sets before his readers many concrete applications of this principle,

[3] Summa Theol. III.86.4.

## ALLEGORICAL PUNISHMENTS

to enable them to see the divine justice in its various manifestations.

In so representing each punishment as an allegory, Dante is obliged to adapt each one to the sin involved.[4] Some attempt at this had been made in the older visions of hell, as when the avaricious are punished with molten gold, the lustful are forced to lie on burning beds, and the gluttons are fed with loathsome reptiles.[5] But such punishments as this are hardly more than suggestive of the nature of the sins, and are purely physical. Though sometimes Dante does not do much more than this, he often attempts an allegory of the spiritual or social effects of the various crimes, and may not give any direct indication of their physical aspects. He is obviously limited by the necessity of giving material representations of spiritual things. On this Dionysius the Carthusian remarks:

By these and similar figures of speech the sufferings of the souls detained in purgatory or in hell are shown under images and similitudes of corporal things, since they can be better

---

[4] The explanation of this fitness had received little systematic attention until Professor Grandgent undertook it in the arguments prefixed to the cantos of the Inferno in his edition of La Divina Commedia, Boston, 1913. Much of my work is illustrative and confirmatory of his brief statements.

[5] The following description, though much later than Dante, preserves the older tradition:

> There are gluttons fed
> With toads and adders; there is burning oil
> Poured down the drunkard's throat; the usurer
> Is forced to sup whole draughts of molten gold;
> There is the murderer for ever stabbed,
> Yet can he never die; there lies the wanton
> On racks of burning steel, whiles in his soul
> He feels the torment of his raging lust.
> —Ford, 'Tis Pity She's a Whore, III, vii.

understood, and spirits returned to the body can be more useful in speaking to the living, to whom spiritual things ought to be declared through corporal things.

—De Quatuor Noviss. 3.20.

Milton, whose problem was somewhat like that of Dante, speaks in Paradise Lost 5.573 of "likening spiritual to corporal forms" in order to make them intelligible to "human sense."

In addition to making his punishments suitably allegorical, Dante naturally makes them such as to exemplify the principles of justice he had learned from his masters. One of the chief of these, as regards penalties, is that of the counterpassion, that is, that the penalty should be of the same sort as the injury inflicted. Aristotle and Aquinas explain that this is often insufficient, for the circumstances may require a heavier penalty. A man who injures the person of a prince should receive not merely equal personal injury, but something further, in that he has injured the state over which the prince rules. Counterpassion must take into account not merely the injury inflicted on the person, but the nature of the action. When thus interpreted, "counterpassion," says St. Thomas, "is in accordance with commutative justice."[6] Dante keeps this principle in mind. His penalties start with the counterpassion, but he does not stop with the external aspect of an offence; he enquires into its effects on society, and devises the penalty with the ultimate importance of the sin in view.

[6] Summa Theologica II.ii.61.4; see also p. 26, above.

## THE FIRST CIRCLE

When Dante and Virgil begin their journey, they come among the spirits who were neither cold nor hot in life, and hence were displeasing to God and to his enemies. It is fitting that they should be excluded from both heaven and hell, yet since "justice disdains them" they need not detain us.

Dante sees next those who because of positive evil are to enter hell itself. They cry out against their fate, blaspheming God, their parents, the human species, the place, the time, and the seed of their engendering and their birth. Here Dante gives us the habitual behavior of the impious, who having made selfish use of their free will, complain because of what their actions have brought on them. Virgil tells Dante that they are ready to pass the river into hell

> Because celestial Justice spurs them on,
> So that their fear is turned into desire.
> —Inferno 3.125-6.

At first sight it appears arbitrary that divine justice causes these sinners to desire the torments at the prospect of which they cry out, but it is the truth of life, for men choose torment and the company of the tormented by choosing darkness rather than light, being driven by concupiscence to do evil.[7] In life, however, they had commonly thought that they were obtaining good for themselves, but here the truth is apparent.

Entering the first circle, Dante sees those condemned to hell because they had died in infancy

---

[7] Cf. the quotation from Aquinas, p. 52, above.

without baptism, "which is the portal of the Faith," and those noble pagans who lived before the time of Christ. As himself one of the latter, Virgil says:

> Without hope we live on in desire.
> —Inferno 4.42.

This to Dante was the state of the best men before the coming of Christ; in hell they live as they had lived on earth.

From Limbo Dante comes to Minos, the judge of hell. He is "discriminator of transgressions," and the sinners who come before him confess all; hence the assignment of penalties in hell is always in accord with the truth, and there can be no complaint against the judge.

Beyond the seat of Minos are regions of darkness and the bellowing of tempests, where fierce winds blow the shades continually hither and thither. These are carnal sinners, whose emotions swayed them hither and thither, and to whom rest never came. Most of them had therefore been inconstant in love. In this penalty Dante abandons the material associations of the sin. As these sinners have confused their own lives and those of others, so they here justly suffer confusion.

In the next circle are the gluttons, lying on the stinking earth like dogs, and exposed to continual hail, discolored rain, and snow, from which they endeavor to protect themselves by continually turning, while Cerberus, the great worm, rends them. In this description Dante relinquishes the mediæval habit of punishing the gluttons with loathsome food, turning from so crude a device to the moral state of the glutton. His description of the squalor of these sinners represents the truth about gluttony, though in life this vice may have been surrounded with the splendor of great banquets.

The justice of their punishment perhaps appears most plainly in the conduct of the dog Cerberus. In Dante's century the glutton was conventionally described as neglecting the poor, and throwing to the dogs the fragments of his feast.[8] By an exaggeration of the punishment, they are themselves thrown to a demoniac dog. Still further, the gluttons had grossly abused the products of the earth by their gluttony. Consequently the rain, which commonly enables the earth to bring forth food, makes it for them vile and a means of torture. Even the monotony of the rain is a turning back on them of the monotony of their sin, one requiring little physical or intellectual activity.

The poets pass on to the circle of the avaricious and the prodigal. The kind of avarice punished here, though ruinous to the character, is not the aggravated form that deliberately steals or in some way injures other men for gain. Hence St. Thomas distinguishes it from the avarice opposed to justice, as follows:

[Avarice] denotes immoderation in the interior affections for riches; for instance, when a man loves or desires riches too

[8] Petrarch, Confessional Psalms, in the *Romanic Review* 2, (1911), 434.

much, or takes too much pleasure in them, even if he be unwilling to steal. In this way covetousness is opposed to liberality.

—Summa Theol. II.ii.118.3.

The description of this circle is prefaced by a reflection apparently not spoken at the time of the descent, but springing up in the mind of the poet as he committed his imaginary experience to writing:

> Justice of God, ah! who heaps up so many
> New toils and sufferings as I beheld?
> And why doth our transgression waste us so?

—Inferno 7.19-21.

By these lines Dante calls attention to the strange character of the punishment of these sinners, and leads us to ask in what way it is especially just. The company, greater than any he has yet seen, is divided into two parts, moving around the circle in opposite directions and pushing great stones before them. On opposite sides of the circle they meet, and turn back, one group, that of the prodigal, shouting, "Why keepest?" and the other, that of the niggardly, "Why squanderest thou?" This heavy but useless, Sisyphus-like toil shows the state of men who in life incessantly labor for "empty treasures." For riches are in themselves of no avail to man; if an avaricious man could heap up all the gold in the world he could not secure rest. As Dante says of riches,

> these false traitresses promise, if any one rightly regards them, that they will take away all thirst and all deficiency, and will bring satiety and sufficiency. And this they hold out to every man at the outset, guaranteeing the fulfilment of

this promise when they have increased up to a certain measure; and after they are amassed to that extent, in place of satiety and refreshment, they produce and set up feverish and intolerable thirst within the breast; and instead of satisfying a man, they set before him a fresh goal, that is to say, a greater amount to be desired, and, coupled with this, fear and anxiety for what is already gained; so that in truth 'they cannot give rest, but bring more care', which before, in their absence, was not felt.
—Convivio 4.12.39-54.

The sinners in this circle are so deformed by their unintelligent life that they cannot be recognized. This is in accord with the thought of St. Thomas, who writes that we may rank sins according to the good

to which the human appetite is inordinately subjected; and then the lesser the good, the more deformed is the sin: for it is more shameful to be subject to a lower than to a higher good. Now the good of external things is the lowest of human goods: since it is less than the good of the body, and this is less than the good of the soul, which is less than the Divine good. From this point of view the sin of covetousness [avaritia], whereby the human appetite is subjected even to external things, has in a way a greater deformity.

—Summa Theol. II.ii.118.5.

Similarly we read about riches in the Convivio 4.13.142-7:

Wherefore the vileness of riches is made sufficiently manifest by all these indications of it; and therefore the man of right desire and of true knowledge never loves them; and not loving them he does not unite with them, but wishes always to keep them at a distance from him except so far as they are adapted to serve some necessary purpose.

Indeed the best men are unlikely to secure even lawful gains, because "much anxious thought is required for it, and the good generally bestow anxious thought on more important matters,"⁹ such as the perfection of the intellect.

The conventional mediæval punishment for the avaricious in hell is torture with molten gold. Dante, abandoning any attempt at direct suggestion of the physical aspects of the vice, shows by symbol the state the sinners have by their own free will brought on themselves. The punishment also exhibits the correspondence demanded by justice. As they labored on vain things, vain toil punishes them. They deformed their souls by their sins, so their shades in hell, as the representatives of the soul, receive deformity as punishment.

Continuing on their way, the poets come to the Stygian swamp within which are men covered with mud and of angry appearance, who smite themselves and one another not with their hands alone, but with their heads, their breasts, and their feet, and rend themselves and each other with their teeth.¹⁰ This injury both to their neighbors and themselves represents the life the wrathful had lived, for, as Chaucer in the Parson's Tale says of wrath: "Certes, this cursed synne anoyeth bothe to the man hymself and eek to his neighebor." Similarly in Petrarch's Confessional Psalms the wrathful man confesses: "My life was hateful to me, and in my rage I wished

---

⁹ Convivio 4.11.105-7.

¹⁰Inferno 7.112-4. The passage is sometimes interpreted to mean that each one strikes and tears the others, but Scartazzini, in his edition of La Divina Commedia, Milan, 1903, quotes Buti as saying: "Coloro . . . hanno stracciato nel mondo lo prossimo e ancora sè medesimi."

myself to be lost as well as every other man."[11] The injury that the angry man does to himself has been recognized by Aristotle, who writes in Ethics 7.7 that "anybody who acts in anger feels pain in his action." This reproduction of the life on earth in the punishments of hell seems to be indicated when Virgil says of Filippo Argenti:

> That was an arrogant person in the world;
> Goodness is none, that decks his memory;
> So likewise here his shade is furious.
>
> —Inferno 8.46-8.

Dante expresses his wish to see Filippo subjected to his proper punishment, and sees his wish so carried out that he thanks God for its fulfilment.[12] This is in accord with the principle of St. Thomas, who says that "to wish evil to some one under the aspect of justice may be according to the virtue of justice, if it be in conformity with the order of reason," and that it is praiseworthy to desire that vengeance should correct vice and maintain justice.[13] The justice of the counterpassion seems here to be exercised, for the other wrathful shades set on Filippo, as he when alive had attacked other men in his wrath. In addition he turns his teeth on himself, as though to exemplify the state of the wrathful soul. This characteristic action is later seen in the angry Minotaur, who, on seeing Virgil and Dante,

[11] *Romanic Review* 2,434.
[12] Inferno 8.60.
[13] Summa Theol. II.i.46.6; II.ii.158.1, reply 3.

>                   bit himself,
> Even as one whom anger racks within.
>                        —Inferno 12.14-5.

In company with the actively wrathful are the sullen, submerged beneath the waters of the marsh, who say:

>              We sullen were
> In the sweet air, which by the sun is gladdened,
> Bearing within ourselves the sluggish reek;
> Now we are sullen in this sable mire.
>                        —Inferno 7.121-4.

*This again is a plain statement that the punishment of the damned is a continuance of the life they have lived on earth; for St. Thomas writes of the sinners from this type of anger:

> The inordinateness of anger may be considered in relation . . . to the duration of anger, for that anger endures too long; and this may happen . . . because the cause of anger, to wit, the inflicted injury, remains too long in a man's memory, the result being that it gives rise to a lasting displeasure, wherefore he is grievous and sullen to himself.
>                   —Summa Theol. II.ii.158.5.

*The followers of Epicurus, who believed that the soul perished with the body, are punished in just travesty of their false belief by unending enclosure in tombs like those beyond which they chose to believe they would have no existence. As they had inflicted the tomb—that is, the lack of hope of eternal life—on all men, so in strict justice the tomb is inflicted on them. This punishment is just, even to making the tombs more or less hot according to the sin, yet it is inferior in art to some others of Dante's punishments, in that it indicates nothing of the moral state of the sinners.

In the course of the passage of this sixth circle, Virgil explains to Dante the general arrangement of hell. Above are the sinners through incontinence; below those who sinned through malice.[14] Their malicious acts had as their end injury to some other person; that is, they were deliberate acts of injustice, since justice is the virtue that especially deals with the relation of man to others, and the malicious sinner does not act through passion, but deliberately. Some of the actions of the incontinent had been unjust, but since their minds were not fixed in the intention of injuring others, even the avaricious among them are not, as we have seen, to be reckoned with the unjust. The sinners by violence and fraud are, however, all to be classified as sinners against justice, having their minds clear on the subject of the injuries they did to others.[15]

For Dante justice was not merely the foremost of the virtues, more admirable than Hesperus or Lucifer, but it took high rank in another way. Following his teachers, he says that it is the most human of virtues, existing "only in the rational or intellectual part of a man, that is, in his will."[16] Dante

---

[14] Inferno 11.22. I shall not attempt to decide whether bestiality (line 83) is represented in Dante's hell. Torraca, in his note on the passage, says that it is not. Mr. W. H. V. Reade (The Moral System of Dante's Inferno, Oxford, 1909, chap. 24) finds a small place for it.

[15] This subject has been worked out in detail, with a wealth of references to the Latin text of Aristotle, and to the works of St. Thomas, by Mr. Reade (op. cit., chapter 20).

[16] Convivio 1.12.72-4.

here uses the word *intellectual* rather loosely, though the main idea, that justice is in the will, is from St. Thomas.[17] Injustice, as Dante goes on to say in the Convivio, is worthy of hate in proportion as justice is worthy of love, and the sins connected with injustice are inhuman. This explains why the sinners of the seventh, eighth, and ninth circles are worthy of more severe punishments than those above them. Dante, however, as though he were dwelling on the relation of the words *intellectual* and *inhuman,* speaks of fraud alone as "man's peculiar vice," seeming to leave out of the reckoning for the moment the less obviously intellectual injustice by violence.[18] It is true that all but one of the sins against justice mentioned in the Convivio are sins of fraud.[19] Rapine, however, is a sin of violence, and is punished in the seventh circle.

In populating the lower inferno with sinners against justice, Dante was able to develop his views of man and the social organism. These sinners were not merely vile in themselves, but guilty of dragging down all human nature by sinning against the public order, in which alone human virtue can reach its perfection. Hence the part of hell given over to these sinners may be said to represent society at its worst, or society as it would be if injustice were altogether prevalent. The Inferno represents the world wholly deprived of the good government, with

---

[17] Summa Theol. II.ii.58.4. See p. 6, above.

[18] Mr. Reade (pp. 349 ff.) points out that here Dante is not in agreement with either St. Thomas or Cicero.

[19] For the list, see p. 53, above.

its restraint of injustice, for which the author of the De Monarchia longed. It reveals, too, the roots of bad government in personal injustice.

The first sinners encountered after Dante is prepared to observe the varieties of injustice represent rapine. Here are the men who "through violence" have injured others, led in part by "blind cupidity." They have fulfilled the Thomistic conception of injustice, injury to another inflicted because of cupidity. In this circle are the opposites of the just ruler of the De Monarchia,

> Tyrants are these,
> Who dealt in bloodshed and in pillaging.
> —Inferno 12.104-5.

As a penalty they are plunged in boiling blood. To emphasize the propriety of their sufferings, one of the centaurs remarks:

> Justice divine, upon this side, is goading
> That Attila, who was a scourge on earth.
> —Inferno 12.133-4.

Their punishment is striking in its just gradation. The greatest tyrants and conquerors are plunged to the eyebrows in their sanguine bath, while those responsible for less bloodshed rise higher in the stream. The principle of counterpassion is here well observed. The tyrants had driven their victims into rivers of blood; the same treatment is accorded them by the centaurs. Yet in spite of its justice this is one of Dante's less imaginative punishments, founded on the penalty paid by homicides in other mediæval visions, such as that of Alberic of Monte Cassino, part 7. Only the external qualities of the sin are considered.

The next punishment is also strikingly appropriate. The suicides do not appear in the bodily form of which they have deliberately deprived themselves, and even after the last judgment will not be clad in their bodies, which will merely be hung on the trees in which their spirits dwell.

In the words of Peter of Vinea, however, appears a curious contradiction of the principles of Aristotle. He says of his suicide:

> My spirit . . .
> Made me unjust against myself, the just.
>
> —Inferno 13.70-72.

On its face this is impossible, for Aristotle held that a man could not willingly suffer injustice and positively states that the suicide does not treat himself unjustly.[20] Mr. Reade remarks that the "one wholly inadmissible explanation is that [Dante] had forgotten his Aristotle."[21] If this is true, Dante must have had Aristotle's belief in mind when disregarding it. Mr. Reade's assertion is supported by Peter's gnomic words:

> For 'tis not just to have what one casts off.
>
> —Inferno 13.105.

[20] Pp. 51, 63, above.
[21] The Moral System of Dante's Inferno, p. 424.

# THE SUICIDES

They almost echo St. Thomas' statement:

A man's ownership depends on his will, so there is no disproportion if he forfeit something of his own free-will, either by his own or by another's action.

—Summa Theol. II.ii.59.3.

The suicide can lay no just claim to his body since not unjustly deprived of it, hence it is right that he should not have it. When Dante is basing the punishment of the canto on such a principle, it is the more amazing that Peter's first reference to justice should violate it.

Indeed, Dante's whole treatment of the suicides is curious. Having said in Canto 11 that the man with injury as an end "afflicteth others" with force or fraud, Dante here apparently classes injury to oneself with injury to others. St. Thomas says that the suicide "does an injury, not indeed to himself, but to the State and to God,"[22] supporting the latter idea by I Cor. 3.17: 'If any man defile the temple of God, him shall God destroy.' Is it possible that Dante assumed that his readers knew this, and hence neglected to make it clear, but did not intend to indicate that the injury as well as the violence of the suicides was directed against themselves? On such an interpretation the suicides, as sinners against society and God, would make an excellent transition from the tyrants of the first round, to the sinners against God of the third.

Lano and Jacomo are placed here because of the violent excess of their prodigality, which brought

[22] Summa Theol. II.ii.59.3, reply 2.

Lano to his death by suicide. Their violent lives are typified by the wounds they receive as they plunge naked through the forest. This punishment is fitting in its justice, and gives a picture of the evil state of Jacomo and Lano in life, so far as the whole man, including his mind and even his property, can be typified by the body.

Proceeding, the poets come to a place

> where
> A horrible form of Justice is beheld.
> —Inferno 14.5-6.

Here are punished those who have done violence against the Diety by denying and blaspheming him and contemning nature, which is the art of God. The just vengeance of the Almighty, which Dante invokes as he recalls the torments of these souls, shows itself here by giving those who despised his goodness, and perverted it into something vile and hateful, a punishment which is a horrible perversion of nature; the air is thick with flakes that fall like snow on a mountain, but are of fire and ignite the sand of the plain, rather than give any possibility of fruitfulness. Yet this punishment is not sufficient for Capaneus, who appears to care not for the fire, and exclaims: "Such as I was living, am I, dead." And he defies the utmost vengeance of Jove. His chief punishment is that his pride is not abated; indeed no suffering save his own madness could be proportionate to his fury;

> his own despites
> Are for his breast the fittest ornaments.
> —Inferno 14.71-2.

# SINS AGAINST NATURE

Here we have expressed at its clearest the principle that governs the punishments of the whole Inferno; every sinner is in death as he has been in life, and his own wickedness is its own suitable penalty.

Dante next beholds those who by the sin of sodomy have shown their contempt for the processes of nature. They are obliged to keep continually in motion, thus reminding us of those who, having sinned carnally, though in accord with nature, are kept continually in movement by winds. If one of these sinners makes any pause, he is condemned to lie on the burning sand for a hundred years without protecting himself from the fiery snow. This may mean that the sinner through unnatural lust is ever in danger of the sin of blaspheming God directly, and hence of receiving the punishment of the blasphemers.

Unnatural vice is explained by St. Thomas as follows:

Worst of all is the corruption of the principle on which the rest depend. Now the principles of reason are those things that are according to nature because reason presupposes things as determined by nature, before disposing of other things according as it is fitting. . . . In matters of action it is most grave and shameful to act against things as determined by nature. Therefore, since by the unnatural vices man transgresses that which has been determined by nature with regard to the use of venereal actions, it follows that in this matter this sin is gravest of all. . . . The order of nature is from God himself. Wherefore in sins contrary to nature, whereby the very order of nature is violated, an injury is done to God, the Author of nature.

—Summa Theol. II.ii.154.12.

Next Dante beholds the usurers, sitting on the fiery sand and looking fixedly at purses suspended around their necks.[23] These, perhaps because of their relation to the avaricious, whose sin had deprived them of human semblance, Dante cannot recognize, though they are Florentines.

It is commonly said that these are sinners against art, as those preceding them were sinners against nature. However, it seems hardly proper to make this unqualified division. In Canto 11, where Virgil gives the plan of this part of the Inferno, he speaks of the sins of Sodom and Cahors as "disdaining Nature and her bounty," without mentioning art. After a brief interval Dante asks for an explanation of this saying, and is told that nature comes from the divine intellect and from its art. In the De Monarchia 1.3.18 he says that nature is the art of God. Hence violence against nature is violence against the goodness of God. Virgil continues to explain that human art, being founded on nature, is as it were a grandchild of God, and that from art and nature man must gain his bread, and prosper. Then he adds that because the usurer takes another way, he despises nature in herself and in art her follower, since he does not put his trust in nature.[24] Hence the sin of the usurers is primarily against nature and only secondarily against art. Moreover, the art of

[23] Inferno 17.45 ff.
[24] Inferno 11.110-11.
    Per sè natura, e per la sua seguace
    Dispregia, poichè in altro pon la speme.
*Altro* seems to refer to *natura* (in some other than nature), rather than to *la sua seguace* (in some other than art).

# THE USURERS

agriculture, referred to in Genesis 1.28, the passage indicated by Dante, is one of those which, in Convivio 4.9, he puts among the instruments of nature, and hence makes an art in but a minor degree. We may remember also the common belief that while the increase of animals was a proper source of wealth, it was unnatural to receive increase from money, and hence sinful to receive a "breed for barren metal," as Shakespeare calls interest on money. Aquinas plainly says that usury is unnatural.[25] The usurers, then, are primarily sinners against nature, and hence are justly punished in the same circle with those who have done violence directly against God and his methods of showing his goodness.

St. Thomas regarded usury as a sin directly against justice,—

> To take usury for money lent is unjust in itself, because this is to sell what does not exist, and this evidently leads to inequality which is contrary to justice.
>
> —Summa Theol. II.ii.78.1.

The group of sinners in this round show Dante's development of counterpassion. In their perversion these men did not sin against themselves or other individuals alone, but ultimately against God himself. Consequently their punishment, though a just retaliation for their perversion, yet is not a perversion in the particular matter in which each had sinned, but is the same for each, and affects fundamental processes of nature.

[25] See p. 30, above.

Having been carried by Geryon to Malebolge, the two poets see the panders and seducers in the first bolgia. The two kinds are in separate columns, moving in opposite directions. They do not, however, interfere with each other, and the punishment of both is the same; horned demons hurry them on with fierce blows of their whips. One inclines to say that the demons represent the evil passions of both. The panders are said, however, to have been incited by avarice, which can hardly be generally attributed to the seducers. The passions of the two classes would, it seems, not be represented in the same way. As to the justice of the penalty, Virgil's last speech seems significant; after telling of the sorrowful case of Hypsipyle, he says of Jason:

> Such sin unto such punishment condemns him.
> —Inferno 18.95.

One is tempted to render this: Such a sin condemns him to suffering that is like it. The striking thing about the sin seems to be the injury done to Hypsipyle and that done to Medea. On the theory of the counterpassion, then, Jason suffers torment because he has inflicted it on others.[26] The same might be said of the panders. If this be true, Dante seems in this instance to have abandoned the attempt to give an allegory of the lives of the panders and seducers, and to have shown only their punishment.

[26] Reade (p. 340) holds that "the sin of Jason consists in the *nocumentum proximi* [injury to one's neighbor] involved in the false promises made to Isifile."

# THE FLATTERERS AND SIMONISTS

The flatterers of the next bolgia are also held by St. Thomas to oppose the justice of God, when they encourage sin by flattery,—

> for this is contrary to the love of God, against Whose justice he speaks, and contrary to the love of his neighbor, whom he encourages to sin.
> —Summa Theol. II.ii.115.2.

Aquinas also deals with flattery as a fraudulent sin, saying that it is mortal "when one man flatters another, so that by deceiving him he may injure him in body or in soul."

As to their punishment, the flatterers might well cry out with Capaneo, "As I was in life, so I am in death," for the bolgia is foul with the filth of the flatteries in which the sinners are bemired.[27]

Passing to the description of the next bolgia, Dante apostrophizes the Divine Wisdom in admiration of the art it displays in heaven, on earth, and in hell, and of the justice with which it measures out what is fitting. This leads on to expect some special fitness in the punishment. The conduct of the simonists has been marked by perversion of things to their opposites:

---

[27] I have noted two later parallels: "fowle corruption of flatterers" (Barclay, Ship of Foods, 'Of flaterers and glosers'), and "vile and filthier flatteries" (Jonson, Sejanus I, i). The justice of punishing them in filth

> That out of human privies seemed to flow
> (Inferno 18.114)

is emphasized by Swift's idea, in the last part of Gulliver's Travels, chap. 7, that the employment of the sycophant of the Yahoo king was "to lick his master's feet and posteriors."

> Ye who the things of God, which ought to be
> The brides of holiness, rapaciously
> For silver and for gold do prostitute.
>
> —Inferno 19.2-4.

Here we have the antithesis of "brides" and "prostitute," of "holiness" and "rapaciously." Dante in his address shows the utter contrast between the conduct of the pope and that of Jesus and the disciples; he declares that the pope, by doing the opposite of what might be expected of him, trod down the good, and raised up the evil; that instead of worshipping God he has worshipped gold and silver. This recalls to us the conduct of the usurers, avaricious like the pope, who contemned nature and put their trust elsewhere. With this thought of the utter contrast of the simoniac's behavior to his duty as a Christian, Dante exclaims to him, as though in reference to the inverted posture of the pope, thrust head-first into a hole in the ground, and waving his blazing feet in the air:

> Therefore stay here, for thou art justly punished.
>
> —Inferno 19.97.

And he continues with reference to the gains in which the "wealthy Father" was in contrast with St. Peter:

> And keep safe guard o'er the ill-gotten money.

The full propriety of his position, inverted in his "purse" in the earth, is apparent to the pope himself, for he says, as though to indicate that his penalty is the allegory of his life and exhibits counterpassion:

# THE DIVINERS

> Wealth
> Above, and here myself, I pocketed.
> —Inferno 19.72.

To go farther in developing the fitness of this punishment is perhaps fanciful. It has been suggested, however, that the eyes they did not raise to the sky can now behold only the interior of the earth, and that by burrowing in the earth they come in contact with the metals they loved when alive.[28] It is possible to think that the flame which burns the soles of their feet is a perversion of that which rested on the heads of the disciples when they received the gift of the Holy Spirit and Simon Magus offered gold for it.

Looking into the next bolgia, Dante sees men who move backward, with their necks so twisted that their faces are above the middle of their backs. This deformity of the image of man appears to Dante one of the most severe punishments he has seen, and he is moved to tears, but Virgil, who had commended him for desiring the just punishment of Filippo Argenti, rebukes his sentimentality by exclaiming:

> Here pity lives when it is wholly dead.
> —Inferno 20.28.

He adds that no one is baser than he who is troubled by acts of the divine justice. In this he follows St. Thomas, who declares that the righteous should rejoice at the execution of the divine decrees.[29]

---

[28] Scartazzini, *ad loc.*
[29] Summa Theol. III. supp. 94.3.

Those so twisted from human shape are the diviners, who attempted to learn the future by unlawful means, and practised fraud on those who trusted them. St. Thomas, in discussing divination, says that men may know future events in two ways, first, through their causes, and second, through themselves. To foretell the future by the study of causes, as astronomers do eclipses, is lawful, but to try to foretell events whose causes cannot be studied is to arrogate a function

> proper to God, who alone in His eternity sees the future as though it were present. . . . Therefore if any one presumes to foretell or foreknow suchlike future things by any means whatever, except by divine revelation, he manifestly usurps what belongs to God. It is for this reason that certain men are called divines [diviners]: wherefore Isidore says (Etym. viii): They are called divines, as though they were full of God. For they pretend to be filled with the Godhead, and by a deceitful fraud they forecast the future to men.  —Summa Theol. II.ii.95.1.

It seems, then, that Dante thought of the magicians as abandoning the proper form of human mental activity (signified by the normal posture of man) for a kind of activity improper to man (signified by the distorted bodies of the soothsayers). This improper activity is an attempt to usurp the functions of God. So far from being successful, it has led the diviner into "magical illusions" or frauds, where genuine knowledge of the future is impossible. Consequently retaliatory justice has decreed that

> Because he wished to see too far before him
> Behind he looks, and backward goes his way.
>   —Inferno 20.38-9.

# THE BARRATORS AND HYPOCRITES

As the sinner perverted his mind and deprived it of its proper activity, so his body is perverted. In its symbolism of the mental state of the superstitious man, this is one of Dante's most admirably conceived penalties.

In the next bolgia, the punishment is less skillfully devised; rather than presenting the moral condition of the sinners, it gives their material activity. The barrators, or grafters, are concealed beneath boiling pitch. The propriety and justice of the punishment of those who sinned in concealment is well expressed by the demon, who shouts:

> It here behoves thee to dance covered,
> That, if thou canst, thou secretly mayest pilfer.
> — Inferno 21.53-4.

The next bolgia is distinguished by two forms of punishment. The common hypocrites wear gilded leaden mantles, like those of monks, which in retributive justice force on them the appearance of piety, dignity, and splendor that they falsely assumed in life. On their moral qualities and the effects of hypocrisy nothing is said. They are alone among the sinners in wearing clothing to secure the concealment secured by the barrators in a less cleanly way. Even plainer in the exactness of its justice is the crucifixion of Annas, Caiaphas, and their companions in the condemnation of Jesus. As by their conduct toward him they had made themselves the arch hypocrites, they fittingly hear the weight of the punishment of all the other hypocrites, who tread on their prostrate bodies.

Next in order are the thieves, whose crime is one of those mentioned in the Convivio as opposed to justice. First is Vanni Fucci, who is transfixed with a serpent, and as a result burns to ashes; immediately his members are restored as before. The serpents suggest the cunning and slyness of theft, and the burning of Vanni to ashes signifies his violent character, revealed by the sacrilegious nature of his theft, and still preserved in hell, as appears in his defiance of God and Dante's comment thereon:

> Through all the sombre circles of this Hell,
> Spirit I saw not against God so proud.
> —Inferno 25.13-14.

His sacrilege may properly be punished with his theft, for St. Thomas remarks in the Summa Theologica II.ii.66.6 that as a penalty for theft the punishment of death is not inflicted in contemporary courts of law, unless the theft be aggravated by some grave circumstance, as in sacrilege. Altogether the punishment of Vanni is so fully in harmony with his life that Dante might well have written:

> Justice of God! O how severe it is,
> That blows like these in vengeance poureth down![30]

Apparently a significant part of the canto is that telling that some of the sufferers are in human form and some in the form of serpents. Two of them, Cianfa and Agnello, one with the body of a serpent and the other with that of a man, exchange their shapes. Their transformations into serpents un-

[30] Inferno 24.119-20. The more usual reading is *potenzia* (power) instead of *giustizia* (justice).

doubtedly are in harmony with the fraudulent character of their deeds. We may suspect that Cianfa and Agnello had together engaged in a transaction such that by reason of their combination their thefts had been successfully carried on. This seems to appear in Dante's comment:

> Two and yet none did the perverted image
> Appear.
> —Inferno 25.77-8.

Partial loss of human appearance, as we have observed of the avaricious and the usurers, is a suitable penalty for those sinners who set their minds on property rather than on higher things. A few of the thieves lose human semblance more completely than do either of the other classes, for they wholly give it up for that of brutes. This is explained by the following passage from St. Thomas:

A mortal sin is one that is contrary to charity as the spiritual life of the soul. Now charity consists principally in the love of God, and secondarily in the love of our neighbor, which is shown in our wishing and doing him well. But theft is a means of doing harm to our neighbor in his belongings; and if men were to rob one another habitually, human society would be undone.
—Summa Theol. II.ii.66.6.

Stealing tends to bring about the dissolution of society, on which, as the De Monarchia shows, man as a social animal depends for a good life. Hence, since the thief is sinning against human nature, justice requires that he should be punished by loss of human nature, typified by his human form. The allegory represents both the low moral state of the thief, and that of society when theft is not restrained. Dante, with his political interests, is especially impressed by this punishment, and by its connection with his own ill-governed and unjust Florence, from which come five of the thieves. This penalty is not merely one of the most vivid in the Inferno, but one of the most successful in representing the moral state of the unjust man, and the effect of his sin on the social order.

In the next bolgia are punished those who can say of themselves:

> The deeds I did
> Were not those of a lion, but a fox.
> The machinations and the covert ways
> I knew them all.
> —Inferno 27.74-7.

Their covered ways, like those of the barrators and the hypocrites, are expressed by concealment. It is, however, more complete, as their intellectual power had been greater. They are wholly enwrapped by flames that conceal the identity of each, and yet make a display as striking as their deeds had done on earth. Their counterpassion is expressed by saying that the flames make booty of them, for they have made booty of other men and their goods, as when Ulysses craftily took Troy from the Trojans, Achilles from Deidamia, and the Palladium from the temple. A view of the minds of these sinners is afforded not by the nature of their punishment so much as by their narratives. In these, and in the description of their means of communication—the

# THE SOWERS OF DISCORD

sound of the flame reproducing the voice of the sinner[31]—lies much of the art of the canto.

The next bolgia is that

> where is paid the fee
> By those who, sowing discord, win their burden.
> —Inferno 27.135-6.

Further, it is said that they are

> Disseminators of scandal and of schism.
> —Inferno 28.35.

Scandal, according to St. Thomas, exists when,

> while going along the spiritual way, a man may be disposed to spiritual downfall by another's word or deed, in so far, to wit, as one man by his injunction, inducement or example, moves another to sin.
> —Summa Theol. II.ii.43.1.

The kind of ruin to which these sinners have furnished incitement is here limited; they have not encouraged others to any large number of vices, but only to the rupture of the unity of the church, the

---

[31] I cannot believe that the tongues of the sinners are allegorically represented by the flames, as is often suggested (e.g., by Scartazzini and Grandgent). It is true that when Ulysses speaks, the point of the flame does move "as if it were the tongue that spake" (26.89); and when Guido speaks, the point of the flame gives the words the same guise as does the speaking tongue. In other words, the sound of the flames becomes articulate, since the sinners cannot speak directly to Dante. Aside from this comparison to the tongue, in which the flames are not actually called tongues, the idea of tongues of fire may have come from the account of the descent of the Holy Spirit, where the little flames on the heads of the disciples are called tongues in the original, and consequently in the translations. It is said that Dante's flames represent the eloquence with which the false counsellors put forward their plans. It is true that Guido gave false counsel, but judging from his account of the pressure exerted on him, the eloquence was all on the other side. As for Ulysses, he is damned for wiles and tricks, but not for false counsel. This bolgia may properly be called that of the tricksters or strategists, but not that of the fraudulent counsellors.

state, or the family. The first is represented by Mahomet, Ali, and Fra Dolcin, the second by Pier da Medicina, Curio, and Mosca, the third by Bertram dal Bornio. Aquinas says that schism is opposed to both peace and charity; hence it would be opposed to justice. He also writes:

> The sin of schism is, properly speaking, a special sin, for the reason that the schismatic intends to sever himself from that unity which is the effect of charity: because charity unites not only one person to another with the bond of spiritual love, but also the whole church in unity of spirit. Accordingly schismatics properly so called are those who wilfully and intentionally separate themselves from the unity of the Church, for this is the chief unity, and the particular unity of several individuals among themselves is subordinate to the unity of the Church, even as the mutual adaptation of each member of a natural body is subordinate to the unity of the whole body.
> —Summa Theol. II.ii.39.1.

Incidentally the illustration with which the quotation concludes might have furnished Dante with a hint for the allegorical punishment of the schismatics, who have dismembered the Church.

Dante's sinners against the state might have been listed under sedition, which like schism is said by Aquinas to be opposed to peace. They differ in that while schism is opposed to the spiritual unity of the multitude, sedition is opposed to "the temporal or secular unity of the multitude, for instance of a city or kingdom."[32] As St. Thomas says in the following article, "it follows manifestly that sedition is opposed to justice and the common good." The man

[32] Summa Theol. II.ii.42.1, reply 2.

whose injustice takes the form of sedition can properly appear among the fraudulent, for St. Thomas says, in words that remind us of Dante's, that the sin of sedition is "in him who sows discord." Apparently the idea of sowing discord rather than that of schism in its narrow sense is to be taken as the key of this canto.

Emphasis on the political as well as the religious aspect helps one to understand why Dante was so powerfully affected by the sight of these sinners that his eyes became as though drunken, and he longed to stand and weep. The exiled citizen of Florence and author of the De Monarchia was of all men the one to be affected by a sight of the truth about the causers of injustice and misgovernment. The mangled bodies, while representing the moral state of the sinners, without perception of natural and fitting unity, still more clearly signify the state to which they had brought man, as a social being, dependent on organization. In his hatred for such sins, Dante seems to have taken special pains to show how just their punishment is. They "pay their fee"[33] as though in exact recompense; they were sowers of division, and therefore are in the same way divided;[34] and finally Bertram dal Bornio says:

> Because I parted persons so united,
>   Parted do I now bear my brain, alas!
>   From its beginning, which is in this trunk.
> Thus is observed in me the counterpoise.
>
> —Inferno 28.139-42.

[33] Inferno 27.135.
[34] Inferno 28.36.

His concluding line practically says that he is an illustration of the Aristotelian theory of punishment.[35]

The sinners next visited are punished by loathsome diseases, graphically described. Dante lingers over them, as over those in the preceding bolgia, so long as to be rebuked by Virgil. He also twice speaks of justice in connection with them, once as

> the ministress
> Of the high Lord, Justice infallible.
> —Inferno 29.55-6.

and in the next canto as "rigid justice." Hence one expects this sin to be punished with peculiar fitness. Among the falsifiers who occupy the bolgia Dante first encounters the alchemists, suffering from itching leprosy. They appear to him not as men of science, but rather as swindlers who made one metal seem like another, imitating the true with the false. The fraudulent aspect of alchemy, well described by Chaucer in the Canon's Yeoman's Tale, was also familiar to St. Thomas, who writes:

> If the gold and silver produced by alchemists have not the true specific nature of gold and silver, the sale thereof is fraudulent and unjust, especially as real gold and silver can produce certain results by their natural action, which the counterfeit gold and silver of alchemists cannot produce.
> —Summa Theol. II.ii.77.2.

The swindling alchemists are, then, properly placed among the unjust.

After the alchemists are those who deceived by

---

[35] See p. 26, above.

impersonating some one else. They suffer from a mental rather than a physical disease, and are unlike the others in that they are not prostrated by sickness, but able to move freely about. The counterfeiters and liars are punished by dropsy and fever respectively. On lying, which probably generally includes the other types of falsehood, St. Thomas writes thus:

> A lie is evil in respect of its genus, since it is an action bearing on undue matter. For as words are naturally signs of intellectual acts, it is unnatural and undue for anyone to signify by words something that is not in his mind. . . . A lie is sinful not only because it injures one's neighbor, but also on account of its own inordinateness.
> —Summa Theol. II.ii.110.3.

The inordinateness of the lie and the unnatural state of the mind of the living liar are allegorically represented by the disorder of the physical and mental powers of the sufferers in this bolgia. Since the lie is a violation of the order of nature, the punishment is properly sickness or a violation of the natural order of the body, rather than something from without.

In the next article Aquinas says that lying is a mortal sin when its purpose is "to injure one's neighbor, in his person, his possessions or his good name." Obviously this describes the lies of Sinon and Potiphar's wife, and shows their injustice.

St. Thomas also proves that truth is part of justice:

> Truth does not regard legal debt, which justice considers, but rather the moral debt, in so far as, out of equity, one man

owes another a manifestation of the truth. Therefore truth is a part of justice. . . .

Since man is a social animal, one man naturally owes another whatever is necessary for the preservation of human society. Now it would be impossible for men to live together, unless they believed one another, as declaring the truth to one another.

—Summa Theol. II.ii.109.3.

The quotation furnishes another strong reason for Dante's interest in the falsifiers. Falsehood appears in the Convivio[36] in the list of inhuman vices opposed to justice, or the proper organization of society. The deformed and helpless minds and bodies of the falsifiers are symbols not merely of their own state, but of the state of human society that results from falsehood. The crippling of the social life of man which these sinners have brought about is retorted on themselves.

In the last and deepest pit of hell are the sinners most like Satan. The closest human ties have not held them, but they have violated the natural feelings of brothers, patriots, hosts, and beneficiaries. They have betrayed without scruple those who had every reason to trust them, and displayed complete lack of gratitude. By such betrayal and ingratitude they have committed two of the sins that Dante classes as inhuman and especially opposed to justice. Aristotle and St. Thomas also associate gratitude with the proper return of favors required by justice, being of the opinion that the proper requital of benefits is necessary to hold society together. Altogether,

[36] 1.12.80. See p. 54, above, in connection with this and the following paragraph.

## THE ICE OF PRIDE

the sinners in this pit have departed as far from natural human feelings and obligations as is possible for man. Such departure from natural feelings of dependence on and obligation to one's fellows is the result of the capital sin of pride, or *superbia,* which leads the proud man to scorn God, parents, rulers, and friends, as Satan himself scorned his obligations to God.[37] *Superbia* is a sort of gigantic selfishness or surpassing egotism that puts its possessor above all restraint. With it is naturally associated envy, the next of Satan's peculiar vices, which acts against those in any way superior to the proud man, whose undaunted wickedness is excited by the prosperity and goodness of those whose excellence he cannot endure to have greater than his own. So Satan, when envious of God, turned against him in pride. Likewise Cain, whose name is given to one of the parts of the lowest hell, could not endure the goodness of his brother, but being loosed by pride from all restraints, murdered him. The great distinction between the sinners in the lowest pit and those in the higher parts of hell is that those in the pit felt wholly emancipated from the laws necessary to the life of man in society—that is, from the laws of God. St. Thomas thus explains the sin of *superbia:*

On the part of the conversion to a mutable good, there is no reason for pride being the greatest of sins, because uplifting which pride covets inordinately is not essentially most incompatible with the good of virtue. But on the part of

[37] Petrarch, Confessional Psalms, 'Superbia,' in the *Romanic Review* 2, (1911), 432.

the aversion from the immutable good pride has extreme gravity, because in other sins man turns away from God, either through ignorance or through weakness, or through desire for any other good whatever; whereas pride denotes aversion from God simply through being unwilling to be subject to God and His rule. Hence Boethius says that while all vices flee from God, pride alone withstands God; for which reason it is especially stated (James iv.6) that God resisteth the proud. Wherefore aversion from God and His commandments, which is a consequence as it were in other sins, belongs to pride by its very nature, for its act is the contempt of God. And since that which belongs to a thing by its nature is always of greater weight than that which belongs to it through something else, it follows that pride is the most grievous of sins by its genus, because it exceeds in aversion [from the immutable good] which is the formal complement of sin.

—Summa Theol. II.ii.162.6.

So these sinners are justly punished. Their icy arrogance is inflicted on themselves, for the ice that grips them typifies the state of their hearts in life, without warm natural feeling. Indeed the world for them was an utterly cold and unloving place, frozen by winds stirred from the wings of Satan. St. Augustine makes plain the fitness of their punishment:

The devil and his angels, having turned away from the light and warmth of charity, and having advanced very far into pride and envy, are as it were torpid in icy hardness. And hence through a figure they are put in the north.[38]

The propriety of the penalty of Judas, Brutus, and Cassius is evident. In life they gave themselves

[38] Epistle 140, sect. 55. See also Confessions 10.59. Bromiardus (Sermon 8, on 'Pena') says that the envious are cold, for their minds freeze on seeing the prosperity and happiness of others. For Satan in the north, see Milton's Paradise Lost 5.686.

over to Satan as no other men had ever done; so they receive punishment directly from him. Judas is the greatest sinner against God and the spiritual life of man; Brutus and Cassius are the greatest sinners against the political life so necessary to man's perfection. Hence this trio can be punished by no less worthy demon than the author of evil himself.

As for Satan, having attempted to overthrow God, he has himself been overthrown. Made as foul as once he was fair, he has been hurled from the highest heaven, to which he aspired, to the lowest hell, and the complete power for which he strove has resulted in helplessness, save that he can aid in tormenting his own followers.

Dante has now completed one stage of his journey. He has seen that in spite of their apparent power and prosperity on earth, in spite of their success in perverting the best life of man by corrupting society, the forces of evil are not free to act as they will, but are finally subject to God. The evil man receives full and exact punishment for all the evil he does. However his life may appear, it is in the grasp of the divine justice, which is continually exacting the proper fee from all living men who set themselves to do evil. For them life itself is hell.

# CHAPTER V

### THE PURGATORIO: JUSTICE IN HUMAN SUFFERING

From hell, the allegory of the life of the thoroughly wicked, Dante passes to purgatory, the allegory of those who, though not without spot, are not deliberate and constant in evil. They bear their sufferings with content because thereby they are purified from sin. Their world is a world of affliction, but of the affliction that works out an eternal weight of glory. The Purgatorio sets out from the question: Why did God make suffering and affliction part of the daily life of man? Dante's answer is that these sufferings counteract man's tendency to evil, and keep him disciplined to the good life. The sufferings of the literal purgatory are in fulfilment of the penalties for sins committed in the flesh. If, however, a man while alive bears with patience sufficient affliction, he may escape the pains of purgatory. The connection between the sufferings of this life and those of purgatory is so close that Dante can easily make the Purgatorio the allegory of living men who patiently bear the divine penalties.

On punishments which are inflicted by God, and yet do not contradict the sufferer's own will, St. Thomas writes as follows:

The act of sin makes man deserving of punishment, in so far as he transgresses the order of Divine justice, to which he cannot return except he pay some sort of penal compensation, which restores him to the equality of justice; so that, according to the order of Divine justice, he who has been too indulgent to his will, by transgressing God's commandment, suffers, either willingly or unwillingly, something contrary to what he would wish. This restoration of the equality of justice by penal compensation is also to be observed in injuries done to one's fellow men. Consequently it is evident that when the sinful or injurious act has ceased there still remains the debt of punishment.

But if we speak of the removal of sin as to the stain, it is evident that the stain cannot be removed from the soul, without the soul being united to God, since it was through being separated from Him that it suffered the loss of its brightness, in which the stain consists. Now man is united to God by his will. Wherefore the stain of sin cannot be removed from man, unless his will accept the order of Divine justice, that is to say, unless either of his own accord he take upon himself the punishment of his past sin, or bear patiently the punishment which God inflicts on him; and in both ways punishment avails for satisfaction. Now when punishment is satisfactory, it loses somewhat of the nature of punishment; for the nature of punishment is to be against the will; and although satisfactory punishment, absolutely speaking, is against the will, nevertheless in this particular case and for this particular purpose, it is voluntary.

—Summa Theol. II.i.87.6.

In this passage Aquinas deals with sin that has actually been committed, but elsewhere we learn that affliction may also be medicine against not only the sins of the past, but also those of the present and the future.[1] Hence the pains of the Purgatorio may denote all the spiritual afflictions that may come to any who has a tendency to error that needs correction. This aspect of purgatory, as the allegory of the hard things of life rooting out from man the sin

---

[1] See p. 62, above.

that became his lot as a son of the fallen Adam, explains at least why the Purgatorio is little concerned with the social effects of sin; the question is that of the individual spirit. For the social aspects of this *cantica* one must go to the visions of the latter part. The sins of the Inferno, on the contrary, are those that became manifest in human society, often as acts of injustice. Hence specific sinful acts are usually selected for punishment. In the Purgatorio the roots of sin rather than its effect on the social order are in question. Consequently the Purgatorio deals directly with the seven capital sins, which lie at the bottom of all acts of sin, and are potential in every heart, though they may never come to the surface.

The justice of the afflictions of purgatory is plain. They are the direct result of something in man that requires the remedy provided by the punishment. In fact, the desire of the sufferers to endure is of itself almost enough to establish the justice of the penalties, for, as we have seen,[2] Aristotle believed that no one could voluntarily suffer injustice.

It is not, however, sufficient that there be justice in the infliction alone, but the penalty must correspond with the sin with the exactness demanded by justice. The retaliation must be as fitting as it was in hell. In purgatory, however, the allegory is that of opposition to sin. "The hurt that had been caused by self-indulgence must be cured by self-denial." The punishments are not for eternal torment, but for medicinal effect, to purge the sinner of his sin,

[2] P. 51, above.

as St. Thomas puts it in his remarks on purgatorial punishment.³ As has been observed, Aquinas mentions this aspect of punishment in his commentary on the Ethics; the same idea is found elsewhere and was evidently common.⁴ Another metaphor for the punishments of purgatory is that they make straight what was crooked,⁵ as by a bending in the direction contrary to that caused by the sin. Consequently, with the account of each sin naturally comes the remedy against it, somewhat as in Chaucer's Parson's Tale, where the analysis of each sin is followed by a section with a heading in the form Remedium Contra Peccatum Superbiæ (Remedy against the Sin of Pride). Chaucer in every case thinks of the virtues most opposed to the sin in question. Dante does not neglect this aspect, in the examples of virtue presented to the sinners, yet he also thinks much of the remedy provided by affliction. The various afflictions must be remedies calculated to purge the heart of the vice in question, and hence opposed to it.

The notion of punishments opposed to sins was current in Dante's century. Indeed, Bromiardus, a

³ Summa Theol. III. supp. 97.1. Compare Robertus Holkot: "Purgatory is the hospital of God, where the sick are placed to be cured" (Opus, lectio 193). St. Bernard of Clairvaux writes of purgatory: "I will go into this region, and I will see this great vision of the way in which the pious Father leaves his sons who are to be glorified in the hands of the tempter, not that they may be killed, but that they may be purged" (Sermones de Diversis 42).

⁴ See p. 62, above.

⁵ Purgatorio 23.126, quoted on p. 135, below. In his commentary on Ethics 2, lectio 11, St. Thomas writes of effort against sin that Aristotle "uses the simile of those who straighten crooked pieces of wood; who when they wish to straighten them, bend them the other way, and so they are brought to the mean." Some of Dante's Italian words echo the Latin of the passage. See Appendix.

late contemporary of Dante's, says there are penalties of two sorts, those opposed to sins, and those similar to them. Some of his examples of opposite penalties are like those of Dante's Purgatorio:

The effeminate and slothful, who on earth seek how they may live without bodily exertion, in hell have no rest. The gluttons who here eat to excess, there suffer hunger.
—Sermon 6, 'Pena.'

Bromiardus is discussing hell, yet since Augustine, followed by Gregory and Aquinas,[6] makes no distinction between the punishments of hell and those of purgatory, there is no reason why his classification should not be carried over to purgatory. But Dante had already used in hell the type of punishment similar to the offence, or suggesting it; hence, in presenting a definite and consistent allegory of hell and purgatory, he must employ in purgatory a kind of penalty unlike that of hell, as the meaning of the two regions is different.

The law of the contrary penalty in medicinal punishment is also stated by St. Thomas, though not in relation to purgatory, which is not much discussed in the Summa Theologica. It seems, none the less, that his words should be decisive for Dante's allegorical practice:

When the stain is removed, the wound of sin is healed as regards the will. But punishment is still requisite in order that the other powers of the soul may be healed, since they were disordered by the sin that was committed, so that, to wit, the disorder may be remedied by the contrary of that

[6] Summa Theol. III, app. 2, art. 2. Contrast Summa Theol. III supp. 97.1, reply 2.

which caused it. Moreover punishment is requisite in order to restore the equality of justice, and in order to remove the scandal given to others, so that those who were scandalized at the sin may be edified by the punishment.

—Summa Theol. II.i.87.6.

Having in some instances clearly adopted punishments opposite to the sins, like those of Bromiardus, it seems unlikely that Dante would have shifted his method of purging other sins, and given penalties imitative of the sins, like those of hell. If he has done so, the exact and careful structure characteristic of his work has been in this instance abandoned; and the punishments, while just, have no special significance in themselves, or definite relation to the sin. Indeed an imitative punishment, being like those of hell, might be supposed to immerse the sinner more deeply in evil rather than to free him from it. If the penalties of the entire Purgatorio are not of the same nature, no consistent allegory for this part of the Commedia can be found. Purgatory would sometimes resemble hell, sometimes differ from it; it could not represent a different aspect of man's earthly life. It is, however, highly probable that Dante did intend a consistent allegory of the justice of God in sending afflictions especially suited to purge the hearts of men from specific vices, and consequently that the punishments of purgatory are all of one nature, and opposed to the vices on which they act.[7]

---

[7] The idea that the penalties of purgatory are opposed to the sins they punish is briefly set forth by R. Fornaciari in an article entitled *Sulla pene assegnate da Dante alle anime del Purgatorio*, in *Giornale Dantesco* 1 (1894), 366. Nicola Zingarelli (*Bulletino della Società*

Before Dante and Virgil, in their passage through purgatory, encounter any of the spirits undergoing punishment, they have various experiences that prepare them for what they are to see. First they meet a group of spirits who have just arrived in purgatory. In contrast with the weeping souls by the River Styx, they are singing a psalm of deliverance. Seeing among them his friend Casella, Dante expresses surprise that he has not been earlier brought by the angel to the mount. Casella replies in words which show the desire of all the souls in purgatory to submit themselves to the divine justice, as those in hell are in rebellion against it:

> No outrage hath been done me,
> If he who takes both when and whom he pleases
> Has many times denied to me this passage,
> For of a righteous [just] will his own is made.
> —Purgatorio 2.94-8.

In ante-purgatory Dante encounters Manfred, who repented at the very end of his life and died unreconciled with the Church. He illustrates the possibility of hope for man, for, as he tells us, his escape from the hopeless inferno, even though his sins were horrible, shows that

> is not so lost
> Eternal Love, that it cannot return,
> So long as hope has anything of green.
> —Purgatorio 3.133-5.

Man's lot is in his own hands so long as he does not wholly give over the mastery of himself to evil.

*Dantesca Italiana*, n.s., 1 (1894), 132) does not wholly accept the idea. It is also very briefly stated by Franz Hettinger, Die Göttliche Komödie (Freiburg, 1889), p. 342.

## LOVE SATISFIES JUSTICE

Further on are a group of active men whose lives were suddenly cut off by violence, and who repented with their last gasps. Buonconte of Montefeltro, one of these, tells how at the moment of his death a demon came for him and shrieked to the angel of God who bore him away:

> Thou bearest away the eternal part of him,
> For one poor little tear, that takes him from me.
> —Purgatorio 5.106-7.

This reaffirmation of the thought of Manfred, joined with the large number of those who secured hope of heaven by delayed repentance, suggests that Dante is emphasizing his idea by repetition. It lies near the heart of his work, for he is declaring that a man is not condemned by God for any number of evil deeds, but only for a character in which evil wholly rules. Here is the influence of Aristotle's doctrine of the moral bent. So long, Dante thinks, as there is a spark of good left in a man, something of the good and happy life may be possible. A little good, giving man something of hope, has in it power for the overthrow of a great amount of evil, for good is the power for victory in the world. One who in any degree desires righteousness has potency to become altogether righteous. Virgil, in explaining why the prayers of the living avail the dead, shows the propriety of this:

> For top of judgment doth not vail itself,
> Because the fire of love fulfills at once
> What he must satisfy who here installs him.
> —Purgatorio 6.37-9.

Justice is not abandoned; it is satisfied by love.

When Dante arrives at the gate of purgatory, the angel who guards it explains that he received the keys from St. Peter, who commanded him to err rather in admitting the unworthy, if they kneeled and asked admission, than in shutting out the deserving. He adds, also, that he who looks back, after having entered purgatory, is forced to return. His words restate what Dante has already said in this *cantica:* that the desire for good always receives its full due from eternal justice and that no external test is imposed. The desire to live the good life, bearing affliction, is ever granted. Yet there is no absolute escape from condemnation. To look back with longing from the cleansing pains imposed by the divine justice is to be thrown beyond the gates.

Dante and Virgil first enter the circle where pride, or *superbia,* the chief of the seven capital sins, is punished. The sinners are crushed almost to the earth by heavy burdens of rocks. Moved to pity even by the memory of this sight, the poet writes in apostrophe to Christians who in pride—another name for infirmity of mind—trusted in their own misguided steps. In a similar strain St. Thomas writes:

Knowledge of truth is twofold. One is purely speculative, and pride hinders this indirectly by removing its cause. For the proud man subjects not his intellect to God, that he may receive the knowledge of truth from Him, according to Matth.xi.25, 'Thou hast hid these things from the wise and prudent,' i.e. from the proud, who are wise and prudent in their own eyes, 'and hast revealed them to little ones,' i.e. to the humble: nor does he deign to learn anything from man, whereas it is written (Ecclus.vi.34): 'If thou wilt incline

## THE CONTRADICTORY OF PRIDE

thine ear, thou shalt receive instruction.' The other knowledge of truth is affective, and this is directly hindered by pride, because the proud, through delighting in their own excellence, disdain the excellence of truth; thus Gregory says (Moral.xxiii.10) that the proud, although certain hidden truths be conveyed to their understanding, cannot realize their sweetness: and if they know of them they cannot relish them. Hence it is written (Prov.xi.2): 'Where humility is there also is wisdom.'

—Summa Theol. II.ii.162.3.

Dante continues his apostrophe by asking if men did not remember that they were but worms of the dust, and that for all their pride their souls must go naked before the eternal justice. But now, in contrast to the unjustified self-confidence of their lives, the faces of even the more lightly punished seem to say: "I can do no more." As they pass, they repeat, in amplified form, the Lord's Prayer, expressing man's utter dependence on God:

> Come unto us the peace of thy dominion,
> For unto it we cannot of ourselves,
> If it come not, with all our intellect.
>
> —Purgatorio 11.7-9.

They give over their wills as sacrifices to God, and humbly ask for the daily food without which they could not live. As for their own merit, they pray that, because of its lack of value, God will not consider it in judging them. This is the utter contradiction of pride, which consists, as St. Thomas says, in "aversion from God simply through being unwilling to be subject to God and His rule."[8]

[8] Summa Theologica II.ii.162.6.

Among the proud, Dante talks with Odersi, who disclaims the high reputation Dante gives him, and says that in life he would have been less courteous, because of his "great desire of excellence"—that is, because of his pride, for St. Thomas says that "pride covets excellence inordinately," and that "pride denotes immoderate desire of one's own excellence," which leads a man to think that "he has from himself that which he has from God," or that what he has received from above is "due to his own merits."[9] Odersi indicates as much in the next line:

> Here of such pride is paid the forfeiture.[10]

The price rendered to justice is that he now does among the dead what he would not, before his repentance, do among the living.

The burden of rocks may indicate any affliction, such as failure to succeed in an enterprise, that could break down pride. Eyes bent on the ground are appropriate for those who desire to escape pride, for the reverse is the attitude usual to the sin, as Dante indicates when he writes:

> Now wax ye proud, and on with looks uplifted,
> Ye sons of Eve, and bow not down your faces
> So that ye may behold your evil ways!
> —Purgatorio 12.70-2.

Petrarch in his Confessional Psalms makes the proud man say: "I raised up my horns, and looked

---

[9] Summa Theol. II.ii.162.4 and 8.

[10] Purgatorio 11.88. The same idea of a just price appears in lines 125-6:
> Such money renders back
> In payment he who is on earth too daring.

on the sky." There is also in Proverbs 21.4 the association of "a high look and a proud heart." By a punishment that turns the eyes to the opposite extreme, the balance of justice is restored.

The poets next stand on the terrace appropriated to the punishment of envy. The garments of the penitents are so like their rocky background that Dante cannot at first distinguish them, as they sit like beggars against the rocks. They represent the sort of affliction which a penitent man could use as an aid against envy. He whose condition is so bad that it cannot be improved is not tempted by envy as is the rising, ambitious man. Drawing still nearer, Dante sees that the eyelids of the sufferers are sewed together with wire and they are totally blind. The reason of this is apparent; unless one sees, either literally or figuratively, the goods of others, one can hardly be envious. Since envy is caused chiefly by material possessions, as St. Thomas points out,[11] the eye is often the gate of envy. We have at present such expressions as "to look with envious eyes," and something of the sort was evidently current in Dante's time, for in Petrarch's Confessional Psalms the prayer against envy runs: "Oh Lord, remove from me envious eyes, that I may see and do what is straight and right." At a later time Bacon wrote:

Envy and love come easily into the eye, especially upon the presence of the objects, which are the points that conduce to fascination, if any such thing there be. We see likewise the Scripture calleth envy an evil eye; . . . so there still

[11] Summa Theol. II.ii.36.2.

seemeth to be acknowledged, in the act of envy, an ejaculation or irradiation of the eye.[12]

This recalls the original meaning of the Latin *invidia*, coming from *invidere* (*in* + *videre*, to see), which meant *to look askance at, to look maliciously or spitefully at*. By derivation, then, envy is a matter of sight. In addition to Mark 7.22, the passage Bacon refers to, there is another Biblical passage in which envy is also a matter of the eye, for the Vulgate version of 1 Samuel 18.9 relates that the envious Saul, after David had been praised above him, "was accustomed to look at David with eyes that were not straightforward."

The justice of Dante's conception is clear. The envious are redressing the balance by giving up the faculty through which they had especially sinned. The loss of sight may signify retirement from the world through sickness or exile, so that the victim is less tempted to envy, and more certain, because blind to the world, "of beholding the high light" of heaven.[13]

On the next ledge, that of wrath, Dante and Virgil encounter a cloud of smoke or vapor, so dense that the darkness it causes is deeper than that of hell itself; moreover, it is so painful to the eyes that Dante is obliged to keep his closed.[14] He hears

[12] Of Envy. In the Sylva Sylvarum 944 Bacon remarks that envy is of greatest force when the cast of the eye is oblique. For "obliquo oculo" (oblique eye) meaning *envy* see Horace, Epistles 1.14.37. Bacon's Sylva, and to some extent his essays, are collections of matter of considerable antiquity.

[13] Purgatorio 13.86.

[14] Proverbially, an annoyance is "as smoke to the eyes" (Peele, Old Wives' Tale 271). This proverb is said to appear also in Italian.

spirits passing by and praying to the peaceful Lamb of God for peace and mercy. These prayers are most appropriate, for peace would not be the usual possession of the angry man, and mercy or clemency, as St. Thomas explains, diminishes anger.[15] In this prayer there is among the spirits "all harmony"; hence their condition is opposite to that of the angry and contentious. The penalty of the smoke is the more difficult to understand because it is not described at length, and because only a single penitent, of whose sins we know nothing, is mentioned; he, moreover, does not say anything of the sin from which he is purifying himself. From Marco's own statement that he was a lover of virtue, we can only infer that Dante did not regard anger as the most serious of the sins he describes. In this he is in agreement with St. Thomas,[16] who shows its connection with justice and explains that it is more reasonable, more dependent on bodily constitution, more open, and brought about by a more definite cause than sins of concupiscence.

In explanation of the penalty, Perez writes:

The smoke which issues from fire is a part which the fire separates from itself that it may heat better and be clearer, and is something that does not furnish either greater heat or softer light, but merely deadens and darkens the fire. Hence it is just that in the midst of very dense smoke they should think on their peculiar sin who once from the fire of wrath obtained smoke to put out or to deaden with thoughts of vengeance the fire of charity, and to cloud with dark appearances the light of truth. . . . This smoke is likened by

---

[15] Summa Theol. II.ii.157.4.
[16] Summa Theol. II.i.46.6,7; 47.3; II.ii.156.4; 158.

the poet to fog, and to thick and humid mists, because, perhaps, just as the fog and the mists make objects appear much larger than they are, so wrath increases beyond their proper size the forms of wrongs and injuries, and increases the causes of one's own pains. It is compared to night without stars, and to the gulf of the inferno, because no one is wise enough to foresee to what perils and enormities we can be conducted in the midst of the clouds of wrath.[17]

Charles Eliot Norton writes: "The gloom and the smoke symbolize the effects of anger on the soul."[18] And Dean Plumptre remarks: "To be conscious of wrath is to be in hell, with all its blackness of darkness, its bitterness and foulness."[19]

The suggestion made explicit in the last quotation is implied in the others, and seems to be the common interpretation. But is it a possible one? To accept it is to assume that in purgatory Dante has represented another hell. But, as has been observed, the principles governing purgatory are quite unlike those governing hell, though in both regions the punishments are not arbitrary, but are fitted to the nature of the place and to the character of the sinner and of his sin. To assume anything else is to overlook the carefully elaborated significance of the various parts of Dante's creation, and bring the whole to confusion. In hell the sinners are in the presence of the sins in which they lived, but in purgatory the former sinners are in the presence of the corrective for their sins. In the Inferno the

---

[17] I Setti Cerchi del Purgatorio di Dante, Verona, 1867, p. 151.

[18] Translation of the Divine Comedy, Boston, 1902, *ad loc.*

[19] Translation of the Divina Commedia, Boston, 1907, note on Purgatory 16.1.

## THE SWIFTNESS OF WRATH

wrathful are as furious against each other and against themselves as ever they have been in life, but this cannot be true of the Purgatorio. We do read of smoke in the description of the wrathful in hell, and of smoke in the account of the third ledge of purgatory, but the smoke of hell is not the essential part of the punishment there. Hence it seems hardly possible to say that the smoke of the third ledge represents the blinding effect of anger. The punishment is caused by anger and is the penalty for it, but is not, if purgatory is distinct in meaning from hell, an allegory for the sin itself.

Perhaps the irritating quality of the smoke, which affects Dante, furnishes training in patience. Something further is suggested by observing that the penitent are cut off from the sight of their fellows and from all easy contact with them, and that they are obliged to move very slowly and with great care; Dante tells how he himself walked behind Virgil—

> E'en as a blind man goes behind his guide,
>   Lest he should wander, or should strike against
>   Aught that may harm or peradventure kill him,
> So went I through the bitter and foul air.
> —Purgatorio 16.10-13.

Such caution is quite the opposite of the conduct of the angry man, who rushes to do injury to his fellows. St. Thomas remarks that "anger would seem to have a certain pre-eminence on account of the strength and quickness of its movement," and that it is characterized by "impetuosity, whereby it precipitates the mind into all kinds of inordinate action."[20] He perhaps derived this from Aristotle's Ethics, 7.7, where it is said that "wrath, on account of the heat and swiftness of its nature, when it hears something, does not stop to understand it, and goes on to inflict punishment." On the other hand, complete lack of the passion of anger, which is also a vice, occurs when the movement of the will is altogether lacking or weak.[21] As Dante explains of the avaricious and the prodigal, opposite vices receive their punishments on the same ledge of purgatory. He cannot, however, easily show the punishment of the opposite of anger, for it would require a penalty something like that of sloth, on the next ledge. So characteristic is rapid movement of the sin of anger that even in virtuous and commendable wrath,

the movement of anger should not be immoderately fierce, neither internally nor externally, and if this condition be disregarded, anger will not lack sin, even though just vengeance be desired. —Summa Theol. II.ii.158.2.

St. Thomas also suggests that separation from the object of anger soon causes anger to subside; the isolation of the sinners on this terrace is part of their punishment. Dante seems here to be representing the enforced and painful opposites necessary to redress the balance of justice that has been weighed down by anger, or as he puts it, to untie the knot that anger has tied.[22]

[20] Summa Theol. II.ii.158, 4 and 6; see also II.i.46.5.
[21] Summa Theol. II.ii.158.8.
[22] Purgatorio 16.24. Professor Grandgent makes this penalty something of an opposite, saying that the smoke is "a symbol of the energetic stifling of angry passion" (Argument to Canto XV, in his edition of La Divina Commedia, Boston, 1913).

## SLOTH AND AVARICE

On the next terrace, in the punishment of sloth, the penalty is obviously intended to restore the balance of justice by means of the opposite. Those who have been slow are moving at their best speed. This compensatory haste is called justice by the penitents themselves.[23] It typifies the painful necessity for exertion which helps the man who desires to overcome a tendency to sloth. The full heart of these men is in their retribution, for they say:

> So full of longing are we to move onward,
> That stay we cannot; therefore pardon us.
>
> —Purgatorio 18.115-6.

Dante next passes to the terrace where avarice receives its punishment, which is the most bitter in purgatory. We remember that avarice, according to St. Thomas, is the sin which, because it subjects the human heart to external things, "has in a way a greater deformity" than the rest.[24] As we learn from the treatise De Monarchia, this is probably the sin which Dante hated more than any other, because it opposed justice and so prevented the full realization of the good of man.[25] Hence it is especially appropriate that Dante should not only mention the justice of the punishment of this sin, but should also say that by justice it was made "less hard."[26] The penitent avaricious, having been especially opposed to justice, are in penitence especially devoted to it.

[23] Purgatorio 18.117.
[24] Summa Theol. II.ii.118.5. See p. 81, above.
[25] See pp. 16 ff., above.
[26] Purgatorio 19.77.

They are bound hand and foot, with their faces to the earth:

> Even as our eye did not uplift itself
> Aloft, being fastened upon earthly things,
> So justice here has merged it in the earth.
> As avarice had extinguished our affection
> For every good, whereby was action lost,
> So justice here doth hold us in restraint,
> Bound and imprisoned by the feet and hands;
> And so long as it pleases the just Lord
> Shall we remain immovable and prostrate.
> —Purgatorio 19.118-26.

Commentators on this passage usually say that the punishment of avarice is imitative of the sin. This opinion is founded chiefly on the first three lines of the quotation, which represent as brought to earth the eyes which did not elevate themselves to heaven, but were fixed on earthly things. Perez[27] and, apparently, Professor Grandgent[28] believe that the penitent are bound because they were not active in doing good when alive.[29] This interpretation first

---

[27] *Op. cit.*, p. 201.

[28] "Those whose eyes were fixed on vile earthly goods must lie with their faces in the dust; those who eschewed useful activity are now tight bound and motionless" (Argument to Canto XIX). But see notes 31 and 32, below.

[29] Torraca, in his edition of La Divinia Commedia (Rome, 1905), seems also to indicate that the binding of the penitents signifies avarice, for he rejects the generally accepted reading *spense,* in line 121, and apparently quite on his own authority, proposes *strinse,* to correspond with *stretti, legati,* and *presi.* This emendation violates the principle that of two readings the more difficult is to be preferred; and there is danger in making unsupported changes in text to support an interpretation. The reading *spense* is not contradictory to the passage in which St. Thomas suggests that the love of riches may lead a man to act against the love of God and of his neighbor (Summa Theol. II.ii.118.4). In Convivio 4.13 Dante himself points out that the possession of riches is a deprivation of good, and makes the assertion positive, calling riches vile. To be sure riches are, as

leads us to examine lines 115-7:

> What avarice does is here made manifest
> In the purgation of these souls converted,
> And no more bitter pain the Mountain has.

Do they mean that the penalty shows, by its nature, just what the sin of avarice does? that is, do the penalties imitate avarice? We may answer that these lines, with those immediately preceding, give the announcement, such as we are accustomed to find in the description of each terrace, of the sin there punished. For example, that telling of the nature of the first ledge runs:

> Here of such pride is paid the forfeiture.
> —Purgatorio 11.88.

Hence the simplest meaning here would be: Avarice is the sin for which the souls in this circle are punished. More literally it would be: What avarice causes is shown here by the purgation of the converted souls. The next line, saying that the punishment here is heavier than elsewhere, suggests that the speaker, Pope Adrian, means that avarice is a more serious sin than any of the others. It seems, then, that it is hardly necessary to think that lines 115-7 indicate that what follows gives a picture of avarice as it is, rather than a representation of a

St. Thomas and Dante knew, in a sense good. However, if in that sense the avaricious man is not deprived of "every good," he certainly cannot be represented as eagerly desiring "every good," for at most he desires only lesser and material goods. Hence it would seem that the emendation should be rejected, even by those who accept the usual interpretation of the meaning of the passage. Does an interpretation which needs the assistance of a change in text give Dante's meaning?

penalty resulting from avarice and suited to purge it from the heart. It is evident that the announcement of the sin punished, and of the quality of the punishment, in lines 115-7, is naturally followed by details of the nature of the sin and the penalty, lines 118-24.

In lines 118-20 the play on words is evident. The eyes which were not raised to heaven are now plunged to earth; the eyes once fixed on things of the earth now regard the earth itself. The question arises: Are earthly things and the earth substantially identical? or can we feel that there is instead a contrast in meaning? Earthly things are the good things of this earth which the eyes of those who are now groveling in the dust no longer look upon.[30] In fact we have here a condition not unlike that of the envious; they did not look upward, but made bad use of their eyes, and hence they are wholly deprived of the use of them; so the avaricious are now unable to look with longing eyes upon the good things of the world. It might seem that the proper corrective would have been to look upward, but purgatory is a place of remorse, and not of joy.

In lines 121-6 the parts beginning with *As* and *So* are connected by an evident play on words. The connection in idea seems to be between "whereby was action lost" (which might freely be rendered: they labor in vain) and the immovable state of the tightly bound penitents. In life they had labored inces-

---

[30] Professor Grandgent writes: "Allegorically the discipline signifies the averting of the mind from worldly things and the humble renunciation of glory and power" (Arg. to Canto XIX).

santly to obtain riches; now they are prevented from entering upon any sort of activity.[31] This is quite in harmony with Dante's thought. In the Convivio 4.12,13 and 14 he sets forth the continual care, and yet the complete lack of proper satisfaction, which attends the possession of wealth. In the Inferno he is even plainer, for where can a better example of vain labor be found than in the Sisyphus-like toil of the avaricious and the prodigal, uselessly rolling their heavy stones around the circle?

We may also observe that the prodigal, as Statius tells us, are associated with the avaricious in purgatory as they were in hell. He indeed makes the assertion of all purgatory,

> that the transgression which rebuts
> By direct opposition any sin
> Together with it here its verdure dries.[32]

Dante, however, specifically mentions the opposite vice here only, perhaps because only on this terrace can he show contrary vices punished by the same penalty. The punishment is evidently enough opposed to the sins of the inordinately wasteful, who have devoted as great energy to spending as have the avaricious to the business of getting.

Such suffering as Dante pictures was known in his age as the just opposite of the sin of avarice. Bromiardus, in giving a list of penalties inflicted in

[31] Professor Grandgent explains: "Those who spent their energy on pelf . . . lie prostrate on the ground" (Dante, New York, 1921, p. 364).

[32] Purgatorio 22.49-51. Do the last two words imply opposition of sin and penalty? They may be rendered: "withers its green leaves."

hell as the contraries of certain sins, writes as follows:

> The covetous who get and keep great estates and many beautiful mansions, and gold and silver, avidly accumulating personal and real property, and getting rich through ill-got profits, in hell lie in a very narrow pit, lacking everything good, and without hope of consolation lamenting and quoting from the fifth chapter of the Wisdom of Solomon: What good hath riches with our vaunting done us? All those things are passed away like a shadow.
> —Sermon 8, 'Pena.'

It seems, then, that the punishment of the avaricious represents the proper opposite and corrective of the sin, rather than imitates the sin itself. As Statius puts it, the desire of those punished in purgatory is not for the sin, but, through divine justice and contrary to the will, for the torment that frees them from it.[33] If the sinner is still living with his sin, it is difficult to see that purgatory is in this respect unlike hell in allegorical significance—but this is to reduce Dante's careful allegory to chaos. If the avaricious exhibit the *remedium contra peccatum avariciæ* (remedy against the sin of avarice), their lot is full of instruction.

As in the circle immediately below that of avarice the nature of the purgation is strikingly opposite to that of the sin, so it is on the terrace just above—that of the gluttons, who suffer the pangs of unsatisfied desire for the food which they had taken in sinful excess in their lives. When alive they had doubtless shown all the signs of their over-indul-

[33] Purgatorio 21.64-6.

gence; but in purgatory they are so emaciated as not to be recognizable. Yet their sufferings are as though self-inflicted, for Forese Donati explains:

> All of this people who lamenting sing,
>   For following beyond measure appetite
>   In hunger and thirst are here re-sanctified.
> Desire to eat and drink enkindles in us
>   The scent that issues from the apple-tree,
>   And from the spray that sprinkles o'er the verdure;
> And not a single time alone, this ground
>   Encompassing, is refreshed our pain,—
>   I say our pain, and ought to say our solace,—
> For the same wish doth lead us to the tree
>   Which led the Christ rejoicing to say *Eli,*
>   When with his veins he liberated us.
>
> —Purgatorio 23.64-75.

Here we have the fullest expression of the will to suffer for the sake of escaping sin. The allegorical interpretation, as it applies to the life of a man who desires above all to escape from the dominion of his besetting sin, is too obvious to need explanation.

We also have here a statement of the general nature of purgatory, in the reference to it as

> the mount
> That you doth straighten, whom the world made crooked.[34]

This indicates that the mountain is a place where the sinful conduct of the souls is reversed, and they are quite unlike what, as sinners, they were in life. Or, allegorically, the penitent is diametrically opposed in his desires to the sinner. This is in accord with justice, which strikes men, as Dante tells us, in the place most connected with their sins, and which cor-

[34] Purgatorio 23.125-6. See p. 115, above.

rects every excess or defect, so that the penitent do not have "too great desire" but hunger only "so far as is just."[35]

But though purgatory represents desire in just measure and proportion, it does not show all of life. It is a place for penance and purgation, not for construction. Hence we see the gluttonous, like the other penitents of purgatory, engaged only in ridding themselves from gluttony, but not as engaged in active and constructive exercise of the opposite virtue, which would be abstinence or sobriety according to reason, and for some high end.[36] The constructive force is not, however, wholly lacking in purgatory, but appears in the examples of virtue given in every circle. In this one the most striking is that of Daniel, who for religious reasons rejected the attractive food offered him.

The three poets pass from the ledge of gluttony to that of lust. This is occupied, save at the very edge, with flames of the most intense heat, from which the penitent are careful not for an instant to issue. The punishment here also is a matter of free will, and may be taken to signify allegorically that the penitent man on earth does not desire for an instant to give up his attempt to escape from his sin. The general significance of fire which purifies from sin as gold and silver are purified in refining is obvious and is reinforced by the use of the phrase "beati mundo corde" (blessed are the pure in heart). The word *mundus*—unlike *purus*—does not, how-

[35] Purgatorio 24.38,153-4.
[36] Summa Theol. II.ii.146.1, reply 2; 149.4.

## THE FLAME OF LUST

ever, have more relation to purity from lust than to purity from any other sin. In fact the most orthodox ideas of purgatory contemplate no other purifying agency than fire, being based chiefly on the passage:

> If any man's work shall be burned, he shall suffer loss: but he himself shall be saved; yet so as by fire.
>
> —1 Corinthians 3.15.

Hence Dante could hardly represent purgatory at all without making use of fire, which nevertheless appears only on this seventh ledge. Yet general fitness in relation to sin hardly explains why fire is especially appropriate in the punishment of the lustful.

Butler[37] refers to Philalethes as believing that the discipline is here imitative of the sin, as, in his opinion, it also is on the third and fifth ledges. Perez[38] says that the sinners here are appropriately punished by fire, as were the sodomites in hell, and we remember that fire from heaven was the punishment of licentious Sodom and Gomorrah.[39] Scartazzini[40] writes that the lustful are wrapped in the hottest flames, "because they burned in the flame of lust," and Torraca[41] quotes from the Book of Sidrach CLXXI: "Lust is a dangerous fire." He then, like most of the commentators, develops Dante's reference to the hymn beginning *Summæ Deus clemen-*

---

[37] *The Purgatory of Dante*, London, 1892, note on 19.117.
[38] *Op. cit.*, p. 241.
[39] Cf. also Leviticus 20.14; 21.9.
[40] *Op. cit.*, on Purgatorio 25.109-26.
[41] *Op. cit.*, on Purgatorio 25.122.

*tiæ* (God of clemency supreme) which contains the appropriate stanza:

> Scorch with fitting flames my loins and diseased liver, that my limbs may be ready and active, with all pestilent lust removed.

It must be observed, however, that purifying fire is quite different from lust itself as a fire. There may be a fire of lust, and there may be a purifying fire, but the two are hardly identical. Torraca suggests this by his: "Fire for fire," and Plumptre makes it clearer by saying: "The new fire must burn out the old." This ingenious explanation at least avoids the idea that the punishment of the lustful is imitative of their sin, and is supported by Dante's statement that the sinners "add unto their burning by their shame."[42] Purifying fire is opposed to lust in Mark 9.47-9, where we read:

> And if thine eye offend thee, pluck it out: it is better for thee to enter into the kingdom of God with one eye, than having two eyes to be cast into hell fire: where their worm dieth not, and the fire is not quenched. For every one shall be salted with fire, and every sacrifice shall be salted with salt.

Here the eye is interpreted as referring to lust, and the fire with which every man shall be salted is not that of hell, but that which makes possible entrance into the kingdom.

The force opposed to lust must be considerable, for the early theologians lay strong emphasis on the power of this vice. St. Thomas quotes from Augustine:

---

[42] Purgatorio 26.81.

# THE FIRE OF CHARITY

"Of all a Christian's conflicts, the most difficult combats are those of chastity; wherein the fight is a daily one, but victory rare."[43]

Yet opposition sufficient to overcome lust can be provided by the fire of love. This idea was current in Dante's century. We read in an English homily:

> This fir calle I charite,
> That brinnand in us au to be.
> It clenses man of sinful lust,
> Als fire clenses iren of rust,
> Opon this fir au we to lai
> Gastli recles, that es at sai,
> God praier, that ful suet smelles,
> And Goddes wreth swages and felles,
> And geres him grant man his bon,
> Haf he never sli sin don.[44]

This at least shows that in mediæval times it was possible to think of the flames of charity as instruments of penance.[45] Such charity is obviously that which suffereth long and beareth all things, endureth all things.

In the Earthly Paradise justice appears in a different fashion. The responsibility for man's suffering because of the fall of Adam is laid on man

---

[43] Summa Theol. II.ii.154.3, reply 1.

[44] English Metrical Homilies from Manuscripts of the Fourteenth Century, ed. by John Small, Edinburgh, 1862, p. 104, Hom. in Epiphania Domini. Cf. also the Fioretti of St. Francis, 40.

[45] "By fire the tribulation and calamities of this life are signified, since God tests the elect like gold in a furnace. Yet those who do not purge their sins by adversities patiently borne, nor in this life produce acts of contrition and above all of love (which are equally signified by fire, of which it is said: I came to send fire on the earth) —these, I say, must pass through purifying flames in purgatory" (Joseph Mansus, De Purgatorio). This is a modern compilation, yet much of its contents is of early origin. Any idea found in it has probably been used in homilies for centuries. For example, love of one's neighbor appears as purifying fire in the commentary of Euthymius Zigabenus (fl.1110) on Mark 9.49.

himself, who by sin brought suffering down upon him. Dante listens to the explanation:

> The Good Supreme, sole in itself delighting,
>   Created man good, and this goodly place
>   Gave him as hansel of eternal peace.
> By his default short while he sojourned here;
>   By his default to weeping and to toil
>   He changed his innocent laughter and sweet play.
> —Purgatorio 28.91-6.

This is an affirmation of the original and essential goodness of man and his freedom to stand or fall. This freedom is inseparable from the justice of God. Having sinned, man must in free will show penitence; in strict justice the sin and the sorrow for it must be "of one measure"—as it were the counter-passion of Aquinas. Yet confession and penitence can save man from the full consequence of sin. Confession is for the sake of the sinner, not of the judge, for Dante receives the warning:

> Shouldst thou be silent, or deny
> What thou confessest, not less manifest
> Would be thy fault, by such a Judge 'tis known.
> —Purgatorio 31.37-9.

The divine justice sees things as they are; no concealment is possible, and values are determined with absolute correctness. This is the fundamental teaching of the Purgatorio as of the Inferno. But Beatrice says further:

> But when from one's own cheeks comes bursting forth
>   The accusal of the sin, in our tribunal
>   Against the edge the wheel doth turn itself.
> —Purgatorio 31.40-2.

Since divine justice is tempered with mercy, man can hope to throw off evil and rise to perfection.

## THE DE MONARCHIA IN ALLEGORY

Though man's individual salvation be secured, that is not enough. The highest spiritual and social life can be secured only through Church and Empire. Of these Dante sees a marvelous vision, the allegorical presentation of the De Monarchia. The world cannot be in a state of justice while these great powers are out of harmony and either is unjustly encroaching on the sphere of the other. But on the contrary, as we are told when the Griffon fastens the car, signifying the Church, to the tree that signifies the Empire, in the proper coöperation of the two "is preserved the seed of all the just."[46] The Empire is, however, in a special sense the guardian of justice on earth, and consequently under the protection of the divine justice. Human frailty prevents the recognition of this truth; as Beatrice says to Dante,

> And if thy vain imaginings had not been
> Water of Elsa round about thy mind,
> And Pyramus to the mulberry, their pleasure,
> Thou by so many circumstances only
> The justice of the interdict of God
> Morally in the tree wouldst recognize.
> —Purgatorio 33.67-72.

Consequently mankind, resting in the justice of the divine order, may hope for a time when, under proper spiritual teaching and just government, it may actualize its highest end. Indeed even in the midst of our broken society individuals of vision may in their own hearts live the perfect life for which all men were created.

[46] Purgatorio 32.48.

## CHAPTER VI

### THE PARADISO: THE JUSTICE OF VARIATION IN HUMAN TALENTS

In his Tenth Epistle, which deals primarily with the Paradiso, Dante insists on the practical value of this part of his work, saying that it is intended to "remove those now living on earth from a state of misery and conduct them to a state of felicity." He also applies the general purpose of the Commedia to its last part, saying that while its subject literally is the state of the souls of the blessed after death, allegorically it deals with man, as by meriting he is liable to the rewards of justice. The Paradiso is concerned, then, with the life of man in this world. Yet even without the Tenth Epistle, this truth would be hardly less clear. Dante's grip on this world is firm; he no more needs in the Paradiso than he did in the Inferno to escape from the life of man as he knew it. His heaven is in man's conscience, and he is too sure of the unity of God's creation to need to escape from the present into some other world that can be set over against this one. However firmly Dante may have held the literal beliefs of his poem, or however nobly he may have set them forth, he is always certain that the kingdom of God has its best reality in the heart of man.

Yet it has been difficult for commentators to keep

this in mind. The allegorical meaning of the third part, as a picture of the good life on earth, has been comparatively neglected, partly, it may be, because Dante himself has given rather less space to allegory and more to various excursuses, than in the other *cantiche*. These digressions, however, frequently emphasize the poet's interest in mundane affairs and his feeling of their close connection with those of heaven. Commentators have seemed to hesitate to bring heaven down to earth, as it were, by an allegory of paradise. Yet that is what Dante intended to do. He may be said to have written the Paradiso to show that heaven is on earth, as in the Inferno he showed that hell is on earth.

Consequently the problem of the Paradiso with respect to justice is analogous to those of the preceding *cantiche*. The distribution of rewards and honors is a part of Aristotelian justice quite as much as that of punishments and is governed by the same general laws. The rewards of paradise must be appropriate, must exhibit the fit proportion of justice, and must signify by allegory the life of the blessed man on earth. The blessings of heaven are all alike in that they consist of the union of the spirit with God, and consequently of a perfect life for the individual. This perfection is not, as the De Monarchia indicates, an isolated spiritual experience of the individual, but a life in society. The evil of society makes the perfect life difficult, yet not wholly impossible; with all its evil, society is the only place where man can live well. The lives of various righteous men are, however, quite different from one another in their condition in society. The perfect life for one is not the perfect life for another. Hence arises the question of the justice of the lot of any righteous individual. Under the guise of the distribution of rewards in paradise Dante sets himself to this question.

In his constant thought of society as necessary to humanity and his belief in the differing natural gifts of men, the poet was inevitably led to a union of the two not unlike the theory of justice on which Plato's Republic is based: that is, that the just state is one in which all the individuals are working according to their gifts and are put in the places for which they are best fitted. No man does or desires to do that for which another is better fitted than himself, but with content applies himself to his own peculiar task. Some are more honored than others, yet every man, no matter how humble, is necessary to the well-being of society. From this vital relation to the great organism, even the humblest office acquires a dignity that enables it to sustain a comparison with any other. In St. Thomas, and hence in Dante, the emphasis is somewhat shifted, and justice is not so much that of the state as that of God as the great artificer of a properly articulated society. The care with which God has distributed gifts and graces to the worthy is proof of his justice.

Hence St. Thomas concludes that even if sin had not entered the world, variation in the conditions of men would have appeared:

# THE STATE OF INNOCENCE

We must needs admit that in the primitive state there was some inequality, at least as regards sex, because generation depends upon diversity of sex: and likewise as regards age; for some would have been born of others; nor would sexual union have been sterile.

Moreover, as regards the soul, there would have been inequality as to righteousness and knowledge. For man worked not of necessity, but of his own free-will, by virtue of which man can apply himself more, or less, to action, desire, or knowledge; hence some would have made a greater advance in virtue and knowledge than others.

There might also have been bodily disparity. For the human body was not entirely exempt from the laws of nature, so as not to receive from exterior sources more or less advantage and help: since indeed it was dependent on food wherewith to sustain life.

So we may say that, according to the climate, or the movement of the stars, some were born more robust in body than others, and also greater, and more beautiful, and in all ways better disposed; so that, however, in those who were thus surpassed, there would have been no defect or fault either in soul or body.

—Summa Theol. I.96.3.

Though in the state of innocence there would have been no tyranny or servitude, yet man as a social animal must have had rulers fitted to oversee the common weal:

A man is the master of a free subject, by directing him either towards his proper welfare, or to the common good. Such a kind of mastership would have existed in the state of innocence between man and man, for two reasons: First, because man is naturally a social being, and so in the state of innocence he would have led a social life. Now a social life cannot exist among a number of people unless under the presidency of one to look after the common good; for many, as such, seek many things, whereas one attends only to one. Wherefore the Philosopher says, in the beginning of the Politics, that wherever many things are ordered to one, we shall always find one at the head directing them. Secondly, if one man surpassed another in knowledge and virtue, this would not have been fitting unless these gifts issued to the benefit of others, according to I Pet. iv. 10. 'As every man hath received grace, ministering the same to one another.' Wherefore Augustine says (De Civ. Dei xix.): 'Just men command not by the love of domineering, but by the service of counsel. The natural order of things requires this; and thus did God make man.'

—Summa Theol. I.96.4.

The last words indicate the position on human inequality which Dante exhibits concretely throughout the allegory of the Paradiso.

The theme of unequal distribution of the divine influence appears in the first three lines of the *cantica:*

> The glory of Him who moveth everything
> Doth penetrate the universe, and shine
> In one part more and in another less.

Such inequality is not the result of chance or partiality, but an indication of divine justice:

The order of the universe, which is seen both in effects of nature and in effects of will, shows forth the justice of God. Hence Dionysius says (Div.Nom.viii.4): "We must needs see that God is truly just, in seeing how He gives to all existing things what is proper to the condition of each; and preserves the nature of each one in the order and with the powers that properly belong to it." . . . Thus also God exercises justice, when He gives to each thing what is due to it by its nature and condition. This debt however is derived from the former; since what is due to each thing is due to it as ordered to it according to the divine wisdom. And although God in this way pays each thing its due, yet He Himself is not the debtor, since He is not directed to other things, but rather other things to Him. Justice, there-

fore, in God is sometimes spoken of as the fitting accompaniment of His goodness.
—Summa Theol. I.21.1.

Equality of justice has its place in retribution, since equal rewards or punishments are due to equal merit or demerit. But this does not apply to things as at first instituted. For just as an architect, without injustice, places stones of the same kind in various parts of a building, not on account of any antecedent difference in the stones, but with a view to securing that perfection of the entire building which could not be obtained except by the different positions of the stones; even so, God from the beginning, to secure perfection in the universe, has set therein creatures of various and unequal natures, according to his wisdom, and without injustice, since no diversity of merit is presupposed.
—Summa Theol. I.65.2.

In explaining how she and Dante have ascended to the heaven of the moon, Beatrice carries on the thought of the opening lines of the Paradiso:

> All things whate'er they be
> Have order among themselves, and this is form,
> That makes the universe resemble God.
> Here do the higher creatures see the footprints
> Of the Eternal Power, which is the end
> Whereto is made the law already mentioned.
> In the order that I speak of are inclined
> All natures, by their destinies diverse,
> More or less near unto their origin.
> —Paradiso 1.103-11.

This diversity is the cause of the real unity of the whole, as Dante may have learned from St. Thomas:

This opinion [that the distinction of things is not from God] cannot stand . . . because, according to this opinion, the universality of things would not proceed from the intention of the first agent, but from the concurrence of many active causes; and such an effect we can only describe as being produced by chance. Therefore, thus the perfection

of the universe, which consists of the diversity of things, would be a thing of chance, which is impossible. Hence we must say that the distinction and multitude of things come from the intention of the first agent, who is God. For he brought things into being in order that his goodness might be communicated to creatures, and be represented by them; and because his goodness could not be adequately represented by one creature alone, he produced many and diverse creatures, that what was wanting to one in the representation of the divine goodness might be supplied by another. For goodness, which in God is simple and uniform, in creatures is manifold and divided; and hence the whole universe together participates in the divine goodness more perfectly, and represents it better than any single creature whatever.
—Summa Theol. I.47.1.

As the divine wisdom is the cause of the distinction of things for the sake of the perfection of the universe, so it is the cause of inequality. For the universe would not be perfect if only one grade of goodness were found in things.
—Summa Theol. I.47.2.

This thought seems to have been in Dante's mind when he wrote on the capacity of the human race to perform its function of actualizing the whole capacity of its possible intellect:

And since this capacity as a whole cannot be reduced to action at one time through one man, or through any one of the societies discriminated above, multiplicity is necessary in the human race in order to actualize its capacity in entirety. Likewise multiplicity is necessary in creatable things in order to exercise continually the capacity of primal matter.
—De Monarchia 1.3.66-76.

This passage echoes the commentary of Aquinas on Ethics 1, lectio 1. According to the same principle of diversity and unity Beatrice explains the spots of the moon:

## THE HEAVEN OF THE MOON

> And even as the soul within your dust
>   Through members different and accommodated
>   To faculties diverse expands itself,
> So likewise this Intelligence diffuses
>   Its virtue multiplied among the stars,
>   Itself revolving on its unity.
> Virtue diverse doth a diverse alloyage
>   Make with the precious body that it quickens,
>   In which, as life in you, it is combined.
>                 —Paradiso 2.133-41.

Thus preparation is made for the later development of the theme of the inequality and diversity, but complete harmony and satisfaction, of the blessed.

The first heaven visited is that of the "inconstant moon," fit abode for those whose vows have been broken. Here Dante makes specific in a question to Piccarda the problem which in general has already been discussed, that of the unequal distribution of the divine favor. He asks if the lowly lot awarded by divine justice is acceptable to her and her companions:

> Are you desirous of a higher place,
>   To see more or to make yourselves more friends?
>                 —Paradiso 3.65-6.

The reply is that she has no thirst for anything save what is assigned to her, for her desires are all in harmony with the will of God, as are the desires of all the inhabitants of heaven. The allegorical reflection of this upon the life of men on earth is evident. Let each be contented with the lot for which he is fitted, not by the laws of men but by his nature as it was created. This is harmonious with free will, as Piccarda points out, because it is what every one should desire for himself. The human and the divine wills meet.

> And his will is our peace.
> —Paradiso 3.85.

In allegory this means that the blessed life on earth is possible for righteous men of whatever station, as Dante indicates by saying that then it became clear to him

> how everywhere
> In heaven is Paradise, although the grace
> Of good supreme there rain not in one measure.
> —Paradiso 3.88-90.

In the succeeding canto Beatrice affirms that all souls dwell in the same heaven:

> But all make beautiful the primal circle,
> And have sweet life in different degrees,
> By feeling more or less the eternal breath.
> They showed themselves here, not because allotted
> This sphere has been to them, but to give sign
> Of the celestial which is least exalted.
> —Paradiso 4.34-9.

She proceeds to explain that they appear in the various spheres only to make their varying degrees of blessedness plain to Dante—that is, we might say, for the sake of making more easy Dante's task of poetical construction. Dante does not intend his pictures of the heavens to be taken literally.

The next piece of exposition, of great importance for the theme of the whole Commedia, treats of the reasons why the justice of God appears unjust in the eyes of mortals, and there is the admission that

## THE HEAVEN OF MERCURY

this appearance of injustice may actually be an argument of faith. The possibility that even the devout might find difficulty in the perception of justice in all the circumstances of the ordering of the universe, and that the discussion of the subject might tend to edification, is in truth one of the chief reasons why Dante undertook such a poem as the Divine Comedy. The explanation of the low position given to those who have broken vows because violence was used against them by others is that they submitted to the violence and did not have the strength of will to return to their cloisters when they had opportunity. This leads easily to further discussion of the importance of freedom of the will, and Beatrice explains that nothing can take the place of a failure to keep vows, because a vow is a sacrifice of freedom of the will, which is the greatest gift of God to man. This tells why free will is of great significance in Dante's entire poem. It is indeed a gift which God allows not merely to the blessed, but even, in a measure, to the damned. That is, Dante is sure that man is still an individual, whether living a good or an evil life.

In the heaven of Mercury, to which Dante and Beatrice next ascend, the blessed who approach Dante immediately announce their participation in the general blessedness of heaven:

> With light that through the whole of heaven is spread
> Kindled are we.           —Paradiso 5.118-19.

In his reply Dante also refers to the place in heaven assigned to his interlocutor:

> [I] know not why thou hast,
> Spirit august, thy station in the sphere
> That veils itself to men in alien rays.
> —Paradiso 5.127-9.

At these words the soul addressed, evidently completely satisfied with its "grade," becomes more lucent than before. It is the soul of Justinian, and speaks on the great theme which Dante deals with in the De Monarchia. As we might expect, the discourse contains something specifically on justice, for the sake of which the Empire existed. Justinian speaks of "the living justice which inspires" him,[1] and indicates that it was the power behind all the actions by which the Empire rose to its place as the representative and protector of justice on earth. Indeed the Empire is properly such only when it stands for justice; it is true of the Imperial ensign that

> this ever
> Ill follows he who it and justice parts.
> —Paradiso 6.104-5.

This ensign can be called the arms of God, so necessary to the right conduct of the world is justice among men.

Returning then to his initial subject, Justinian explains his "grade." Mercury is appropriate to the spirits who have lived lives of labor that honor and fame might be theirs. It is proper that, since their desires have paused there, they should have no higher station, and desire no higher one than they have deserved, because they can say, in complete accord with Aristotelian and Thomistic justice:

[1] Paradiso 6.88.

## THE CRUCIFIXION WAS JUST

> In commensuration of our wages
> With our desert is portion of our joy,
> Because we see them neither less nor greater.[2]

Diversity of level is necessary to the justly ordered society, in which each performs his function. As Justinian puts it,

> Voices diverse make up sweet melodies;
> So in this life of ours the seats diverse
> Render sweet harmony among these spheres.
> —Paradiso 6.124-6.

This appears in more prosaic form in St. Thomas:

It is the part of the best agent to produce an effect which is best in its entirety; but this does not mean that he makes every part of the whole the best absolutely, but in proportion to the whole; in the case of an animal, for instance, its goodness would be taken away if every part of it had the dignity of an eye. Thus, therefore, God also made the universe to be best as a whole, according to the mode of a creature; whereas he did not make each single creature best, but one better than another.
—Summa Theol. I.47.2.

In the variations of station in heaven there is respect for free will; those desirous of fame live in heaven on the level they have chosen, and wish no other or higher blessedness.

The words of Justinian indicating both that the crucifixion of Christ was just and that the Jews were justly punished for it are unintelligible to Dante; this problem is solved by Beatrice according to the methods of St. Thomas.[3] The conception involved is that of just proportion between sin and

---
[2] Paradiso 6.118-20. See p. 21, above, for St. Thomas' expression of this idea.
[3] Summa Theol. II.i.109.7.

punishment, that is, the counterpassion,[4] the filling of the measure emptied by sin:

> Man in his limitations had not power
> To satisfy, not having power to sink
> In his humility obeying then,
> Far as he disobeying thought to rise;
> And for this reason man has been from power
> Of satisfying by himself excluded.
> —Paradiso 7.97-102.

When Adam and Eve ate of the forbidden fruit, they hoped to become as gods,[5] and, as we have seen, man by his sin of pride, or supreme selfishness, has made himself equal to God by disdaining subjection. Hence no other method could reduce the sufferer low enough to satisfy the demands of justice, except that the Son of God should descend from his position in the Godhead to man's estate, thus descending the exact distance which man had aspired to ascend. The Jews were obviously sinful in their wish to crucify the innocent Christ, and hence properly punished by the destruction of their city. But here, as ever, even at the gate of hell, God's love is combined with his justice, for, as Dante says—

> For God more bounteous was himself to give
> To make man able to uplift himself,
> Than if he only of himself had pardoned.
> —Paradiso 7.115-17.

Nor is the free will of man here forgotten, for, as Adam was "sufficient to have stood, though free to fall," so by the sacrifice of Christ man is not raised, but merely made sufficient to raise himself if he will.

[4] See pp. 26 f., above.
[5] Genesis 3.5.

## THE HEAVEN OF VENUS

From the heaven where the justice of man's redemption appears, Dante ascends to the heaven of Venus, appropriated to the lovers. Here Charles Martel explains how the providence of God, acting through the heavenly bodies, disposes all things to their foreseen end. Thus the order of nature appears not like a ruin, but a work of art. From this the speaker passes to the analogous topic of the diversity of men's functions on earth, and discusses it in the spirit of Aristotle and Aquinas. First he inquires from Dante:

> Now say, would it be worse
> For men on earth were they not citizens?

On receiving an unhesitating assent, he continues:

> And can they be so, if below they live not
> Diversely unto offices diverse?
> No, if your master writeth well for you. . . .
> Therefore it behooves
> The roots of your effects to be diverse.
> Hence one is Solon born, another Xerxes,
> Another Melchisedec, and another he
> Who, flying through the air, his son did lose.
> —Paradiso 8.115-26.

If all these natural endowments were put in their appropriate places, the world "would have the people good." That is, the affairs of the world would be properly and justly carried on, as Plato dreamed they might be. The propriety of the subordination of the gifts of the individual to the welfare of society is illustrated by St. Thomas as follows:

In the constitution of things there is no inequality of parts through any preceding inequality, either of merits or of the disposition of the matter; but inequality comes from the perfection of the whole. This appears also in works done by art; for the roof of a house differs from the foundation, not because it is made of other material; but in order that the house may be made perfect of different parts, the artificer seeks different material; indeed he would make such material if he could.

—Summa Theol. I.47.2.

Such proper disposition of the human material of the world is exemplified by the conduct of the contented souls in heaven, who live in meet proportion, and turn ever

> to the Sun which fills it,
> As to that good which for each thing sufficeth.

—Paradiso 9.8-9.

In this heaven we have two whose life on earth had been marked by evil love, atoned for by repentance and good deeds. However much of evil there may have been in the loves of Cunizza and Rahab, their tendency to love was in itself the disposition given them by God, and hence to be respected in heaven. This recognition of the quality in these two women which at first seems connected chiefly with their sins furnishes illustration for the general discussion on the spheres of activity proper to various men. Cunizza and Rahab had at least united their wills with that of God in acting in accord with their natures, though in an evil fashion. By putting them in the planet of love Dante shows the same respect for human individuality which we have previously observed, and again tells us that the justice of God is not a thing apart from the will and nature of man.

## THE HEAVEN OF THE SUN

Dante next passes into the heaven of the sun, so far removed from earth that even the shadow of the earth does not reach it. Here he finds, as is fitting, the great doctors of the Church who have illuminated the world with their wisdom. In speaking with them there is no mention of their "grade," for it seems as though this and the succeeding spheres are equal, and hence position is a matter depending not on degree of holiness, but on natural abilities. In the three spheres below the sun the effects of an imperfect life as well as of a certain kind of nature had appeared, but here the only distinctions are those within the sphere itself, and not in relation to the other spheres. First we learn of the full liberty of the saints, who in their charity tell Dante all he desires to know as freely as water flows to the sea. Then we are told that the different lights that appear vary in size and beauty according to the merits of the soul within. Next we observe that there is perfect concord among the blessed, as at the beginning of the canto we have read of the concord of nature. They are arranged in a circle, and as they sing Dante sees

> the glorious wheel move round,
> And render voice to voice, in modulation
> And sweetness that can not be comprehended,
> Excepting there where joy is made eternal.
> —Paradiso 10.145-8.

Evidently each is exactly fulfilling his proper duty here, as each had done so in the world below; they are continuing to do in heaven what they did on earth. In the full description of the life of St.

Francis we have again a concrete and detailed presentation of the justice of God. The saint has of his own free will chosen the great good divinely allotted to him, and hence continues to enjoy in heaven the same good which he possessed on earth. Earthly humility is heavenly exaltation.

Next comes St. Bonaventura's praise of St. Dominic, who, like St. Francis, carried out the divinely implanted tendencies of his own nature.

Then St. Thomas proceeds to explain what he meant when he said of Solomon:

> To see so much there never rose a second.
> —Paradiso 10.114.

The saying was a qualified one, having relation to Solomon only as compared with other kings. Thus the discussion brings before us in another way the diversity of talents given to men. It also deals with the inequality in ability of men within any group, through Dante's favorite figure of the wax and the seal. The idea, representing the seal, is the same for all, but the heaven which influences a man may operate imperfectly, and the man himself, the wax, may be imperfect. Hence he is less perfectly stamped with the divine idea than are others. This accounts for the inequality of the souls in heaven by a relative rather than an absolute superiority and inferiority, a difference not in kind, but in degree. It is obvious that Dante intends this explanation to account satisfactorily for genuine inequality among living men, and that we may learn from it that all are created for thorough happiness in the exercise of their gifts, that no one should feel either unduly exalted or unduly cast down by his lot, and that the highly gifted, though properly respected for superiority, have no right to occupy a different sphere—literally or allegorically—from that of the less well dowered.

In concluding this discussion of the various abilities of men and the distinctions, but not absolute differences, among them, St. Thomas touches on another topic likewise connected with that of the justice of God. Men, he declares, should not be hasty in judging in those things that they see not. The concern of the saint is not here with the inferiority of man's vision to that of God but rather with the powers of the human intellect. He believes that often current opinion is wrong, and that few are able to understand the truth, so few that men should not assume that they can understand the divine counsel, for the man whom they condemn may be exalted by divine justice, and it is possible that he whom they praise is worthy of divine condemnation. Something of the same thought of the imperfect vision of most men appears in the next canto in the words:

> Whoso lamenteth him that here we die
>   That we may live above, has never there
>   Seen the refreshment of the eternal rain.
>        —Paradiso 14.25-7.

If men saw clearly how the good are rewarded by divine justice, in heaven or on earth, they would see that they should often felicitate the good instead of pitying them, because part of their bliss is "just reward" for all their merit.⁶ `Indeed the vision of the blessed has grace "above its worth." And, as Solomon, touching the theme of correlated function and ability, explains, when the blessed finally assume their bodies,

> Nor can so great a splendour weary us,
> For strong will be the organs of the body
> To everything which hath the power to please us.
> —Paradiso 14.58-60.

In the next heaven, that of Mars, are found men whose deeds were fit subjects for heroic song. In the description of the souls in this heaven, there is nothing said directly of their special suitability to the lot given them, though the recital of their names makes plain their greatness. But in the long discourse of Cacciaguida there are some suggestions that Dante was still thinking on the theme of the propriety of God's dealings with men. First, he speaks incidentally on the subject of contingency and the effect on man's fate of the foreknowledge of God. This is a topic of great importance in relation to the justice of God's ways to man, as was understood by Milton, who devotes many lines to it in Paradise Lost, for he, like Dante, is a champion of the freedom of man, without which justice is not possible. Cacciaguida also bids Dante himself to be confident in the justice of God, as a defense against the sufferings of exile and of persecution by successful enemies:

⁶ Paradiso 14.33.

## THE HEAVEN OF JUPITER

> Yet would I not thy neighbours thou shouldst envy,
> Because thy life into the future reaches
> Beyond the punishment of their perfidies.
> —Paradiso 17.97-9.

In conclusion Cacciaguida points out the personal duty of Dante in respect to what he had seen in his journey. Only dark consciences will find offense in the poet's representations of the world as it is, with the deformity of every sort of evil, whether generally condemned or not, and with the punishment of evil by the righteous judgment of God. Dante feels that world under God is so justly constituted that only by speaking the truth can a poet gain the reality of fame.

The heaven of Jupiter, into which Dante next passes, is that of the good rulers, whose distinguishing characteristic, as we might suppose from the suggestions about the function of rulers given in the De Monarchia, is justice. When Dante first looks upon the spirits, they form themselves into letters which spell the words "Diligite justitiam qui judicatis terram" (Love justice ye that are judges of the earth). Soon they are shaped into the imperial eagle, the sign of the Roman Empire, which was to Dante the highest representative of human justice. Only the justice maintained by the Empire can make possible the best human life, which is the life most in accord with God's will; in short, human justice is in accord with divine justice. Hence Dante exclaims:

> O gentle star! what and how many gems
> Did demonstrate to me, that all our justice

> Effect is of that heaven which thou ingemmest!
> Wherefore I pray the Mind, in which begin
> Thy motion and thy virtue, to regard
> Whence comes the smoke that vitiates thy rays;
> So that a second time it now be wroth
> With buying and with selling in the temple
> Whose walls were built with signs and martyrdoms!
> —Paradiso 18.115-23.

In the last lines we have the thought, already familiar, that greed is the greatest enemy of justice among men. Soon the eagle speaks:

> Being just and merciful
> Am I exalted here unto that glory
> Which cannot be exceeded by desire;
> And upon earth I left my memory
> Such, that the evil-minded people there
> Commend it, but continue not the story.
> —Paradiso 19.13-18.

Dante observes that all the just rulers united in the eagle speak as one man, thus typifying, unobtrusively, the harmony essential to justice. The poet is aware that divine justice is especially mirrored in the heaven of Saturn, yet he knows that in the heaven of Jupiter it is seen without a veil and asks that certain doubts be resolved. It is fitting that these souls famous for justice on earth should speak on divine justice, for the two are alike in nature. The reply of the eagle is prefaced by the statement that the mind of man is not adequate to see the full extent of divine justice:

> Therefore into the justice sempiternal
> The power of vision that your world receives,
> As eye into the ocean, penetrates;

> Which, though it see the bottom near the shore,
> Upon the deep perceives it not, and yet
> 'Tis there, but it is hidden by the depth.
>
> —Paradiso 19.58-64.

Indeed, eternal justice cannot be understood without the illumination of eternal light. But now Dante can have that light:

> Amply to thee is opened now the cavern
> Which has concealed from thee the living justice.
>
> —Paradiso 19.67-8.

It seems that the adjective *living* applied to justice has some special significance for Dante, and that by it he intends to indicate the divine justice as actually at work in the world. It is an active and positive virtue engaged in making the world genuinely better, and not a mere assignment of proper rewards for what has already been done. The same expression is used by Justinian, who in the sixth canto speaks of "the living Justice" as the force which drove on the Roman emperors in their divinely appointed course. Dante is then to learn something of that force which supports and governs the world justly, and not merely of that which passes on the acts of men after they are completed. This conception of a great moving force, rather than a legal circumscription, is needed at the moment by Dante to enable him to hold a wider conception through which he can represent as just something hardly allowed by a narrow statutory definition. As the eagle says,

> Now who art thou, that on the bench wouldst sit
> In judgment at a thousand miles away,
> With the short vision of a single span?
> —Paradiso 19.79-81.

The need here is for the inclusive judgment of the Primal Will, which never has moved from the highest good, and is of ineffable justice:

> So much is just as is accordant with it.
> —Paradiso 19.88.

Then the eagle begins to sing, and says:

> As are
> My notes to thee, who dost not comprehend them,
> Such is the eternal judgment to you mortals.
> —Paradiso 19.97-9.

Then comes the explanation that no one who does not believe in Christ can enter heaven. We have a list of unjust kings and learn the names of some of those whose souls are included in the eagle. The second mentioned is Trajan, who lived a heathen, but was permitted to return to earth from hell, that he might repent. After a few names to be expected, we read:

> Who would believe, down in the errant world,
> That e'er the Trojan Ripheus in this round
> Could be the fifth one of the holy lights?
> Now knoweth he enough of what the world
> Has not the power to see of grace divine.
> —Paradiso 20.67-71.

Ripheus is the Trojan of whom Virgil wrote that he was "the justest man and the most mindful of equity among the Trojans."[7] He was saved because

[7] Aeneid 2.426.

# PREDESTINATION

of his love for the right, through faith, hope, and charity, more than a thousand years before Christ. This is a great mystery, for predestination cannot be understood save by those who see the first cause in its completeness, and even the saints in heaven do not know all who shall be with them. Hence mortals should hold themselves from judging, merely remembering that the kingdom of God suffereth violence from love and living hope, which overcome the divine will not to the overthrow but to the fulfilment of justice, for the will of God is overcome because it wills to be overcome, and in being overcome it overcomes.

Such is Dante's illustration of the workings of the living justice that controls the universe, far above the dogmas or interpretations of dogmas of even the wisest and most spiritual of mortals. This justice is all-powerful, merciful, flexible, and meets every occasion that arises. Man cannot and need not understand it; he need only trust that his will when inspired by love and hope is in agreement with the primal will, and hence that he is in a position to obtain the greatest blessedness possible to mankind. However the conduct of the world may appear to his imperfect vision, he can be sure that in reality the judgments exercised upon him and his fellows are true and righteous altogether. Thus under the veil of his allegory Dante shrouds the great truths of the justice of the world of living men.

The eagle's presentation of the mystery of predestination is in harmony with the belief of St. Thomas, who asserts its justice:

The reason for the predestination of some, and reprobation of others, must be sought in the goodness of God. Thus he is said to have made all things through his goodness, so that the divine goodness might be represented in things. Now it is necessary that the divine goodness, which in itself is one and undivided, should be manifested in many ways in his creation; because creatures in themselves cannot attain to the simplicity of God. Thus it is that for the completion of the universe there are required different grades of being; some of which hold a high and some a low place in the universe. That this multiformity of grades may be preserved in things, God allows some evils, lest many good things should never happen, as was said above (Q. XXII). Let us then consider the whole of the human race, as we consider the whole universe. God wills to manifest his goodness in men; in respect to those whom he predestinates, by means of his mercy, in sparing them; and in respect of others, whom he reprobates, by means of his justice, in punishing them. This is the reason why God elects some; and rejects others. . . . Thus too, in the things of nature, a reason can be assigned, since primary matter is altogether uniform, why one part of it was fashioned by God from the beginning under the form of fire, another under the form of earth, that there might be a diversity of species in things of nature. Why this particular part of matter is under this particular form, and that under another, depends upon the simple will of God, as from the simple will of the artificer it depends that this stone is in this part of the wall, and that in another; although the plan requires that some stones should be in this place, and some in that place. Neither on this account can there be said to be injustice in God, if he prepares unequal lots for not unequal things. This would be altogether contrary to the notion of justice, if the effect of predestination was granted as a debt, and not gratuitously. In things which are given gratuitously a person can give more or less, just as he pleases (provided he deprives nobody of his due) without any infringement of justice.

—Summa Theol. I.23.5.

## THE HEAVEN OF SATURN

From the heaven where the justice of the kings of the earth so easily passes over into the justice of God, Dante ascends to the heaven of Saturn, where he sees the spirits of the contemplative. Here the word justice is not used, yet the subject of the preceding cantos—the inability of mortals to understand the workings of the divine providence—is continued, and other topics relating to justice are mentioned. St. Peter Damien first approaches Dante, and, in answer to a question, says:

> But the high charity, that makes us servants
> Prompt to the counsel which controls the world,
> Allotteth here, even as thou dost observe.

Dante replies:

> I see full well, . . . O sacred lamp!
> How love unfettered in this court sufficeth
> To follow the eternal Providence.[8]

In these two speeches we have, as it were, charity substituted for justice, and love for will, marking the complete union of the souls here with the love and will of God. But Dante still does not see the reason why the function which St. Peter is now performing was by predestination assigned to him rather than to some other. The saint explains that he has a vision of the Supreme Essence, and that the brightness of the splendor with which he flames is in just proportion with his vision. Yet even the seraph of clearest vision cannot fathom the abyss of the eternal law. Hence Dante should, when he

---

[8] Paradiso 21.70-5. For the connection of love and justice see De Monarchia 1.11, and p. 5, above.

returns to earth, warn men against fruitless investigations. The saint then speaks of the corruption of modern pastors, whereat the souls near by give a shout that overcomes Dante like thunder. Beatrice comforts him and explains that if he were able to understand it, he would have learned from it of the workings of the divine vengeance, of which he may know that

> The sword above here smiteth not in haste
>    Nor tardily.
>                        —Paradiso 22.16-17.

In this heaven under the charge of the Thrones, the order of angels who especially reflect "God Judicant,"[9] it is especially fitting that not merely the charity and free love of man and God should appear, but that the vengeance represented by the Inferno should also be touched upon, as though to show that the divine protection of righteousness was more than passive, and that the perversion of free will received its exact and proper recompense. But this suggestion of vengeance in punishment for the sins of the monks, though necessary, is only incidental, for the possible union of man's desires with the plans of the eternal providence is the great lesson of this heaven.

In the next heaven also Dante is not forgetful of the divine vengeance, but declares that

> the high Providence, that with Scipio
> At Rome the glory of the world defended,
>                         —Paradiso 27.61-2.

[9] Paradiso 9.62.

will aid the Church against the wickedness of the unworthy popes. That which Dante here calls "high Providence," in its care for the good of the world as exhibited in the progress of the Roman Empire and the Church, he has before called "living Justice."

But though Heaven has ever its righteous sword in readiness, there are more attractive aspects of the workings of providence. In the heaven of the fixed stars Dante is especially examined on the three fundamental virtues of faith, hope, and love. And he who understands these has no further doubts concerning the justice of God, for he is whole-hearted in accepting the universe as good, and in trusting that it brings good to all who are in accord with its goodness, that is, in accord with the goodness of God, who shows himself to man's understanding through the workings of the universe. This state of mind in which Dante fully accepts what he can see as good and trusts in the just ordering of what he cannot understand and what seems to him unjust, is in part the result of "philosophic arguments." Indeed, the good can kindle love only as it is understood, and only when the mind of man grasps the fundamental truth is it moved toward the Being from whose goodness all other goodness gains its light. Yet, Dante tells us, this intellectual perception is possible to men on earth only in the form of belief, though in paradise profound things freely show "lor parvenza"—their apparition.[10] Here we have the meeting of the literal and the allegorical

[10] Paradiso 24.71.

in the poem. Dante in reality, as the result of his observation of life, has come to a condition such that he understands directly the profound matters of eternal providence, and he represents himself in his poem as having come to such a stage by divine illumination after the experience of his journey. The things he sees in heaven are, allegorically, the things he saw on earth; and because he saw them on earth he wrote his poem to aid other men to see.

In this heaven, where meet souls of every sort, there are again distinctions in degrees of blessedness. As the poet picturesquely puts it,

> And as the wheels in works of horologes
> > Revolve so that the first to the beholder
> > Motionless seems, and the last one to fly,
> So in like manner did those carols, dancing
> > In different measure, of their affluence
> > Give me the gauge, as they were swift or slow.
> > > —Paradiso 24.13-18.

The difference of degree among the blessed is a matter of so much importance to any one who will understand the divine providence, that Dante feels that he must keep it ever before his reader's mind. In this heaven, where souls of diverse natures meet together, their equality and their difference can appear more easily than in the heavens immediately preceding, where the emphasis is as much on the similarity of function of the various souls as on their differences in degree.

The appearance of Adam in this heaven also suggests the problem of the divine justice, for in the relations of God with the "ancient father" are sum-

# ADAM'S SIN

med up, as it were, his relations with all mankind. The theologians have long known this, and Milton followed them when in Paradise Lost he attempted, by telling the story of Adam and Eve, to "justify the ways of God to men." Dante's Adam speaks directly on the subject of his sin and punishment. His crime was not the mere tasting of the apple, but a violation of the nature of justice. As he says,

> The tasting of the tree
> Not in itself was cause of so great exile,
> But solely the o'erstepping of the bounds.
> —Paradiso 26.115-17.

Passing over the mark is not the mere breaking of law, but a violation of what was proper to the nature of man, by the desire through pride to make himself equal to God. St. Thomas explains that Adam's fault was in his desire to be like God above man's measure, and in his unwillingness to occupy his normal place as of God and bound as a servant by the divine commands.[11] The unjust man of Aristotle desires good things that are not fitting for him. Adam was guilty of the inordinateness of desiring what was suitable only to God. By thus abandoning his station and violating his nature, he sinned against all humanity. Hence we see that the sin of Adam involves what Dante has often before represented as the very essence of injustice, namely, the failure to occupy the station and enjoy the rewards proper to the person in question. Adam's sin was that he sought not the highest good of man, but a

[11] Summa Theol. II.ii.163.2.

thing which man could not claim without violating his own God-given nature by aspiring to be something more than human.

On passing to the next heaven, the primum mobile, Dante and Beatrice discourse further on the main theme of the poem—the providence of God and the inability of men to see its workings. Mankind is so miserably absorbed in the "present life" as not to perceive the truth. This "present life" is the life concerned with the things of this world only, like that of the covetous who thought only of "earthly things," and hence had no vision of the divine justice. Dante here inveighs against the sin which he so often attacks, and which he believed was especially opposed to the carrying out of human justice and to the perception of divine justice: the sin of greed, which so holds men under that none can draw their eyes from beneath its waves. Having abandoned their child-like faith and innocence in their desire for the things of this world, men think that there is no one to govern on earth, and thus go astray. Here Dante brings before us the theme of his poem; he wishes to raise the eyes of men above the "present life" to the life of eternal truth, so that they may daily see the order of the divine government. With a similar thought, St. Thomas had written:

God's justice, which establishes things in the order conformable to the rule of his wisdom, which is the law of his justice, is suitably called truth.
—Summa Theol. I.21.2.

# THE ORDERS OF ANGELS

After this general representation of hindrances to the perception of divine justice, Dante passes on to the problem ever renewed in the Paradiso, that of the varying degrees or grades of participation in the divine. This is first discussed in relation to the wonder Dante sees in this heaven, a point of intense light with nine circles of light revolving about it. In proportion as the circles are removed from the point, their motion is slower and their flames less clear, because they receive less of the excellence of the point of light on which depends the heaven and all nature. This is a reversal of the order of the spheres themselves, for they move more rapidly in proportion as they are removed from the center. The meaning is, however, the same, for both show that though all are in perfect accord with love, yet love acts more and less powerfully on various objects. Having in this novel manner reaffirmed a familiar idea, Dante proceeds to apply it to angels and, by allegorical implication, to men. The nine circles of light revolving around the centre are composed of angels arranged according to their nine orders. First are the Seraphim and Cherubim, who resemble the point of light, which signifies God, in proportion as they are able to behold it. Next are Thrones, who similarly have delight in proportion as their view penetrates the divine. Dante then comments, in words which are at once allegorical and literal:

> From this it may be seen how blessedness
>   Is founded in the faculty which sees,
>   And not in that which loves, and follows next;

And of this seeing merit is the measure,
  Which is brought forth by grace, and by good will;
  Thus on from grade to grade doth it proceed.
              —Paradiso 28.109-14.

We may take this as Dante's statement of the cause of the satisfaction of men in ordinary life with the divine justice. In proportion as men are able to see clearly they can advance "from grade to grade" of blessedness. When a man is thus graded in accord with what is within himself, he has no dissatisfaction with his own lot, but accepts it as in harmony with the eternal verities.

Beatrice continues to explain the remainder of the nine orders of angels. Satan's pride led him to aspire above his proper place, and he fell, but others, modest and conscious of their dependence on God, have a vision of the truth. More prosaically St. Thomas explains the reasons for the varying grades of the angels:

It is the saying of the Master of the Sentences (Sent. ii.3) that those angels who were created with more subtle natures and of keener intelligence in wisdom, were likewise endowed with greater gifts of grace.

It is reasonable to suppose that gifts of graces and perfection of beatitude were bestowed on the angels according to the degree of their natural gifts. The reason for this can be drawn from two sources. First of all, on the part of God, who, in the order of his wisdom, assigned various degrees in the angelic nature. As the angelic nature was made by God for attaining grace and beatitude, so likewise the grades of the angelic nature seem to be ordained for the various degrees of grace and glory; just as when, for example, the builder chisels the stone for building a house, from the fact that he prepares some more artistically and more fittingly than others, it is clear that he is setting them apart for the more ornate part of the house. So it seems that God destined those angels for greater gifts of grace and fuller beatitude, whom he made of a higher nature. . . .

It is reasonable to suppose that the angels who had a higher nature were turned to God more mightily and efficaciously. This same thing happens in men, that greater grace and glory are bestowed according to the greater earnestness of their turning to God. Hence it appears that the angels who had the greater natural powers had the more grace and glory.
—Summa Theol. I.62.6.

Beatrice applies to Dante himself the lesson drawn from the varying degrees of the angels:

> I would not have thee doubt, but certain be,
> 'Tis meritorious to receive this grace,
> According as the affection opens to it.[12]

Considering what has gone before, we may interpret the word *affection* here to mean natural inclination, and see again that the natural powers of a man limit the amount of grace he can receive and hence his blessedness. Yet he can have in life all the satisfaction possible to his nature; in other words, what is for him complete and perfect satisfaction. Hence if the willingness unquestioningly to accept his natural allotment can be postulated for any man, he has full possibility of happiness within his own heart. But if his discontent is directed against his natural endowment itself, Dante does not here offer him any aid. A fundamental and thoroughgoing pessimism was something Dante did not feel called on to consider; he begins the consideration of any man's relation to the world with that man as he is—at his best—and does not raise difficulties with which man

[12] Paradiso 29.64-6. Cf. De Monarchia 1.8.8.

cannot deal. He begins where every philosophy inspired with good sense must begin, with man and the world as given, and does not ask whether man and the world could have been or ought to be essentially different. In fact the poet goes even farther than this, and finds in the varying natures of the angels, and hence, we may infer, in those of men, proofs of the goodness of God.

> The height behold now and the amplitude
>   Of the eternal power, since it hath made
>   Itself so many mirrors, where 'tis broken,
> One in itself remaining as before.
>                               —Paradiso 29.142-5.

In the last heaven, the primum mobile, all the saints are gathered together, for here all have their dwelling place, without respect to their grades. All are equally near to God, for in this heaven,

>        where God immediately doth govern,
> The natural law in naught is relevant.
>                               —Paradiso 30.122-3.

Distance does not hinder the light of God from penetrating through the whole. This fact suggests that in spite of the differences in grades about which so much has been said, there is a sense in which the rewards of the saints are equal. This typifies in allegory that the spiritual life of one good man on earth has a certain equality with that of any other, because, in the just ordering of society typified by the heavenly people, the humble man plays as necessary a part as does the great man. So in this part of heaven the light of God is the same for all. Even in the celestial rose the seats are not assigned ac-

## THE ARRANGEMENT OF THRONES

cording to such divisions as have determined the arrangement of the blessed in the spheres. There seems no reason to suppose that one throne is more honorable than any other. There is, however, some sort of arrangement; Beatrice possesses "the throne her merits have assigned her," and Francis, Benedict, and Augustine are assigned by lot. The seat of Beatrice may be especially suited to her merits, but one can hardly assume this for the others. Nothing more is clear than that each saint has his individual seat, in the full light of the divine splendor. The reference to the lot perhaps also refers to predestination and is intended to show that the assignment of Beatrice and of the three saints rests on the divine wisdom, as inscrutable to men as the operation of chance. But it carries no suggestion that the division of the saints is in any way the result of chance. This is the realm where fitness and due proportion everywhere appear:

> Within the amplitude of this domain
>     No casual point can possibly find place,
>     No more than sadness can, or thirst, or hunger;
> For by eternal law has been established
>     Whatever thou beholdest, so that closely
>     The ring is fitted to the finger here.
> And therefore are these people, festinate
>     Unto true life, not *sine causa* here
>     More and less excellent among themselves.
> The King, by means of whom this realm reposes
>     In so great love and in so great delight
>     That no will ventureth to ask for more,
> In his own joyous aspect every mind
>     Creating, at his pleasure dowers with grace
>     Diversely; and let here the effect suffice.
>                         —Paradiso 32.52-66.

Dante is here speaking especially of the infants he saw in paradise, yet since the problem of the varying gifts and graces of men has been in his mind throughout the Paradiso, it seems proper to think that, under the veil of the allegory, he is speaking of all men, and stating his final opinion on the problem. Even here he furnishes no solution; the fact is stated, let that suffice. But if Dante does not attempt a solution, he has advanced far beyond the attitude of questioning and wonder of the earlier part of the poem. He is now matured by experience and sees the fact in its setting as part of the order of the world as it is given to man. Natural inequality, he now is sure, is not a thing at which man need have any surprise, or over which he can properly repine. It is, in fact, unnatural for man to desire that the powers allotted to him or to any other man should be different, because inequality is part of the very constitution of things. It is man's problem to enjoy the blessedness appropriate to him. Dante brings himself and us, then, to the conception of a world thoroughly acceptable in its natural constitution, and one which perfectly exemplifies its nature, except when perverted by the sins of man. When the world is once accepted in this way, the problem of divine justice is solved, and the problem remaining is that of the injustice of man, who is moved by greed to attempt to force the ring on a finger not rightly adapted to it.

But this may be considered an evasion of the question. Ought we not to go behind the natural

## THE ALLEGORY

constitution of the world and ask whether it is as it should be? Two answers may be given. First, Dante was a poet, and as such was not obliged to give a categorical solution. His business was rather to represent the world as it appeared to him. However much use any poet may make of philosophy, his first concern is with presentations rather than with arguments. Dante looked upon the life of men, believed that to man at his best the matter was as he has put it, and so represented it in his Commedia. Second, to go behind the world as it is, in its natural constitution, is impossible. Man's mind is conditioned by this world; it can observe the workings of it, but can hardly escape from it to look upon it from without. Like Archimedes, it has no *pou sto*. Even the words good or bad, when applied to the nature of the world, lose their meaning, for with what shall we compare the world that we may see whether it is good or bad? Some men live and look upon the world in discouragement; Dante's experience permitted him to look upon it with faith and hope and love, as under the care of a king through whom, so far as man permits, it exists in perfect love and happiness. And as for man's capacity for happiness, Dante in his vision was assured of that. When he speaks of heaven as a kingdom "most just and merciful," the allegory means that the world we live in is at its best "most just and merciful," and that man in the spirit of love can be like the ruler of that realm.

The last canto of the Paradiso is given up to the

affirmation of Dante's faith in the relation of the human and the divine, culminating in the vision of the three circles, representing the Trinity, of which one is painted with the image of man. Here Dante's power fails, but with it disappears also the least shadow of doubt, and he knows beyond peradventure of the justice and love of the universe. To this conclusion he comes not as a result of a fully explicable rational process alone. Rational processes are necessary, but insufficient. He who would solve the riddle of the universe and perceive the justice of life on this earth must himself be moved to justice by love.

> The Love which moves the sun and the other stars

must have complete control over the desires and the will, and move them

> Even as a wheel that equally is moved.
> —Paradiso 33.144-5.

The three parts of the Commedia represent justice under three aspects. In the Inferno we see men who have been thrown by sin wholly out of harmony with the organization of the world. They are not under the dominion of love, they do not act justly, and they continually undergo well-merited punishment. In the Purgatorio we see those who have also been thrown out of proportion by sin, but who have seen their condition and are striving to compensate for their excesses or defects by a strong overbending in the contrary direction, that strict justice may find no fault in them, and that they may merit happiness. The interpretation of the Paradiso is less obvious.

Here the question is not that of evil, but of adjustment to the world of the varying natures with which men are endowed. The Paradiso more than either of the preceding parts considers man in his relations with his fellows. Dante asks: What of the justice of a fabric in which there is unlikeness and inequality of nature? He answers that the blessedness of man essentially depends not on the quality of his natural endowment, but on the use he makes of it. Man's place is in society, and society cannot exist without members of various powers and capacities. The just world is that in which every individual performs the duties proper to him.

Yet the Paradiso does not stop with the concept of society, but furnishes also an escape from the seeming personal injustice of life. Hell is misery; so—though mingled with hope—is purgatory. Is the effort to avoid hell worth making? Is the burden of purgatorial affliction to be borne with patience? Can man be happier if during his lifetime he escapes hell or passes through purifying affliction, or is life itself essentially unjust? To these questions Dante, the exile, answers that the world is not at bottom unjust, and that man need not live always in the shades of sin and suffering, but may undergo severe discipline with confidence. To resort to evil to escape the inequalities of the world and of nature is fatal. Let every man employ well the talents he possesses. Then life has for him all the possibilities which Dante, in his allegory, represents by the justly ordered kingdom of heaven.

# APPENDIX

## THE ORIGINALS OF PASSAGES GIVEN IN ENGLISH IN THE BODY OF THE WORK

Page-numbers refer to the body of the work.

The heading *Commentary* indicates the Commentary of St. Thomas on the Ethics.

P. 3. Convivio 1.12.61-88.

E qui è da sapere che ogni bontà propria in alcuna cosa è amabile in quella. . . . E quanto ella è più propria, tanto ancora è più amabile; onde avvegnachè ciascuna virtù sia amabile nell' uomo, quella è più amabile in esso ch' è più umana; e questa è la giustizia, la quale è solamente nella parte razionale ovvero intellettuale, cioè nella volontà. Questa è tanto amabile, che, siccome dice il Filosofo nel quinto dell' Etica, i suoi nemici l' amano, siccome sono ladroni e rubatori. . . . Di questa virtù innanzi dirò più pienamente nel quattordicesimo Trattato.

P. 3. Convivio 4.27.100-2.

Di Giustizia nel penultimo Trattato di questo volume si tratterà.

P. 3. Convivio 2.15.125-7.

La morale Filosofia, secondochè dice Tommaso sopra lo secondo dell' Etica, ordina noi all' altre scienze.

This is not a direct quotation from St. Thomas. Moreover, his treatment of moral philosophy is found not in the second book of his commentary, to which scholars have supposed the word *secondo* to refer, but in the second lectio of the first book. Here he discusses the last of the three divisions of moral philosophy, political philosophy, which is chief in the realm of practical knowledge, because it deals with the "finem ultimum humanae vitae." He speaks of it in relation to other sciences as follows: "Practicae scientiae praecipit politica, et quantum ad usum ejus ut operetur vel non operetur, et quantum ad determinationem actus. Praecipit enim fabro non solum quod sua arte utatur, sed etiam quod sic utatur, tales cultellos faciens. Utrumque enim ordinatum est ad finem humanae vitae. Sed scientiae speculativae praecipit civilis solum quantum ad usum, non autem quantum ad determinationem sui operis. Ordinat enim politica, quod aliqui doceant vel addiscant geometriam. Hujusmodi enim actus inquantum sunt voluntarii pertinent ad materiam moralis, et sunt ordinabilis ad finem humanae vitae. Non autem praecipit politicus geometriae, quae de triangulo concludat: hoc enim non subjacet humanae voluntati, nec est ordinabile humanae vitae, sed dependet ex ipsa rerum ratione. Et ideo dicit, quod politica praeordinat quas disciplinarum debitum est esse in civitatibus, scilicet tam practicarum quam speculativarum, et quis quam debeat addiscere, et usque ad quod tempus." This evidently is the source of Dante's statement.

P. 3.  Convivio 4.8.3-6.

Siccome dice Tommaso sopra al Prologo dell' Etica, conoscere l' ordine d' una cosa ad altra è proprio atto di ragione.

In St. Thomas' Commentary (book 1, lectio 1) the passage runs: Ordinem tamen unius rei ad aliam cognoscere est solius intellectus aut rationis.

P. 4.  Convivio 4.17.62-4.

Giustizia . . . ordina noi ad amare e operare dirittura in tutte cose.

P. 5.  De Monarchia 1.11.93-110.

Caritas, seu recta dilectio, illam [iustitiam] acuit atque dilucidat. Cui ergo maxime recta dilectio inesse potest, potissimum locum in illo potest habere iustitia. . . . Caritas vero, spretis aliis omnibus, quaerit Deum et hominem, et per consequens bonum hominis. Quumque inter alia bona hominis potissimum sit in pace vivere (ut supra dicebatur), et hoc operetur maxime atque potissime iustitia, caritas maxime iustitiam vigorabit, et potior potius.

P. 5.  Summa Theol. II.ii.25.1.

Manifestum est quod idem specie actus est quo diligitur Deus, et quo diligitur proximus. Et propter hoc habitus charitatis non solum se extendit ad dilectionem Dei, sed etiam ad dilectionem proximi.

P. 6. Summa Theol. II.ii.29.3, ad 3.

Pax est opus justitiae indirecte, inquantum scilicet removet prohibens; sed est opus charitatis directe, quia secundum propriam rationem charitas pacem causat. Est enim amor vis unitiva.

P. 6. Commentary, book 5, lectio 1.

Convenienter notificavit justitiam per voluntatem.

P. 6. Summa Theol. II.ii.58.1.

Justitia est habitus, secundum quem aliquis constanti et perpetua voluntate jus suum unicuique tribuit.

P. 6. Summa Theol. II.ii.58.4.

Non enim dicimur justi ex hoc quod recte aliquid cognoscimus. Et ideo subjectum justitiae non est intellectus, vel ratio, quae est potentia cognoscitiva. Sed quia justi in hoc dicimur quod aliquid recte agimus, proximum autem principium actus est vis appetitiva, necesse est quod justitia sit in aliqua vi appetitiva, sicut in subjecto. Est autem duplex appetitus: scilicet voluntas, quae est in ratione; et appetitus sensitivus. . . . Reddere autem unicuique quod suum est, non potest procedere ex appetitu sensitivo; quia apprehensio sensitiva non se extendit ad hoc quod considerare possit proportionem unius ad alterum; sed hoc est proprium rationis. Unde justitia non potest esse sicut in subjecto in irascibili, vel concupiscibili, sed solum in voluntate.

P. 7. Convivio 1.12.61-74.

E qui è da sapere che ogni bontà propria in alcuna cosa è amabile in quella. . . . E quanto ella è più propria, tanto ancora è più amabile; onde avvegnachè ciascuna virtù sia amabile nell' uomo, quella è più amabile in esso ch' è più umana; e questa è la giustizia, la quale è solamente nella parte razionale ovvero intellettuale, cioè nella volontà.

P. 7. Commentary on Politics 1.1, lectio 1.

Loquutio humana significat quid est utile et quid nocivum. Ex quo sequitur quod significet justum et injustum. Consistit enim justitia et injustitia ex hoc quod aliqui adaequentur vel non adaequentur in rebus utilibus et nocivis. Et ideo loquutio est propria hominibus; quia hoc est proprium eis in comparatione ad alia animalia, quod habeant cognitionem boni et mali, ita et injusti, et aliorum hujusmodi, quae sermone significari possunt.

(The passage is a source of De Vulgari Eloquentia 1.2.)

P. 7.   Commentary on Politics 7.14, lectio 11.

In actu autem partis animae irrationalis omnino non potest consistere ultimus finis vitae humanae; quoniam necesse est ipsum consistere in aliquo quod est proprium hominis, in quo distinguitur ab aliis, quia ultimus finis hominis est proprius ei: . . . ergo . . . consisteret in aliqua perfectione pertinente ad partem . . . animae rationalem.

P. 8.   Aristotle, Politics 7.13.

Utetur autem utique studiosus vir et paupertate et aegritudine et aliis pravis fortuniis bene; sed quod beatum, in contrariis est. Etenim hoc determinatum est secundum morales sermones, quod talis est, qui studiosus, cui propter virtutem bona sunt, quae simpliciter bona. . . . [Fortunam] dominam enim existere ponimus.

P. 10.   Commentary 5.1.

Haec enim illegalitas secundum quam dicitur aliquis illegalis, quae etiam est inaequalitas, inquantum homo non adaequatur regulae legis, continet universaliter omnem injustitiam, et est quoddam commune respectu omnis injustitiae.

P. 10.   Commentary on Politics 3, lectio 7.

Finis propter quem instituta est civitas bene ordinata, est secundum virtutem perfectam vivere vel operari.

P. 10.   Summa Theol. II.i.90.2.

(Unus autem homo est pars communitatis perfectae), necesse est quod lex proprie respiciat ordinem ad felicitatem communem.

P. 11.   De Monarchia 2.5.1-21.

Quicunque praeterea bonum Reipublicae intendit, finem iuris intendit. Quodque ita sequatur, sic ostenditur: Ius est realis et personalis hominis ad hominem proportio, quae servata hominum servat societatem, et corrupta corrumpit. . . . Si ergo definitio ista bene quid est et quare comprehendit, et cuiuslibet societatis finis est commune sociorum bonum; necesse est finem cuiusque iuris bonum commune esse, et impossible est ius esse, bonum commune non intendens. Propter quod bene Tullius in prima Rhetorica: 'Semper,' inquit, 'ad utilitatem Reipublicae leges interpretandae sunt.' Quod si ad utilitatem eorum qui sunt sub lege leges directae non sunt, leges nomine solo sunt, re autem leges esse non possunt.

P. 11. Ethics 5.3.

Virtus perfecta, sed non simpliciter, sed ad alterum.

P. 11. Ethics 5.3.

Neque hesperus neque lucifer ita admirabilis.

P. 11. Commentary 5.2.

Neque hesperus, idest stella praeclarissima vespertina, neque lucifer, idest stella praeclarissima matutina, ita fulget sicut justitia.

P. 12. De Monarchia 1.11.32-4.

Et vere tunc potest dici de illa [justitia], ut Philosophus inquit, 'neque Hesperus, neque Lucifer sic admirabilis est.'

P. 12. Convivio 2.15.127-32.

Siccome dice il Filosofo nel quinto dell' Etica, la giustizia legale ordina le scienze ad apprendere, e comanda, perchè non sieno abbandonate, quelle essere apprese e ammaestrate.

P. 13. Ethics 5.5.

Factiva autem totius virtutis sunt legalium quaecumque lege posita sunt circa disciplinam, quae ad commune.

P. 13. Commentary 5.3.

Est enim manifestum, quod illa quae sunt lege posita, sunt factiva totius virtutis, secundum suam disciplinam, qua instruitur homo in ordine ad bonum commune.

P. 14. Commentary 5.3.

Sic aliae malitiae possunt esse sine avaritia quae est specialis injustitia. Quandoque autem est e converso quod aliquis peccat per avaritiam tollendo aliena, et tamen non peccat secundum unam aliquam aliarum malitiarum, neque secundum omnes, et tamen peccat secundum quamdam malitiam. Quod patet quia propter hoc vituperatur quasi injustus.

## APPENDIX

P. 14. Commentary 5.3.

Ille autem qui moechatur ut accipiat de alieno non videtur esse luxuriosus, per se loquendo, quia non intendit luxuriae finem. Sed magis videtur esse injustus, quia propter lucrum contra justitiam fecit. . . . Si vero aliquis inordinate lucratus est surripiens aliena, hoc non reducitur ad aliquam aliam malitiam, sed ad solam injustitiam. . . . Et dicit quod justitia particularis est circa illa, secundum quae attenditur communicatio inter homines; sicut honor et pecunia et ea quae pertinent ad salutem vel dispendium corporis, et circa alia hujusmodi. Est etiam particularis justitia non solum circa res exteriores, sed propter delectationem quae consequitur ex lucro, per quod scilicet aliquis accipiat aliena ultra quam debeat.

P. 15. Summa Theol. II.ii.118.3, obj. 2, seq.

Peccatum avaritiae in hoc consistit quod homo transcendit mensuram in rebus possessis. Sed huiusmodi mensura statuitur per iustitiam. Ergo avaritia directe opponitur iustitiae. . . . Respondeo dicendum quod avaritia importat immoderantiam quandam circa ipsam acceptionem et conservationem divitiarum: inquantum scilicet aliquis acquirit pecuniam ultra debitum aliena surripiendo vel retinendo. Et sic opponitur iustitiae. Et hoc modo accipitur avaritia Ezech. XXII, ubi dicitur: Principes eius in medio eius quasi lupi rapientes praedam ad effundendum sanguinem, et avare lucra sectanda. . . . Iustitia proprie statuit mensuram in acceptionibus et conservationibus divitiarum secundum rationem debiti legalis: ut scilicet homo nec accipiat nec retineat alienum. . . . Avaritia consistit in plus habendo quam debeat secundum iustitiam.

P. 16. De Monarchia 1.11.69-105.

Ad evidentiam primi notandum est quod iustitiae maxime contrariatur cupiditas, ut innuit Aristoteles in quinto ad Nicomachum. Remota cupiditate omnino, nihil iustitiae restat adversum; unde sententia Philosophi est, ut quae lege determinari possunt, nullo modo iudici relinquantur, et hoc metu cupiditatis fieri oportet, de facili mentes hominum detorquentis. Ubi ergo non est quod possit optari, impossibile est ibi cupiditatem esse; destructis enim obiectis, passiones esse non possunt. Sed Monarcha non habet quod possit optare; sua namque iurisdictio terminatur Oceano solum, quod non contingit principibus aliis, quorum principatus ad alios terminantur. . . . Cupiditas namque, perseitate hominum spreta, quaerit alia, caritas vero, spretis aliis omnibus, quaerit Deum et hominem, et per consequens bonum hominis.

P. 16. De Monarchia 1.13.47-55.

Quum ergo Monarcha nullum cupiditatis occasionem habere possit, vel saltem minimam inter mortales, ut superius est ostensum, quod caeteris principibus non contingit, et cupiditas ipsa sola sit corruptiva iudicii, et iustitiae praepeditiva; consequens est, quod ipse vel omnino, vel maxime bene dispositus ad regendum esse potest.

P. 16. Convivio 4.4.22-44.

Onde conciossiacosachè l' animo umano in terminata possessione di terra non si quieti, ma sempre desideri terra acquistare, siccome per esperienza vedemo, discordie e guerre conviene surgere tra regno e regno. Le quali sono tribulazioni delle cittadi; e per le cittadi, delle vicinanze; e per le vicinanze, delle case; [e per le case], dell' uomo; e così s' impedisce la felicità. Il perchè, a questo guerre e alle loro cagioni torre via, conviene di necessità tutta la Terra, e quanto all' umana generazione a possedere è dato, esser Monarchia, cioè uno solo Principato e uno Principe avere, il quale, tutto possedendo e più desiderare non possendo, li re tenga contenti nelli termini delli regni, sicchè pace intra loro sia, nella quale si posino le cittadi, e in questa posa le vicinanze s' amino, in questo amore le case prendano ogni loro bisogno, il quale preso, l' uomo viva felicemente; ch' è quello per che l' uomo è nato.

P. 17. Epistle 6.150-60.

Nec advertitis dominantem cupidinem, quia caeci estis, venenoso susurrio blandientem, minis frustatoriis cohibentem, nec non captivantem vos in lege peccati, ac sacratissimis legibus, quae iustitiae naturalis imitantur imaginem, parere vetantem; observantia quarum, si laeta, si libera, non tantum non servitus esse probatur, quin immo, perspicaciter intuenti, liquet ut est ipsa summa libertas.

## APPENDIX

P. 18. Commentary 5.3.

Est enim manifestum, quod illa quae sunt lege posita, sunt factiva totius virtutis, secundum suam disciplinam, qua instruitur homo in ordine ad bonum commune. Est autem quaedam alia disciplina secundum quam instruitur homo ad actus virtutis secundum quod competit singulariter sibi, scilicet ad proprium bonum inquantum per hoc homo efficitur bonus in seipso. Potest ergo esse dubitatio, utrum hujusmodi disciplina pertineat ad politicam, vel ad aliquam aliam scientiam. Et hoc dicit, posterius esse determinandum scilicet in libro Politicae. In tertio enim libro Politicae ostenditur quod non est idem simpliciter esse virum bonum, et esse civem bonum, secundum quamcumque politiam. Sunt enim quaedam politiae, non rectae, secundum quas aliquis potest esse civis bonus, qui non est vir bonus; sed secundum optimam politicam non est aliquis civis bonus, qui non est vir bonus.

P. 19. De Monarchia 1.12.63-71.

Quum Monarcha maxime diligat homines, ut iam tactum est, vult omnes homines bonos fieri, quod esse non potest apud oblique politizantes. Unde Philosophus in suis Politicis ait quod in politia obliqua bonus homo est malus civis; in recta vero, bonus homo et civis bonus convertuntur.

P. 19. Aristotle's Politics 3.4.

Dicimus utique principem studiosum, esse bonum et prudentem: politicum autem, necessarium esse prudentem.

Et disciplinam autem mox alteram esse dicunt quidam principis, sicut et videntur regum filii equestrem et bellicam erudiri, ut Euripides ait: Non mihi quae vana altera, sed quorum civitati opus est: tamquam sit quaedam principis disciplina. . . . Itaque eadem principis boni et viri boni.

P. 19. Aristotle's Politics 3.4.

Quoniam impossible similes esse omnes cives, non utique erit virtus una civis et boni viri. Eam quidem enim quae studiosi civis oportet omnibus inesse: sic enim optimam necessarium esse civitatem: eam autem quae viri boni, impossible, si non omnes necessarium bonos esse eos qui in studiosa civitate cives.

P. 21. Commentary 5.4.

In politia aristocratica in qua aliqui principantur propter virtutem, mensuratur dignitas secundum virtutem; ut scilicet ille plus habeat qui plus abundat in virtute.

P. 21. Convivio 4.11.51-6.

Dico che la loro imperfezione primamente si può notare nella indiscrezione del loro avvenimento, nel quale nulla distributiva giustizia risplende, ma tutta iniquità quasi sempre; la quale iniquità è proprio effetto d' imperfezione.

P. 22. Commentary 5.5.

Patet ergo quod conjunctio A cum G, idest rei duplae cum persona duplo digniori, et B cum D, idest dimidii cum dimidio, est justum distributivum et tale justum est medium. . . . Proportionale enim est medium inter excessum et defectum; quia proportionalitas est aequalitas proportionis.

Compare De Monarchia 1.11; 1.14; 3.5 for similar use of letters by Dante.

P. 22. De Monarchia 2.5.3-6.

Jus est realis et personalis hominis ad hominem proportio, quae servata hominum servat societatem, et corrupta corrumpit.

P. 23. Politics 1.2.

Diki enim civilis communitatis ordo est. Diki autem justi judicium.

P. 24. Commentary 5.6.

Quando homines dubitant de hoc medio, refugiunt ad judicem; quod idem est ac si refugerent ad id quod est justum; nam judex debet esse quasi quoddam justum animatum, ut scilicet mens ejus totaliter a justitia possideatur. Illi autem qui refugiunt ad judicem, videntur quaerere medium inter partes, quae litigant; et inde est, quod judices vocant medios, vel mediatores, ac si ipsi attingant medium, et in hoc quod perducunt ad hoc quod est justum.

P. 24. Summa Theol. II.i.92.1.

Intentio ferentis legem tendat in verum bonum quod est bonum commune secundum justitiam divinam regulatum.

## APPENDIX

P. 24.  De Monarchia 2.10.2-7.

Nam ubicumque humanum iudicium deficit, vel ignorantiae tenebris involutum, vel propter praesidium iudicis non habere; ne iustitia derelicta remaneat, recurrendum est ad Illum, etc.

P. 25.  Convivio 4.27.88-95.

Conviensi anche a questa età [Senettute] essere Giusto, acciocchè li suoi giudicii e la sua autoritade sia un lume e una legge agli altri. E perchè questa singolar virtù, cioè Giustizia, fu veduta per gli antichi filosofi apparire perfetta in questa età, il reggimento delle città commisero in quelli che in questa età erano.

P. 25.  Commentary on Politics 7.9, lectio 7.

Prudentia autem et virtus magis vigent in provectis quae magis sunt necessariae ad consilium et judicium; et ideo consiliativum et judicativum attribuenda sunt eis quando sunt provectae aetatis.

P. 25.  Commentary 5.7.

Exemplo a linea sumpto fit manifestum, quomodo ipse judex ad aequalitatem omnia reducat.

P. 25.  Commentary 5.7.

Ex praemissis enim patet quod justum de quo nunc agitur, est medium damni et lucri: quod quidem justum nihil est aliud quam habere aequale ante commutationem et post, etiam praeter voluntatem; ut patet in eo qui judice cogente restituit alteri quod plus habebat.

P. 26.  Ethics 5.8.

Si patiatur quae fecit, vindicta recte sit.

P. 26.  Commentary 5.8.

Manifestum est enim quod majus est nocumentum quando aliquis percutit principem, per quod non solum personam ipsius, sed totam rempublicam laedit, quam si percutit aliquam privatam personam. . . . In vindictis non solum attenditur quod aequalitas justitiae reparetur per hoc quod aliquis restituat alteri quod ei subtraxit; sed etiam quod pro peccato commisso poenam sustineat: et propter hoc lege aliqui puniuntur etiam pro peccatis pro quibus nulla injuria

# APPENDIX

vel damnum alii irrogatur; et fur compellitur non solum restituere quod accepit, per quod aequalitas justitiae reintegratur; sed etiam ulterius punitur pro culpa commissa.

P. 27. Summa Theol. II.ii.61.4.

Utrum justum sit simpliciter idem quod contrapassum.

P. 27. Inferno 28.142.

> Così s' osserva in me lo contrapasso.

P. 27. Purgatorio 30.108.

> Perchè sia colpa e duol d' una misura.

P. 27. Paradiso 7.82-4.

> Ed in sua dignità mai non riviene [l' umana creatura],
> Se non riempie dove colpa vota,
> Contra mal dilettar con giuste pene.

P. 28. Ethics 5.8.

In contrafacere enim proportionale manet civitas.

P. 28. Commentary 5.8.

Per hoc autem homines commanent adinvicem, quod unus retribuat alteri pro his quae ab eo acceperit. . . . Si autem non sic fiat retributio, non erit aequalitas rerum commutatarum, et sic homines non poterunt adinvicem commanere, eo quod nihil prohibet opus unius artificis esse melius quam opus alterius: sicut domus quam calceamentum: et ideo oportet haec adinvicem adaequari, secundum dictam proportionabilitatem, ad hoc, quod fiat justa commutatio.

P. 29. Summa Theol. II.ii.106.6.

Recompensatio gratiae respicit beneficium secundum voluntatem benefacientis. In quo quidem praecipue hoc commendabile videtur, quod gratis beneficium contulit, ad quod non tenebatur. Et ideo qui beneficium accepit, ad hoc obligatur ex debito honestatis, ut similiter aliquid gratis impendat. Non autem videtur gratis aliquid impendere, nisi excedat quantitatem accepti beneficii: quia quamdiu recompensat minus vel aequale, non videtur facere gratis, sed reddere quod accepit. Et ideo gratiae recompensatio semper tendit ut pro suo posse aliquid majus retribuat.

P. 29. Commentary 5.9.

Numisma factum est secundum compositionem, idest secundum conventionem quamdam inter homines, propter commutationem necessitatis, idest rerum necessariarum. Est enim condictum inter homines quod afferenti denarium detur id quo indiget. Et inde est quod denarius vocatur numisma: nomos enim lex est, quia scilicet denarius non est mensura per naturam, sed nomo, idest a lege: est enim in potestate natura[e] transmutare denarios et reddere eos inutiles.

P. 30. Commentary on Politics 1.9, lectio 8.

Ideo quia homo constitutus est ex rebus quae sunt secundum naturam, aliae res quae sunt, sunt ei cibus. Et ideo omnibus hominibus est naturalis pecuniativa, idest acquisitiva ciborum, vel denariorum pro cibo, ex rebus naturalibus, scilicet ex fructibus et animalibus. Quod autem aliquis acquirat pecuniam non ex rebus naturalibus, sed ab ipsis denariis, hoc non est secundum naturam.

P. 30. Commentary 5.10.

Potest autem dici medietas effectiva, inquantum scilicet est constitutiva medii, quia scilicet actus ejus est justa operatio, quae est medium inter injustum facere et injustum pati, quorum duorum alterum tamen, scilicet injustum facere, pertinet ad malitiam, scilicet injustitiam, quae est extremorum, inquantum accipit sibi plus de bonis et minus de malis; sed injustum pati, non pertinet ad aliquam malitiam, sed magis est poena.

P. 31. Convivio 4.17.65-8.

E ciascuna di queste virtù ha due nemici collaterali, cioè vizi, uno *in troppo* e un altro *in poco*. E queste sono i *mezzi* intra quelli.

P. 31. Commentary 5.10.

Virtus moralis est habitus electivus.

P. 31. Convivio 4.17.68-72.

E nascono tutte [di queste virtù] da uno principio, cioè dall'abito della nostra buona elezione. Onde generalmente si può dire di tutte, che sieno *Abito elettivo consistente nel mezzo*.

# APPENDIX

P. 32. Commentary 5.10.

Potest autem aliquis secundum electionem operari justum tam in commutationibus, quam in distributionibus, dupliciter. Uno modo inter se et alterum: . . . Alio modo inter duos alios, quod pertinet ad judicem vel arbitrum. . . . Justus operetur justum. . . . Conferat . . . aequaliter secundum proportionem.

P. 32. De Monarchia 1.11.46-51.

Quantum vero ad operationem, iustitia contrarietatem habet in posse; nam quum iustitia sit virtus ad alterum, sine potentia tribuendi cuique quod suum est, quomodo quis operabitur secundum illam?

P. 33. Commentary 5.11.

Justum de quo quaeritur, est justum simpliciter, quod est justum politicum . . . Justum politicum consistit in quadam communitate vitae, quae ordinatur ad hoc, quod sit per se sufficientia eorum, quae ad vitam humanam pertinent. Et talis est communitas civitatis, in qua debent omnia inveniri, quae sufficiant humanae vitae.

P. 34. De Monarchia 1.3.85-90.

Quod dico propter agibilia, quae politica prudentia regulantur, et propter factibilia, quae regulantur arte; quae omnia speculationi ancillantur tanquam optimo, ad quod humanum genus prima bonitas in esse produxit.

P. 34. De Monarchia 1.12.38-48.

Hoc viso, iterum manifestum esse potest, quod haec libertas, sive principium hoc totius libertatis nostrae, est maximum donum humanae naturae a Deo collatum; quia per ipsum hic felicitamur ut homines, per ipsum alibi felicitamur ut Dii. Quod si ita est, quis erit qui humanum genus optime se habere non dicat, quum potissime hoc principio possit uti? Sed existens sub Monarcha, est potissime liberum.

P. 35. Commentary 5.11.

In recta gubernatione multitudinis non permittimus quod homines principentur, scilicet secundum voluntatem et passiones humanas, sed quod principetur homini lex, quae est dictamen rationis, vel homo qui secundum rationem agat: quia si princeps sequitur passiones humanas, faciet hoc sibi.

scilicet, quod plus accipiet de bonis, et minus de malis, et fiet tyrannus, quum hoc sit contra rationem principis. Ad hoc enim princeps institutus est ut custodiat justitiam, et per consequens aequalitatem quam praeterit, dum sibi usurpat plus de bonis et minus de malis. . . . Quia princeps, si sit justus, nihil plus attribuit sibi de bonis, quam aliis, nisi forte secundum debitam proportionem distributivae justitiae, inde est, quod princeps non laborat ad utilitatem suam, sed aliorum. Et propter hoc supra dictum est, quod justitia legalis, secundum quam princeps gubernat multitudinem, est alienum bonum. . . . Quia ergo princeps laborat pro multitudine, danda est merces a multitudine, scilicet honor et gloria, quae sunt maxima bonorum, quae ab hominibus dari possunt. Si autem sunt aliqui principes, quibus ista non sufficiant pro mercede, sed quaerunt lucra, isti sunt injusti et tyranni. Et super hanc mercedem ab hominibus exhibitam boni principes expectant mercedem a Deo.

P. 36. Aquinas, De Regimine Iudaeorum 6.

Principes terrarum sunt a Deo instituti, non quidem ut propria lucra quaerant, sed ut communem populi utilitatem procurent.

P. 36. De Monarchia 1.11.70-8.

Notandum est quod iustitiae maxime contrariatur cupiditas, ut innuit Aristoteles in quinto ad Nicomachum. Remota cupiditate omnino, nihil iustitiae restat adversum; unde sententia Philosophi est, ut quae lege determinari possunt, nullo modo iudici relinquantur, et hoc metu cupiditatis fieri oportet, de facili mentes hominum detorquentis.

P. 36. Paradiso 6.112-4.

> Questa picciola stella si correda
> > Dei buoni spirti, che son stati attivi
> > Perchè onore e fama li succeda.

P. 37. Paradiso 18.91-3.

Diligite justitiam, qui judicatis terram.

P. 37. De Monarchia 1.11.95-140.

Cui ergo maxime recta dilectio inesse potest, potissimum locum in illo potest habere iustitia. Huiusmodi est Monarcha; ergo eo existente, iustitia potissima est vel esse potest.

... Quanto magis causa est causa, tanto magis effectum diligit, quum dilectio talis adsequatur causam per se. Quum ergo Monarcha sit universalissima causa inter mortales, ut homines bene vivant, quia principes alii per illum, ut dictum est; consequens est, quod bonum hominum ab eo maxime diligatur.

P. 38. De Monarchia 1.12.83-91.

Patet, quod quamvis Consul sive Rex respectu viae sint domini aliorum; respectu autem termini aliorum ministri sunt, et maxime Monarcha, qui minister omnium procul dubio habendus est. Hinc etiam iam innotescere potest, quod Monarchia necessitatur a fine sibi praefixo in legibus ponendis.

P. 38. De Monarchia 1.14.38-41.

Habent namque nationes, regna, et civitates inter se proprietates, quas legibus differentibus regulari oportet.

P. 39. Commentary 5.12.

Nam et Isidorus dicit in libro Ethymologiarum, quod jus dicitur quasi justum. Videtur autem esse contrarietas quantum ad hoc, quod politicum idem est quod civile; et sic id quod apud Philosophum ponitur ut divisum, apud juristas videtur poni ut dividens, nam jus civile ponunt partem juris positivi. Sed attendendum est, quod aliter sumitur politicum vel civile hic apud Philosophum, et aliter apud juristas. Nam Philosophus hic nominat politicum justum vel civile ex usu, quo cives utuntur; juristae autem nominant jus politicum vel civile ex causa, quod scilicet civitas aliqua sibi constituit. Et ideo hoc convenienter a Philosopho nominatur legale, idest lege positum, quod et illi dicunt positivum. Convenienter autem per haec duo dividitur justum politicum. Utuntur enim cives et justo eo quod natura menti humanae indidit, et eo quod est positum lege.

P. 39. Convivio 4.9.87.

La Ragione scritta è arte di bene e d' equità.

P. 40. De Monarchia 2.5.6-9.

Nam illa Digestorum descriptio, non dicit quod quid est iuris, sed describit illud per notitiam utendi illo.

P. 40. Commentary 5.12.

Justum vero ex positione alicujus civitatis vel principis apud illos tantum est virtuosum, qui subduntur jurisdictioni illius civitatis vel principis. Alio modo manifestat hoc justum, secundum causam, cum dicit, quod justum naturale non consistit in videri vel non videri, idest non oritur ex aliqua opinione humana, sed natura. Sicut enim in speculativis sunt quaedam naturaliter cognita, ut principia indemonstrabilia, et quae sunt propinqua his; quaedam vero studio hominum adinventa, et quae sunt propinqua; ita etiam in operativis sunt quaedam principia naturaliter cognita quasi indemonstrabilia principia, et propinqua his, ut malum esse vitandum, . . . et similia. Alia vero sunt per industriam hominum excogitata, quae dicuntur hic justa legalia.

P. 41. Convivio 4.9.150-67.

Regole sono in quella che sono *puri arti,* siccome sono le leggi de' matrimoni, delli servi, delle milizie, delli successori in dignitadi; e di queste in tutto siamo allo Imperadore suggetti senza dubbio o sospetto alcuno. Altre leggi sono, che sono quasi *seguitatrici di Natura,* siccome costituire l' uomo d' etade sufficiente ad amministrare; e di questo non semo in tutto suggetti. Altre sono molte, che *paiono avere alcuna parentela* coll' arte imperiale, e qui fu ingannato ed è chi crede che la sentenza imperiale sia in questa parte autentica: siccome giovanezza, sovra la quale nullo imperiale giudizio è da consentire, in quanto egli è Imperadore: però quello che è di Dio, sia renduto a Dio.

P. 41. Summa Theol. II.i.91.4, ad 1.

Per naturalem legem participatur lex aeterna secundum proportionem capacitatis humanae naturae. Sed oportet ut altiori modo dirigatur homo in ultimum finem supernaturalem. Et ideo superadditur lex divinitus data, per quam lex aeterna participatur altiori modo.

P. 42. Summa Theol. II.i.93.3, ad 2.

Lex humana intantum habet rationem legis, inquantum est secundum rationem rectam; et secundum hoc manifestum est quod a lege aeterna derivatur. Inquantum vero a ratione recedit, sic dicitur lex iniqua; et sic non habet rationem legis, sed magis violentiae cujusdam.

P. 42.  Summa Theol. II.i.94.2.

Hoc est ergo primum praeceptum legis, quod bonum est faciendum et prosequendum, et malum vitandum. . . . Homo habet naturalem inclinationem ad hoc quod veritatem cognoscat de Deo, et ad hoc quod in societate vivat.

P. 42.  Summa Theol. II.i.94.3.

Ad legem naturae pertinet omne illud ad quod homo inclinatur secundum suam naturam. . . . Anima rationalis sit propria forma hominis.

P. 43.  Summa Theol. II.i.95.2.

Omnis lex humanitus posita intantum habet de ratione legis, inquantum a lege naturae derivatur. Si vero in aliquo a lege naturali discordet, jam non erit lex, sed legis corruptio. Sed sciendum est quod a lege naturali dupliciter potest aliquid derivari: uno modo sicut conclusiones ex principiis, alio modo sicut determinationes quaedam aliquorum communium. . . . Derivantur ergo quaedam a principiis communibus legis naturae per modum conclusionum; sicut hoc quod est *non esse occidendum,* ut conclusio quaedam derivari potest ab eo quod est *nulli esse faciendum malum:* quaedam per modum determinationis; sicut lex naturae habet quod ille qui peccat puniatur; sed quod tali poena vel tali puniatur, hoc est quaedam determinatio legis naturae. Utraque igitur inveniuntur in lege humana posita. Sed ea quae sunt primi modi continentur in lege humana, non tamquam sint solum lege posita, sed habent etiam aliquid vigoris ex lege naturali. Sed ea quae sunt secundi modi, ex sola lege humana vigorem habent.

P. 44.  De Monarchia 2.7.1-22.

Et illud quod natura ordinavit, de jure servatur: natura enim in providendo non deficit ab hominis providentia, quia si deficeret, effectus superaret causam in bonitate, quod est impossibile. . . . Propter quod patet, quod natura ordinat res cum respectu suarum facultatum; qui respectus est fundamentum iuris in rebus a natura positum. Ex quo sequitur quod ordo naturalis in rebus absque iure servari non possit, quum inseparabiliter iuris fundamentum ordini sit annexum. Necesse est igitur ordinem de iure servari.

P. 44. De Monarchia 3.2.9-32.

Haec igitur irrefragabilis veritas praefigatur, scilicet quod illud quod naturae intentioni repugnat, Deus nolit. Nam si hoc verum non esset, contradictorium eius non esset falsum, quod est: Deum non nolle quod naturae intentioni repugnat. Et si hoc non falsum, nec ea quae sequuntur ad ipsum. Impossibile enim est in necessariis consequentiis falsum esse consequens, antecedente non falso existente. . . . Manifestum est quod Deus finem naturae vult: aliter coelum otiose moveret; quod dicendum non est.

P. 45. De Monarchia 2.2.39-61.

Ex his iam liquet quod ius quum sit bonum, per prius in mente Dei est: et quum omne quod in mente Dei est, sit Deus (iuxta illud: "Quod factum est, in ipso vita erat"); et Deus maxime seipsum velit, sequitur quod ius a Deo, prout in eo est, sit volitum. Et quum voluntas et volitum in Deo sit idem, sequitur ulterius quod divina voluntas sit ipsum ius. Et iterum ex hoc sequitur quod ius in rebus nihil est aliud quam similitudo divinae voluntatis. Unde fit quod quidquid divinae voluntati non consonat, ipsum ius esse non possit; et quidquid divinae voluntati est consonum, ius ipsum sit. Quapropter quaerere utrum de iure factum sit aliquid, licet alia verba sint, nihil tamen aliud quaeritur quam utrum factum sit secundum quod Deus vult. Hoc ergo supponatur quod illud quod Deus in hominum societate vult, illud pro vero atque sincero iure habendum sit.

P. 45. De Monarchia 2.5.11-23.

Si ergo . . . cuiuslibet societatis finis est commune sociorum bonum; necesse est finem cuiusque iuris bonum commune esse, et impossibile est ius esse, bonum commune non intendens. Propter quod bene Tullius in prima Rhetorica: 'Semper,' inquit, 'ad utilitatem Reipublicae leges interpretandae sunt.' Quod si ad utilitatem eorum qui sunt sub lege leges directae non sunt, leges nomine solo sunt, re autem leges esse non possunt. Leges enim oportet homines devincire ad invicem, propter communem utilitatem.

P. 46. De Monarchia 2.6.7-25.

Quicunque finem iuris intendit, cum iure graditur: Romanus populus subiciendo sibi orbem, finem iuris intendit, ut manifeste per superiora in isto capitulo est probatum; ergo Romanus populus subiciendo sibi orbem, cum iure hoc fecit; et per consequens de iure sibi adscivit Imperii dignitatem. Quae conclusio, ut ex omnibus manifestis illata sit, manifestandum est hoc quod dicitur: quod quicumque finem iuris intendit, cum iure graditur. Ad cuius evidentiam advertendum quod quaelibet res est propter aliquem finem, aliter esset otiosa; quod esse non potest, ut superius dicebatur. Et quemadmodum omnis res est ad proprium finem, sic omnis finis propriam habet rem cuius est finis.

P. 46. De Monarchia 2.6.36-41.

Impossibile est iuris finem quaerere sine iure, quum quaelibet res ad proprium finem se habeat velut consequens ad antecedens: nam impossibile est bonam valetudinem membrorum attingere sine sanitate.

P. 47. De Monarchia 2.6.61-7.

Si aliquid, ut finis ipsius iuris, absque iure obtineretur, ita esset finis iuris, hoc est commune bonum, sicut exhibitio facta de male acquisito est eleemosyna: et sic, quum in propositione dicatur de fine iuris existente, non tantum apparente, instantia nulla est.

P. 47. De Monarchia 3.10.30-40.

Nemini licet ea facere per officium sibi deputatum quae sunt contra illud officium; quia sic idem, in quantum idem, esset contrarium sibi ipsi: quod est impossibile. Sed contra officium deputatum Imperatori est scindere imperium; quum officium eius sit humanum genus uni velle, et uni nolle tenere subjectum, ut in primo huius de facili videri potest: ergo scindere Imperium Imperatori non licet.

P. 48. De Monarchia 1.13.48-50.

Monarcha nullam cupiditatis occasionem habere possit, vel saltem minimam inter mortales.

P. 48. Commentary 5.12.

Rationes rerum mutabilium sunt immutabiles, sic quicquid est nobis naturale quasi pertinens ad ipsam hominis rationem, nullo modo mutantur: puta actiones et dispositiones motus mutantur ut in paucioribus. Et similiter etiam illa quae pertinent ad ipsam justitiae rationem nullo modo possunt mutari, puta non esse furandum, quod est injustum facere. Illa vero quae consequuntur, mutantur ut in minori parte. . . .

Omnes enim leges ponuntur secundum quod congruit fini politicae; sed tamen sola una est optima politia secundum naturam ubicumque sit.

P. 51. Purgatorio 16.67-78.

> Voi che vivete, ogni cagion recate
> Pur suso al ciel, così come se tutto
> Movesse seco di necessitate.
> Se così fosse, in voi fora distrutto
> Libero arbitrio, e non fora giustizia,
> Per ben letizia, e per male aver lutto.
> Lo cielo i vostri movimenti inizia,
> Non dico tutti: ma, posto ch' io il dica,
> Lume v' è dato a bene ed a malizia,
> E libero voler, che, se fatica
> Nelle prime battaglie col ciel dura,
> Poi vince tutto, se ben si nutrica.

P. 51. Paradiso 15.1-3.

> Benigna volontade, in cui si liqua
> Sempre l'amor che drittamente spira,
> Come cupidità fa nell' iniqua.

P. 52. Commentary 5.14.

Incontinens operatur sibi nociva propter voluntatem. Habet enim per se voluntatem boni, sed per concupiscentiam trahitur ad malum. Et hoc quod dictum est, probat per hoc, quod cum voluntas sit apparentis boni, nullus vult id quod non existimat esse bonum. Incontinens autem extra passionem existens non reputat bonum illud quod facit, unde absolute non vult illud; sed tamen operatur illud quod existimat non oportere operari, propter concupiscentiam quae est in appetitu sensitivo, voluntas autem est in ratione.

P. 52. Ethics 5.11.

Neque enim vult nullus, quod non existimat esse studiosum.

P. 53. Convivio 1.12.74-84.

Questa [la giustizia] è tanta amabile, che, siccome dice il Filosofo nel quinto dell' *Etica,* i suoi nemici l' amano, siccome sono ladroni e rubatori: e però vedemo che 'l suo contrario, cioè la ingiustizia, massimamente è odiata; siccom' è tradimento, ingratitudine, falsità, furto, rapina, inganno e loro simili. Li quali sono tanto inumani peccati, che, ad iscusare sè dell' infamia di quelli, si concede da lunga usanza che uomo parli di sè.

P. 53. Summa Theol. II.ii.66.6.

Si passim homines sibi invicem furarentur, periret humana societas.

P. 54. Inferno 11.25-6.

> Ma perchè frode è dell' uom proprio male,
> Più spiace a Dio.

P. 56. Ethics 5.13.

Homines autem in seipsis existimant esse injustum facere, propter quod et injustum esse facile, hoc autem non. Commisceri quidem enim ei, quae vicini, et percutere proximum et dare manu argentum, facile et in ipsis. Sed sic habentes hoc facere neque in ipsis.

P. 56. Commentary 5.15.

Dicit quod multi existimant quod est statim in promptu quod habeant facere etiam injustum; unde reputant quod facile sit aliquem esse habitualiter injustum. Sed hoc non est ita. Facile enim est, et statim in potestate hominis, quod aliquis faciat ea quae sunt injusta, puta quod commisceatur cum uxore vicini sui, et quod percutiat proximum et quod tollat argentum de manu alterius, vel quod de manu sua det aliquis argentum ad procurandum homicidium, vel aliquid hujusmodi. Sed quod homines hujusmodi faciant sic se habentes, scilicet prompte et delectabiliter, non est facile, neque statim in potestate hominis; sed ad hoc pervenitur per longam consuetudinem.

P. 56. Convivio 4.9.65-75.

Sono anche operazioni che la nostra [ragione] *considera nell' atto della volontà,* siccome offendere e giovare; siccome stare fermo e fuggire alla battaglia; siccome stare casto e lussuriare; e queste del tutto soggiacciono alla nostra volontà; e però semo detti da loro buoni e rei, perch' elle sono proprie nostre del tutto; perchè, quanto la nostra volontà ottenere puote, tanto le nostre operazioni si stendono.

P. 57. Commentary 5.15.

Facere injustum per se est praedicta facere sic se habentem, scilicet quod sit volens et promptus ad hoc.

P. 58. Commentary 5.16.

Dubitat de aequitate, an eadem sit cum justitia naturali et legali.

P. 58. Commentary 5.16.

Dicitur autem in graeco epiiches quasi id quod est conveniens vel decens, ab epi, quod est supra, et icos quod est obediens; quia videlicet per epiichiam aliquis excellentiori modo obedit, dum observat intentionem legislatoris, ubi dissonant verba legis.

P. 59. Paradiso 20.121.

> Tutto suo amor laggiù pose a drittura.

P. 59. Paradiso 20. 133-4.

> E voi, mortali, tenetevi stretti
> A giudicar.

P. 60. Commentary 5.16.

Et talia sunt facta humana: de quibus dantur leges.

P. 60. De Monarchia 1.14.35-47.

Leges municipales quandoque deficiant, et opus habeant directivo, ut patet per Philosophum in quinto ad Nicomachum, epiichiam commendantem. Habent namque nationes, regna et civitates inter se proprietates, quas legibus differentibus regulari oportet. Est enim lex regula directiva vitae. Aliter quippe regulari oportet Scythas, . . . et aliter Garamantes.

P. 61. De Monarchia 1.14.52-3.

Secundum sua communia, quae omnibus competunt.

P. 61. Convivio 4.9.75-84.

E conciossiacosachè in tutte queste volontarie operazioni sia equità alcuna da conservare, e iniquità da fuggire; la quale equità per due cagioni si può perdere, o per non sapere qual' essa si sia, o per non volere quella seguitare; trovata fu la Ragione scritta, e per mostrarla e per comandarla. Onde dice Augustino: 'Se questa (cioè equità) gli uomini la

## APPENDIX 205

conoscessero, e conosciuta servassero, la Ragione scritta non sarebbe mestieri.' E però è scritto nel principio del vecchio Digesto: 'La Ragione scritta è arte di bene e d' equità.'

P. 62. Commentary 5.16.

Ponit quamdam proprietatem talis virtuosi: et dicit quod talis non est acribodikaios, idest diligenter exequens justitiam ad deterius, idest ad puniendum, sicut illi qui sunt rigidi in puniendo, sed diminuunt poenas quamvis habeant legem adjuvantem ad puniendum. Non enim poenae sunt per se intentae a legislatore, sed quasi medicina quaedam peccatorum. Et ideo epiiches non plus apponit de poena quam sufficiat ad cohibenda peccata.

P. 62. Summa Theol. II.ii.108.4.

Alio modo potest considerari poena, inquantum est medicina non solum sanativa peccati praeteriti, sed etiam praeservativa a peccato futuro, vel etiam promotiva in aliquod bonum. . . . Non autem punitur aliquis in spiritualibus bonis sine propria culpa, neque in praesenti, neque in futuro: quia ibi poenae non sunt medicinae, sed consequuntur spiritualem damnationem.

P. 63. Commentary 5.17.

Nullus potest sibi injustum facere; nec etiam qui seipsum occidit sibiipsi injustum facere videtur, cum volens patiatur.

P. 64. Summa Theol. II.ii.79.1.

Ad justitiam vero generalem pertinet facere bonum debitum in ordine ad communitatem et ad Deum, et vitare malum oppositum.

P. 64. Summa Theol. II.i.100.2.

Communitas ad quam ordinat lex divina, est hominum ad Deum vel in praesenti vel in futura vita. Et ideo lex divina praecepta proponit de omnibus illis per quae homines bene ordinentur ad communicationem cum Deo. Homo autem Deo conjungitur ratione, sive mente, in qua est Dei imago: et ideo lex divina praecepta proponit de omnibus illis per quae ratio hominis bene ordinata est. Hoc autem contingit per actus omnium virtutum. Nam virtutes intellectuales ordinant bene actus rationis in seipsis, virtutes autem morales ordinant bene actus rationis circa interiores passiones et exteriores operationes. Et ideo manifestum est quod lex divina convenienter proponit praecepta de actibus omnium virtutum.

P. 65. Summa Theol. II.ii.57.1, ad 3.

Quia justitia aequalitatem importat, Deo autem non possumus aequivalens recompensare, inde est quod justum secundum perfectam rationem non possumus reddere Deo; et propter hoc non dicitur proprie jus lex divina, sed fas, quia videlicet sufficit Deo ut impleamus quod possumus. Justitia tamen ad hoc tendit ut homo, quantum potest, Deo recompenset, totaliter animam ei subjiciens.

P. 67. Tenth Epistle 172-5.

Si vero accipiatur opus allegorice, subiectum est homo, prout merendo et demerendo per arbitrii libertatem iustitiae praemiandi et puniendi obnoxius est.

P. 70. De Monarchia 1.4.3-4.

Actuare semper totam potentiam intellectus possibilis.

P. 73. Inferno 3.4.

Giustizia mosse il mio alto fattore.

P. 73. Convivio 2.14.40-4.

La verità . . . ch' è ultima perfezione nostra, siccome dice il Filosofo nel sesto dell' Etica, quando dice che 'l vero è il bene dello intelletto.

P. 74. Summa Theol. III.86.4.

Justum est enim ut qui voluntati suae plus indulsit quam debuit, contra voluntatem suam aliquid patiatur: sic enim erit aequalitas.

P. 74. Summa Theol. II.i.87.3, ad 1.

Justum tamen est secundum Gregorium, quod "qui in suo aeterno peccavit contra Deum, in aeterno Dei puniatur." Dicitur autem aliquis in suo aeterno peccasse, non solum secundum continuationem actus in tota hominis vita durantis; sed quia ex hoc ipso quod finem in peccato constituit, voluntatem habet in aeternum peccandi. Unde dicit Gregorius, quod "iniqui voluissent sine fine vivere, ut sine fine potuissent in iniquitatibus permanere."

## APPENDIX

P. 75. Dionysius the Carthusian, De Quatuor Noviss. 3.20 (from Bautz, Das Fegfeur, Mainz, 1883).

His ergo et consimilibus monstrata sunt animarum in purgatorio aut in inferno detentarum supplicia sub imaginibus et similitudinibus corporalium rerum, secundum quod utilius capere poterant et reversae (animae) ad corpus, *i.e.,* ad pristinum sensum, salubrius recitare viventibus, quibus spiritualia per corporalia declarari oportet.

P. 76. Summa Theol. II.ii.61.4.

Contrapassum est commutativum justum.

P. 77. Inferno 3.125-6.

> Chè la divina giustizia gli sprona
> Sì che la tema si volge in disio.

P. 78. Inferno 4.42.

> Senza speme vivemo in disio.

P. 79. Summa Theol. II.ii.118.3.

Alio modo [avaritia] importat immoderantiam circa interiores affectiones divitiarum; puta cum quis nimis amat vel desiderat divitias, aut nimis delectatur in eis, etiamsi nolit rapere aliena; et hoc modo avaritia opponitur liberalitati.

P. 80. Inferno 7.19-21.

> Ahi giustizia di Dio, tante chi stipa
> Nuove travaglie e pene, quante io viddi?
> E perchè nostra colpa sì ne scipa?

P. 80. Convivio 4.12.39-54.

Promettono le false traditrici, se ben si guarda, di torre ogni sete e ogni mancanza, e apportar ogni saziamento e bastanza. E questo fanno nel principio a ciascuno uomo, questa promissione in certa quantità di loro accrescimento affermando; e poichè quivi sono adunate, in loco di saziamento e di refrigerio, dánno e recano sete di casso febricante e intollerabile; e in loco di bastanza, recano nuovo termine, cioè maggior quantità a desiderio; e con questo paura e sollecitudine grande sopra l' acquisto. Sicchè veramente non *quietano,* ma *dánno più cura,* la qual prima senza loro non s' avea.

P. 81.   Summa Theol. II.ii.118.5.

Potest attendi gradus peccatorum ex parte boni cui inordinate subditur appetitus humanus; quod quanto minus est, tanto peccatum est deformius: turpius est enim subesse inferiori bono quam superiori. Bonum autem exteriorum rerum est infimum inter humana bona; est enim minus quam bonum corporis, quod etiam minus est quam bonum animae, quod exceditur a bono divino. Et secundum hoc, peccatum avaritiae, quo appetitus humanus subjicitur etiam exterioribus rebus, habet quodammodo deformitatem majorem.

P. 81.   Convivio 4.13.142-7.

Assai è manifesta la loro viltà per tutte le sue note; e però l' uomo di diritto appetito e di vera conoscenza quelle mai non ama; e non amandole, non si unisce ad esse; ma quelle sempre di lungi da sè essere vuole, se non in quanto ad alcuno necessario servigio sono ordinate.

P. 81.   Convivio 4.11.105-7.

Molta sollecitudine quivi si richiegga, e la sollecitudine del buono sia diritta a maggiori cose.

P. 82.   Petrarch, Confessional Psalms, Ira, in the Romanic Review (1911) 2.434.

Vita mea mihi odio fuit: et iratum me cum omni homine perdi pariter concupivi.

P. 83.   Ethics 7.7.

Quae autem ira facit, omnis facit tristatus.

P. 83.   Inferno 8.46-8.

> Quei fu al mondo persona orgogliosa;
> Bontà non è che sua memoria fregi:
> Così s' è l' ombra sua qui furiosa.

P. 83.   Summa Theol. II.i.46.6.

Velle enim malum alicujus sub ratione justi, potest esse etiam secundum virtutem justitiae, si praecepto rationis obtemperetur.

P. 84.   Inferno 12.14-5.

> Sè stesso morse
> Si come quei cui l'ira dentro fiacca.

P. 84. Inferno 7.121-4.

> Tristi fummo
> Nell' aer dolce che dal sol s' allegra,
> Portando dentro accidioso fummo:
> Or ci attristiam nella belletta negra.

P. 84. Summa Theol. II.ii.158.5.

Potest autem inordinatio irae ex duobus attendi: . . . alio modo ex ipsa irae duratione, eo scilicet quod ira nimis perseverat: quod quidem potest esse dupliciter. Uno modo, quia causa irae, scilicet injuria illata, nimis manet in memoria hominis: unde ex hoc homo diutinam tristitiam concipit: et ideo sunt sibi ipsis graves et mali.

P. 85. Convivio 1.12.72-4.

Solamente nella parte razionale ovvero intellettuale, cioè nella volontà.

P. 87. Inferno 12.104-5.

> Tiranni
> Che dier nel sangue e nell' aver di piglio.

P. 87. Inferno 12.133-4.

> La divina giustizia di qua punge
> Quell' Attila che fu flagello in terra.

P. 88. Inferno 13.70-2.

> L' animo mio . . .
> Ingiusto fece me contra me giusto.

P. 88. Inferno 13.105.

> Non è giusto aver ciò ch' uom si toglie.

P. 89. Summa Theol. II.ii.59.3, ad 1.

Homo enim per suam voluntatem possidet res, et ita non est praeter proportionem, si ei aliquid subtrahatur secundum propriam voluntatem, vel a seipso vel a alio.

P. 89. Summa Theol. II.ii.59.3, ad 2.

Injuriam quidem facit, non sibi, sed civitati et Deo.

P. 90. Inferno 14.5-6.

> Dove
> Si vede di giustizia orribil arte.

P. 90. Inferno 14.71-2.

> Li suoi dispetti
> Sono al suo petto assai debiti fregi.

P. 91. Summa Theol. II.ii.154.12.

Pessima est principii corruptio, ex quo alia dependent. Principia autem rationis sunt ea quae sunt secundum naturam: nam ratio, praesuppositis his quae sunt a natura determinata, disponit alia secundum quod convenit. . . . In agendis agere contra ea quae sunt secundum naturam determinata, est gravissimum et turpissimum. Quia ergo in vitiis quae sunt contra naturam transgreditur homo id quod est secundum naturam determinatum circa usum venereorum, inde est quod in tali materia hoc peccatum est gravissimum. . . . Ordo naturae est ab ipso Deo. Et ideo in peccatis contra naturam, in quibus ipse ordo naturae violatur, fit injuria ipsi Deo ordinatori naturae.

P. 93. Summa Theol. II.ii.78.1.

Respondeo dicendum quod accipere usuram pro pecunia mutuata est secundum se injustum, quia venditur id quod non est; per quod manifeste inaequalitas constituitur, quae justitiae contrariatur.

P. 94. Inferno 18.95.

> Tal colpa a tal martiro lui condanna.

P. 95. Summa Theol. II.ii.115.2.

Hoc enim contrariatur dilectioni Dei, contra cuius justitiam homo loquitur, et contra dilectionem proximi, quem in peccato fovet.

P. 95. Summa Theol. II.ii.115.2.

Cum quis alicui adulatur ad hoc quod fraudulenter ei noceat vel corporaliter, vel spiritualiter.

P. 95. Inferno 18.114.

> Che dagli uman privati parea mosso.

P. 96. Inferno 19.2-4.

> Le cose di Dio, che di bontate
> Deono essere spose, e voi rapaci
> Per oro e per argento adulterate.

P. 96.  Inferno 19.97-8.
> Però ti sta, che tu se' ben punito;
> E guarda ben la mal tolta moneta.

P. 97.  Inferno 19.72.
> Su l' avere, e qui me misi in borsa.

P. 97.  Inferno 20.28.
> Qui vive la pietà quando è ben morta.

P. 98.  Summa Theol. II.ii.95.1.

Dei proprium, qui solus in sua aeternitate videt ea quae futura sunt, quasi praesentia. . . . Si quis ergo hujusmodi futura praenuntiare aut praenoscere quocumque modo praesumpserit, nisi Deo revelante, manifeste usurpat sibi quod Dei est; et ex hoc aliqui divini dicuntur. Unde dicit Isidorus: "Divini dicti, quasi Deo pleni; Divinitate enim se plenos simulant, et astutia quadam fraudulentiae, hominibus futura conjectant."

P. 98.  Inferno 20.38-9.
> Perchè volle veder troppo davante,
> Diretro guarda, e fa retroso calle.

P. 99.  Inferno 21.53-4.
> Coperto convien che qui balli,
> Sì che, se puoi, nascosamente accaffi.

P. 100.  Inferno 25.13-4.
> Per tutti i cerchi dell' inferno oscuri
> Non vidi spirto in Dio tanto superbo.

P. 100.  Summa Theol. II.ii.66.6, ad 2.

Non infligitur secundum praesens judicium poena mortis, nisi furtum aggravatur per aliquam gravem circumstantiam, sicut patet de sacrilegio.

P. 100.  Inferno 24.119-20.
> O giustizia di Dio quant' è severa,
> Che cotai colpi per vendetta croscia!

P. 101.  Inferno 25.77-8.
> Due e nessun l' imagine perversa
> Parea.

P. 101. Summa Theol. II.ii.66.6.

Peccatum mortale est quod contrariatur charitati, secundum quod est spiritualis animae vita. Charitas autem consistit principaliter quidem in dilectione Dei, secundario vero in dilectione proximi; ad quam pertinet ut proximo bonum velimus et operemur. Per furtum autem homo infert nocumentum proximo in suis rebus; et si passim homines sibi invicem furarentur, periret humana societas.

P. 102. Inferno 27.74-7.

> L' opere mie
> Non furon leonine, ma di volpe.
> Gli accorgimenti e le coperte vie
> Io seppi tutte.

P. 103. Inferno 26.89.

> Come fosse la lingua che parlasse.

P. 103. Inferno 27.135-6.

> In che si paga il fio
> A quei che scommettendo acquistan carco.

P. 103. Inferno 28.35.

> Seminator di scandalo e di scisma.

P. 103. Summa Theol. II.ii.43.1.

In processu viae spiritualis contingit aliquem disponi ad ruinam spiritualem per dictum vel factum alterius inquantum scilicet aliquis sua admonitione vel inductione aut exemplo alterum trahit ad peccandum.

P. 104. Summa Theol. II.ii.39.1.

Et ideo peccatum schismatis proprie est speciale peccatum, ex eo quod intendit se ab unitate separare, quam charitas facit; quae non solum alteram personam alteri unit spirituali dilectionis vinculo; sed etiam totam Ecclesiam in unitate spiritus. Et ideo proprie schismatici dicuntur qui propria sponte et intentione se ab unitate Ecclesiae separant, quae est unitas principalis. Nam unitas particularis aliquorum ad invicem ordinatur ad unitatem Ecclesiae, sicut compositio singulorum membrorum in corpore naturali ordinatur ad totius corporis unitatem.

# APPENDIX

P. 104. Summa Theol. II.ii.42.1, ad 2.

Temporali vel saeculari multitudinis unitati, puta civitatis vel regni.

P. 104. Summa Theol. II.ii.42.2.

Manifestum est ergo quod seditio opponitur et justitiae et communi bono.

P. 105. Inferno 28.139-42.

> Perch' io partii così giunte persone,
> Partito porto il mio cerebro, lasso!
> Dal suo principio ch' è in questo troncone.
> Così s' osserva in me lo contrapasso.

P. 106. Inferno 29.55-6.

> La ministra
> Dell' alto Sire, infallibil giustizia.

P. 106. Summa Theol. II.ii.77.2, ad 1.

Si aurum vel argentum ab alchimicis factum veram speciem non habeat auri et argenti, est fraudulenta et injusta venditio; praesertim cum sint aliquae utilitates auri et argenti veri, secundum naturalem operationem ipsorum, quae non conveniunt auro per alchimiam sophisticato.

P. 107. Summa Theol. II.ii.110.3.

Mendacium autem est malum ex genere: est enim actus cadens super indebitam materiam. Cum enim voces naturaliter sint signa intellectuum, innaturale est et indebitum quod aliquis voce significet id quod non habet in mente. . . . Mendacium non solum habet rationem peccati ex damno quod infertur proximo, sed ex sua inordinatione.

P. 107. Summa Theol. II.ii.110.4.

Nocumentum proximi, quantum ad personam, divitias, vel famam.

P. 107. Summa Theol. II.ii.109.3.

Non enim haec virtus [veritas] attendit debitum legale, quod attendit justitia, sed potius debitum morale, inquantum scilicet ex honestate unus homo alteri debet veritatis manifestationem. Unde veritas est pars justitiae. . . .

Quia homo est animal sociale, naturaliter unus homo debet alteri id sine quo societas humana servari non posset. Non autem possent homines ad invicem convivere, nisi sibi invicem crederent, tamquam sibi invicem veritatem manifestantibus.

P. 109. Summa Theol. II.ii.162.6.

Ex parte autem conversionis non habet superbia quod sit maximum peccatorum; quia celsitudo, quam superbus inordinate appetit, secundum suam rationem non habet maximam repugnantiam ad bonum virtutis. Sed ex parte aversionis superbia habet maximam gravitatem: quia in aliis peccatis homo a Deo avertitur, vel propter ignorantiam, vel propter infirmitatem, sive propter desiderium cujuscumque alterius boni; sed superbia habet aversionem a Deo ex hoc ipso quod non vult Deo et ejus regulae subjici. Unde Boethius dicit quod "cum omnia vitia fugiant a Deo, sola superbia se Deo opponit." Propter quod etiam specialiter dicitur Jacobi IV.6, quod *Deus superbis resistit*. Et ideo averti a Deo et ejus praeceptis, quod est quasi consequens in aliis peccatis, per se ad superbiam pertinet, cujus actus est Dei contemptus. Et quia id quod est per se, semper potius est eo quod est per aliud, consequens est quod superbia sit gravissimum peccatorum secundum suum genus, quia excedit in aversione, quae formaliter complet peccatum.

P. 110. Augustine, Epistle 140, sec. 55, Migne, vol. 33.

Diabolus igitur et angeli ejus a luce atque fervore charitatis aversi, et nimis in superbiam indiviamque progressi, velut glaciali duritia torpuerunt. Et ideo per figuram tanquam in aquilone ponuntur.

P. 112. Summa Theol. II.i.87.6.

Actus enim peccati facit hominem reum poenae, inquantum transgreditur ordinem divinae justitiae, ad quem non redit nisi per quamdam recompensationem poenae, quae ad aequalitatem justitiae reducit, ut scilicet qui plus voluntati suae indulsit quam debuit, contra mandatum Dei agens, secundum ordinem divinae justitiae aliquid contra illud quod vellet, spontaneus vel invitus patiatur. Quod etiam in injuriis hominibus factis observatur, ut per recompensationem poenae reintegretur aequalitas justitiae. Unde patet quod cessante actu peccati vel injuriae illatae, adhuc remanet debitum poenae. Sed si loquamur de ablatione peccati quantum ad maculam, sic manifestum est quod macula peccati ab anima

## APPENDIX 215

auferri non potest, nisi per hoc quod anima Deo conjungitur; per cujus distantiam detrimentum proprii nitoris incurrebat, quod est macula. Conjungitur autem Deo homo per voluntatem. Unde macula peccati ab homine tolli non potest, nisi voluntas hominis ordinem divinae justitiae acceptet, ut scilicet vel ipse sibi poenam spontaneus assumat in recompensationem culpae praeteritae, vel etiam a Deo illatam patienter sustineat; utroque enim modo poena rationem satisfactionis habet. Poena autem satisfactoria diminuit aliquid de ratione poenae. Est enim de ratione poenae quod sit contra voluntatem. Poena autem satisfactoria, etsi secundum absolutam considerationem sit contra voluntatem, non tamen ut nunc; et per hoc est voluntaria.

P. 115. Robertus Holkot, Opus (ed. 1483), cap. 17, lect. 193.

Hospitale Dei est purgatorium de quo suprius dictum est ibi quo ponuntur infirmi ut sanentur.

P. 115. St. Bernard of Clairvaux, Sermones de Diversis 42, Migne 183.663.

Vadam in istam regionem, et videbo visionem hanc grandem, quomodo pius Pater glorificandos filios in manu tentatoris relinquat, non ad occisionem, sed ad purgationem.

P. 115. Commentary 2.11.

Quando damus studium ad hoc quod multum recedamus a peccato, ad quod proni sumus, sic tandem vix perveniemus ad medium. Et ponit similitudinem de illis qui dirigunt ligna distorta; qui dum volunt ea dirigere, torquent in aliam partem et sic reducuntur ad medium. Et est hic considerandum quod haec via acquirendi virtutes est efficacissima; ut, scilicet homo nitatur ad contrarium ejus ad quod inclinatur vel ex natura vel consuetudine.

P. 116. Bromiardus, Sermo 6, 'Pena' (Basel, Johann Amerbach [Hain 3993]).

Lepidi vero et pigri, qui hic semper querunt quomodo carne quiescere possunt, ibi nunquam requiem habebunt. . . . Gulosi etiam qui hic excedunt, ibi esurient.

P. 116. Summa Theol. II.i.87.6, ad 3.

Remota macula sanatum est vulnus peccati quantum ad voluntatem. Requiritur autem adhuc poena ad sanationem aliarum virium animae, quae per peccatum praecedens deordinatae fuerunt, ut scilicet per contraria curentur. Requiritur etiam ad restituendum aequalitatem justitiae, et ad amovendum scandalum aliorum, ut aedificentur in poena qui sunt scandalizati culpa.

P. 118. Purgatorio 2.94-8.
> Nessun m' è fatto oltraggio,
> Se quei, che leva e quando e cui gli piace,
> Più volte m' ha negato esto passaggio;
> Chè di giusto voler lo suo si face.

P. 118. Purgatorio 3.133-5.
> Sì non si perde
> Che non possa tornar l' eterno amore,
> Mentre che la speranza ha fior del verde.

P. 119. Purgatorio 5.106-7.
> Tu te ne porti di costui l' eterno
> Per una lagrimetta che il mi toglie.

P. 119. Purgatorio 6.37-9.
> Cima di giudizio non s' avvalla,
> Perchè foco d'amor compia in un punto
> Ciò che dee satisfar chi qui s'astalla.

P. 120. Summa Theol. II.ii.162.3, ad 1.

Cognitio veritatis est duplex: una pure speculativa; et hanc superbia indirecte impedit, subtrahendo causam. Superbus enim neque Deo intellectum suum subjicit, ut ab eo veritatis cognitionem percipiat, secundum illud Matth. XI.25: *Abscondisti haec a sapientibus et prudentibus,* id est superbis, qui sibi sapientes et prudentes videntur, *et revelasti ea parvulis,* id est, humilibus: neque etiam ab hominibus addiscere dignatur, cum tamen dicatur Eccli. VI.34: *Si inclinaveris aurem tuam,* scilicet humiliter audiendo, *excipies doctrinam.* Alia autem est cognitio veritatis, scilicet affectiva: et talem cognitionem veritatis directe impedit superbia, quia superbi, dum delectantur in propria excellentia, excellentiam veritatis fastidiunt; ut Gregorius dicit, quod "superbi, etsi secreta quaedam intelligendo percipiunt, eorum dulcedinem experiri non possunt; et si noverunt quomodo sunt, ignorant quomodo sapiunt." Unde et Prov. XI.2 dicitur: *Ubi humilitas, ibi sapientia.*

# APPENDIX

P. 121. Purgatorio 11.7-9.

> Vegna ver noi la pace del tuo regno,
> Chè noi ad essa non potem da noi,
> S' ella non vien, con tutto nostro ingegno.

P. 121. Summa Theol. II.ii.162.6.

Superbia habet aversionem a Deo ex hoc ipso quod non vult Deo et ejus regulae subjici.

P. 122. Summa Theol. II.ii.162.4.

Superbia importat immoderatam excellentiae appetitum. . . . Quis a semetipso habere aestimat quod a Deo habet.

P. 122. Purgatorio 11.88.

> Di tal superbia qui si paga il fio.

P. 122. Purgatorio 11.125-6.

> Cotal moneta rende
> A satisfar chi è di là tropp' oso.

P. 122. Purgatorio 12.70-2.

> Or superbite, e via col viso altiero,
> Figliuoli d' Eva, e non chinate il volto,
> Sì che veggiate il vostro mal sentiero.

P. 122. Petrarch, Confessional Psalms, Superbia.

> Errexi cornua et respexi celum.

P. 123. Petrarch, Confessional Psalms, Invidia.

Idcirco domine invidie oculos amove a me ut que recte sint videam et ea agam.

P. 124. I Samuel 18.9.

Non rectis ergo oculis Saul aspiciebat David a die illa.

P. 125. Perez, I Setti Cerchi del Purgatorio di Dante, Verona, 1867, p. 151.

Il fumo ch' esce dal fuoco è quella parte che il fuoco scevera da sè per meglio scaldare e schiarare, è cosa che non dà nè forza di calore, nè dolcezza di lume, ma solo contrista ed accieca. Onde giusto è, che in mezzo a densissimo fumo ripensino al proprio peccato coloro, che un giorno dal fuoco dell' ira trassero fumo a spengere o a illanguidire co' pensieri della vendetta il fuoco della carità, e ad annebbiare con fosche imagini il lume della verità. . . . Questo fumo è assomigliato dal Poeta a *nebbia* e a *vapori umidi e spessi*, forse perchè siccome la nebbia e i vapori fan comparire gli oggetti assai più grandi che non sono, così l' ira aggrandisce oltre il debito le imagini de' torti e delle offese, a accresce i motivi dei propri affanni: è paragonato a *notte* senza stelle, a buio d' inferno, perchè niuno sa prevedere a che perigli ed enormezze possiamo esser condotti in mezzo alle tenebre dell' ira.

P. 127. Purgatorio 16.10-13.

> Sì come cieco va dietro a sua guida
>  Per non smarrirsi, e per non dar di cozzo
>  In cosa che il molesti, o forse ancida,
> M' andava io per l' aere amaro e sozzo.

P. 127. Summa Theol. II.ii.158.4.

Ira habet quamdam excellentiam propter vehementiam et velocitatem sui motus.

P. 127. Summa Theol. II.ii.158.6.

Ex suo impetu, quo mentem praecipitat ad inordinata quaecumque agenda.

P. 128. Ethics 7.7.

Sic ira propter caliditatem, et velocitatem naturae audiens quidem, non praeceptum autem audiens movet ad punitionem.

P. 128. Summa Theol. II.ii.158.2.

Motus irae non immoderate fervescat nec interius, nec exterius: quod quidem si praetermittatur, non erit ira absque peccato, etiamsi aliquis appetat justam vindictam.

P. 129. Purgatorio 18.115-6.

> Noi siam di voglia a moverci sì pieni,
> Che ristar non potem.

P. 130. Purgatorio 19.118-26.

> Sì come l' occhio nostro non s' aderse
>  In alto, fisso alle cose terrene,
>  Così giustizia qui a terra il merse.
> Come avarizia spense a ciascun bene
>  Lo nostro amore, onde operar perdèsi,
>  Così giustizia qui stretti ne tiene

## APPENDIX

>    Ne' piedi e nelle man legati e presi;
>    E quanto fia piacer del giusto Sire,
>    Tanto staremo immobili e distesi.

P. 131. Purgatorio 19.115-7.

>    Quel ch' avarizia fa, qui si dichiara
>    In purgazion dell' anime converse,
>    E nulla pena il monte ha più amara.

P. 131. Purgatorio 11.88.

>    Di tal superbia qui si paga il fio.

P. 133. Purgatorio 22.49-51.

>    La colpa, che rimbecca
>    Per dritta opposizione alcun peccato,
>    Con esso insieme qui suo verde secca.

P. 134. Bromiardus, Sermo 8, 'Pena.'

Cupidi vero qui amplas terras et pulchra maneria et multa et aurum thesauricant et argentum, bona mobilia et immobilia avide cumulantes, et lucra mala lucrantes, ibi erunt in artissimo puteo, omni bono carentes, et sine spe consolationis lamentantes et dicentes illud *Sap.* v. Transierunt omnia velut umbra.

P. 135. Purgatorio 23.64-75.

>    Tutta esta gente che piangendo canta,
>    Per seguitar la gola oltra misura,
>    In fama e in sete qui si rifà santa.
>    Di bere e di mangiar n' accende cura
>    L' odor ch' esce del pome, e dello sprazzo
>    Che si distende su per la verdura.
>    E non pure una volta, questo spazzo
>    Girando, si rinfresca nostra pena;
>    Io dico pena, e dovrei dir sollazzo;
>    Chè quella voglia all' arbore ci mena,
>    Che menò Cristo lieto a dire: "Elì,"
>    Quando ne liberò con la sua vena.

P. 135. Purgatorio 23.125-6.

>    La montagna
>    Che drizza voi che il mondo fece torti.

P. 138. Latin Hymn, attributed to St. Ambrose, Migne 17.1177.

> Lumbos jecurque morbidum
> Flammis adure congruis,
> Accincti ut artus excubent
> Luxu remoto pessimo.

P. 139. Summa Theol. II.ii.154.3, ad 1.

Inter omnia Christianorum certamina duriora sunt praelia castitatis, ubi est quotidiana pugna et rara victoria.

P. 139. De Purgatorio, in Locupletissima Bibliotheca Moralis Praedicabilis . . . P. Josephi Mansi, Congregationis Oratii Romani Presbyteri, Antwerp, 1701.

Per ignem tribulatio et aerumnae huius vitae denotantur, quia Deus tamquam aurum in fornace probavit electos: Qui autem peccata per adversitates patienter toleratas non purgant, neque ullos contritionis et amoris super omnia actus, (qui pariter per ignem figurantur, de quo dicitur: Ignem veni mittere in terram) in hac vita excitant, illis opus est, ut per flammas purgantes pertranseant.

P. 140. Purgatorio 28.91-6.

> Lo sommo Ben, che solo esso a sè piace,
> Fece l'uom buono, e a bene, e questo loco
> Diede per arra a lui d'eterna pace.
> Per sua diffalta qui dimorò poco;
> Per sua diffalta in pianto ed in affanno
> Cambiò onesto riso e dolce gioco.

P. 140. Purgatorio 31.37-9.

> Se tacessi, o se negassi
> Ciò che confessi, non fora men nota
> La colpa tua: da tal giudice sassi.

P. 140. Purgatorio 31.40-2.

> Ma quando scoppia dalla propria gota
> L' accusa del peccato, in nostra corte
> Rivolge sè contra il taglio la rota.

P. 141. Purgatorio 32.48.

> Sì si conserva il seme d' ogni giusto.

# APPENDIX

P. 141.  Purgatorio 33.67-72.

> E se stati non fossero acqua d'Elsa
> Li pensier vani intorno alla tua mente,
> E il piacer loro un Piramo alla gelsa,
> Per tante circostanze solamente
> La giustizia di Dio nello interdetto
> Conosceresti all' arbor moralmente.

P. 142.  Tenth Epistle 267-70.

Removere viventes in hac vita de statu miseriae, et perducere ad statum felicitatis.

P. 145.  Summa Theol. I.96.3.

Necesse est dicere aliquam disparitatem in primo statu futuram fuisse, ad minus quantum ad sexum; quia sine diversitate sexus generatio non fuisset. Similiter etiam quantum ad aetatem; sic enim quidam ex aliis nascebantur, nec illi qui miscebantur, steriles erant. Sed et secundum animam diversitas fuisset et quantum ad justitiam, et quantum ad scientiam. Non enim ex necessitate homo operabatur, sed per liberum arbitrium, ex quo homo habet quod possit magis et minus animum applicare ad aliquid faciendum, vel volendum, vel cognoscendum; unde quidam magis profecissent in justitia et scientia, quam alii. Ex parte etiam corporis poterat esse disparitas. Non enim erat exemptum corpus humanum totaliter a legibus naturae, quin ex exterioribus agentibus aliquod commodum aut auxilium reciperet magis vel minus, cum etiam cibis eorum vita sustentaretur. Et sic nihil prohibet dicere quin secundum diversam dispositionem aeris et diversum situm stellarum, aliqui robustiores corpore generarentur quam alii, et majores, et pulchriores, et melius complexionati; ita tamen quod in illis qui excederentur, nullus esset defectus, vel peccatum, sive circa animam, sive circa corpus.

P. 145.  Summa Theol. I.96.4.

Tunc vero dominatur aliquis alteri ut libero, quando dirigit ipsum ad proprium bonum ejus qui dirigitur, vel ad bonum commune; et tale dominium hominis ad hominem in statu innocentiae fuisset propter duo; primo quia homo naturaliter est animal sociale. Unde homines in statu innocentiae socialiter vixissent. Socialis autem vita multorum esse non posset, nisi aliquis praesideret, qui ad bonum commune intenderet. Multi enim per se intendunt ad multa, unus vero ad unum. Et ideo Philosophus dicit quod quandocumque multa ordinantur ad unum, semper invenitur unum ut principale et dirigens. Secundo, quia si unus homo habuisset super alios supereminentiam scientiae et justitiae, inconveniens fuisset; nisi hoc exequeretur in utilitatem aliorum, secundum quod dicitur: *Unusquisque gratiam quam accepit, in alterutrum illam administrantes.* Unde Augustinus dicit, quod "justi non dominandi cupiditate imperant, sed officio consulendi;" et "Hoc naturalis ordo praescribit; ita Deus hominem condidit."

P. 146. Paradiso 1.1-3.

> La gloria di colui che tutto move
> Per l'universo penetra, e risplende
> In una parte più, e meno altrove.

P. 146. Summa Theol. I.21.1.

Ordo universi, qui apparet tam in rebus naturalibus, quam in rebus voluntariis, demonstrat Dei justitiam. Unde dicit Dionysius: "Oportet videre in hoc veram Dei esse justitiam, quod omnibus tribuit propria, secundum uniuscujusque existentium dignitatem; et uniuscujusque naturam in proprio salvat ordine et virtute." . . . Sic etiam Deus operatur justitiam, quando dat unicuique quod ei debetur secundum rationem suae naturae et conditionis. Sed hoc debitum dependet ex primo; quia hoc unicuique debetur, quod est ordinatum ad ipsum secundum ordinem divinae sapientiae. Et licet Deus hoc modo debitum alicui det, non tamen ipse est debitor; quia ipse ad alia non ordinatur, sed potius alia in ipsum. Et ideo justitia quandoque dicitur in Deo condecentia suae bonitatis.

P. 147. Summa Theol. I.65.2, ad 3.

Aequalitas justitiae locum habet in retribuendo. Justum enim est quod aequalibus aequalia retribuantur. Non autem habet locum in prima rerum institutione. Sicut enim artifex ejusdem generis lapides in diversis partibus aedificii ponit absque injustitia, non propter aliquam diversitatem in lapidibus praecedentem, sed attendens ad perfectionem totius aedificii, quae non esset, nisi lapides diversimode in aedificio collocarentur; sic et Deus a principio, ut esse perfectio in universo, diversas et inaequales creaturas instituit secundum suam sapientiam absque injustitia, nulla tamen praesupposita meritorum diversitate.

P. 147. Paradiso 1.103-11.

> Le cose tutte quante
> Hann' ordine tra loro; e questo è forma
> Che l' universo a Dio fa simigliante.
> Qui veggion l' alte creature l' orma
> Dell' eterno valore, il quale è fine
> Al quale è fatta la toccata norma.
> Nell' ordine ch' io dico sono accline
> Tutte nature, per diverse sorti,
> Più al principio loro e men vicine.

P. 147. Summa Theol. I.47.1.

Sed hoc [quod rerum multitudo et distinctio non sit a Deo] non potest stare, . . . quia secundum hanc positionem non proveniret ex intentione primi agentis universitas rerum, sed ex concursu multarum causarum agentium. Tale autem dicimus provenire a casu. Sic igitur complementum universi, quod in diversitate rerum consistit, esset a casu, quod est impossibile,. Unde dicendum est, quod distinctio rerum et multitudo est ex intentione primi agentis, quod est Deus. Produxit enim res in esse propter suam bonitatem communicandam creaturis, et per eas repraesentandam. Et quia per unam creaturam sufficienter repraesentari non potest, produxit multas creaturas et diversas; ut quod deest uni ad repraesentandam divinam bonitatem, suppleatur ex alia. Nam bonitas, quae in Deo est simpliciter et uniformiter, in creaturis est multipliciter et divisim. Unde perfectius participat divinam bonitatem et repraesentat eam totum universum, quam alia quaecumque creatura.

P. 148. Summa Theol. I.47.2.

Sicut divina sapientia causa est distinctionis rerum, propter perfectionem universi, ita et inaequalitatis. Non enim esset perfectum universum, si tantum unus gradus bonitatis inveniretur in rebus.

P. 148. De Monarchia 1.3.66-76.

Et quia potentia ista per unum hominem, seu per aliquam particularium communitatum superius distinctarum, tota simul in actum reduci non potest; necesse est multitudinem esse in humano genere, per quam quidem tota potentia haec actuetur; sicut necesse est multitudinem rerum generabilium, ut potentia tota materiae primae semper sub actu sit.

P. 149. Paradiso 2.133-41.

> E come l' alma dentro a vostra polve
> Per differenti membra, e conformate
> A diverse potenze, si risolve;
> Così l' intelligenza sua bontate
> Multiplicata per le stelle spiega,
> Girando sè sopra sua unitate.
> Virtù diversa fa diversa lega
> Col prezioso corpo ch' ell' avviva,
> Nel qual, sì come vita in voi, si lega.

P. 149. Paradiso 3.65-6.

> Desiderate voi più alto loco
> Per più vedere, o per più farvi amici?

P. 150. Paradiso 3.85.

> E 'n la sua volontate è nostra pace.

P. 150. Paradiso 3.88-90.

> Chiaro mi fu allor com' ogni dove
> In cielo è Paradiso, e sì la grazia
> Del sommo ben d' un modo non vi piove.

P. 150. Paradiso 4.34-9.

> Tutti fanno bello il primo giro,
> E differentemente han dolce vita,
> Per sentir più e men l' eterno spiro.
> Qui si mostraron, non perchè sortita
> Sia questa spera lor; ma per far segno
> Della celestial ch' ha men salita.

P. 151. Paradiso 5.118-9.

> Del lume che per tutto il ciel si spazia
> Noi semo accesi.

# APPENDIX

P. 152. Paradiso 5.127-9.
> Ma non so chi tu sei, nè perchè aggi,
> Anima degna, il grado della spera,
> Che si vela ai mortal con altrui raggi.

P. 152. Paradiso 6.104-5.
> Mal segue quello
> Sempre chi la giustizia e lui diparte.

P. 153. Paradiso 6.118-20.
> Ma nel commensurar dei nostri gaggi
> Col merto, è parte di nostra letizia,
> Perchè non li vedem minor nè maggi.

P. 153. Paradiso 6.124-6.
> Diverse voci fan giù dolci note;
> Così diversi scanni in nostra vita
> Rendon dolce armonia tra questa rote.

P. 153. Summa Theol. I.47.2, ad 1.

Optimi agentis est producere totum effectum suum optimum; non tamen quod quamlibet partem totius faciat optimam simpliciter, sed optimam secundum proportionem ad totum; tolleretur enim bonitas animalis, si quaelibet pars ejus oculi haberet dignitatem. Sic igitur et Deus totum universum constituit optimum, secundum modum creaturae; non autem singulas creaturas, sed unam alia meliorem.

P. 154. Paradiso 7.97-102.
> Non potea l' uomo nei termini suoi
> Mai satisfar, per non poter ir giuso
> Con umiltate, ubbidiendo poi,
> Quanto disubbidiendo intese ir suso;
> E questa è la cagion per che l' uom fue
> Da poter satisfar per sè dischiuso.

P. 154. Paradiso 7.115-7.
> Più largo fu Dio a dar sè stesso,
> A far l' uom sufficiente a rilevarsi,
> Che s' egli avesse sol da sè dimesso.

P. 155. Paradiso 8.115-26.
> Or di', sarebbe il peggio
> Per l' uomo in terra se non fosse cive? . . .

E può egli esser, se giù non si vive
Diversamente per diversi offici?
No, se il maestro vostro ben vi scrive. . . .
Dunque esser diverse
Convien dei vostri effetti le radici:
Per che un nasce Solone, ed altro Xerse,
Altro Melchisedech, ed altro quello
Che volando per l' aere il figlio perse.

P. 155. Summa Theol. I.47.2, ad 3.

In constitutione rerum non est inaequalitas partium per quamcumque inaequalitatem praecedentem vel meritorum vel dispositionis materiae: sed propter perfectionem totius, ut patet etiam in operibus artis. Non enim propter hoc differt tectum a fundamento, quia habet diversam materiam; sed ut sit domus perfecta ex diversis partibus, quaerit artifex diversam materiam; et faceret eam, si posset.

P. 156. Paradiso 9.8-9.

Al sol che la riempie,
Come quel ben ch' ad ogni cosa è tanto.

P. 157. Paradiso 10.145-8.

La gloriosa rota
Moversi e render voce a voce in tempra
Ed in dolcezza ch' esser non può nota,
Se non colà dove gioir s' insempra.

P. 158. Paradiso 10.114.

A veder tanto non surse il secondo.

P. 159. Paradiso 14.25-7.

Qual si lamenta perchè qui si moia,
Per viver colassù, non vide quive
Lo refrigerio dell' eterna ploia.

P. 160. Paradiso 14.58-60.

Nè potrà tanta luce affaticarne,
Chè gli organi del corpo saran forti
A tutto ciò che potrà dilettarne.

P. 161. Paradiso 17.97-9.

Non vo' però ch' a' tuoi vicini invidie,
Poscia che s' infutura la tua vita
Vie più là che il punir di lor perfidie.

## APPENDIX

P. 161.  Paradiso 18.115-23.

> O dolce stella, quali e quante gemme
> Mi dimostraro che nostra giustizia
> Effetto sia del ciel che tu ingemme!
> Per ch' io prego la Mente, in che s' inizia
> Tuo moto e tua virtute, che rimiri
> Ond' esce il fummo che il tuo raggio vizia;
> Sì ch' un' altra fiata omai s' adiri
> Del comperare e vender dentro al templo,
> Che si murò di segni e di martiri.

P. 162.  Paradiso 19.13-8.

> Per esser giusto e pio
> Son io qui esaltato a quella gloria,
> Che non si lascia vincere a disio;
> Ed in terra lasciai la mia memoria
> Sì fatta, che le genti lì malvage
> Commendan lei, ma non seguon la storia.

P. 162.  Inferno 19.58-64.

> Però nella giustizia sempiterna
> La vista che riceve il vostro mondo,
> Com' occhio per lo mar, dentro s' interna:
> Chè benchè dalla proda veggia il fondo,
> In pelago nol vede, e nondimeno
> È lì, ma cela lui l' esser profondo.

P. 163.  Paradiso 19.67-8.

> Assai t' è mo aperta la latebra,
> Che t' ascondeva la giustizia viva.

P. 164.  Paradiso 19.79-81.

> Or tu chi sei, che vuoi sedere a scranna,
> Per giudicar da lungi mille miglia,
> Con la veduta corta d' una spanna?

P. 164.  Paradiso 19.88.

> Cotanto è giusto, quanto a lei consuona.

P. 164.  Paradiso 19.97-9.

> Quali
> Son le mie note a te, che non le intendi,
> Tal è il giudizio eterno a voi mortali.

P. 164. Paradiso 20.67-71.

> Chi crederebbe giù nel mondo errante,
> Che Rifeo Troiano in questo tondo
> Fosse la quinta delle luci sante?
> Ora conosce assai di quel che il mondo
> Veder non può della divina grazia.

P. 164. Aeneid 2.426.

> Rhipeus, iustissimus unus
> Qui fuit in Teucris et servantissimus aequi.

P. 166. Summa Theol. I.23.5, ad 3.

Ex ipsa bonitate divina ratio sumi potest praedestinationis aliquorum, et reprobationis aliorum. Sic enim Deus dicitur omnia propter suam bonitatem fecisse, ut in rebus divina bonitas repraesentetur. Necesse est autem quod divina bonitas, quae in se est una et simplex, multiformiter repraesentetur in rebus; propter hoc quod res creatae ad simplicitatem divinam attingere non possunt. Et inde est quod ad completionem universi requiruntur diversi gradus rerum, quarum quaedam altum, et quaedam infimum locum teneant in universo. Et ut multiformitas graduum conservetur in rebus, Deus permittit aliqua mala fieri ne multa bona impediantur, ut supra dicitum est (queast. XXII, art. 2). Sic igitur consideremus totum genus humanum, sicut totam rerum universitatem. Voluit igitur Deus in hominibus quantum ad aliquos, quos praedestinat, suam repraesentare bonitatem per modum misericordiae, parcendo; et quantum ad aliquos, quos reprobat, per modum justitiae, puniendo. Et haec est ratio quare Deus quosdam eligit, et quosdam reprobat. . . . Sicut etiam in rebus naturalibus potest assignari ratio, cum prima materia tota sit in se uniformis, quare una pars ejus est sub forma ignis, et alia sub forma terrae a Deo in principio condita; ut sic sit diversitas specierum in rebus naturalibus. Sed quare haec pars materiae est sub ista forma, et illa sub alia, dependet ex simplici divina voluntate; sicut ex simplici voluntate artificis dependet quod ille lapis est in ista parte parietis, et ille in alia; quamvis ratio artis habeat quod aliqui sint in hac, et aliqui sint in illa. Neque tamen propter hoc est iniquitas apud Deum, si inaequalia non inaequalibus praeparat. Hoc enim esset contra justitiae rationem, si

# APPENDIX

praedestinationis effectus ex debito redderetur, et non daretur ex gratia. In his enim quae ex gratia dantur, potest aliquis pro libito suo dare cui vult plus vel minus, dummodo nulli subtrahat debitum, absque praejudicio justitiae.

P. 167. Paradiso 21.70-5.

> 'L' alta carità, che ci fa serve
> Pronte al consiglio che il mondo governa,
> Sorteggia qui, sì come tu osserve.'
> 'Io veggio ben, . . . sacra lucerna,
> Come libero amore in questa corte
> Basta a seguir la provvidenza eterna.'

P. 168. Paradiso 22.16-7.

> La spada di quassù non taglia in fretta,
>   Nè tardo.

P. 168. Paradiso 27.61-2.

> L' alta provvidenza, che con Scipio
> Difese a Roma la gloria del mondo.

P. 170. Paradiso 24.13-8.

> E come cerchi in tempra d' oriuoli
>   Si giran sì, che il primo, a chi pon mente,
>   Quieto pare, e l' ultimo che voli,
> Così quelle carole differente-
>   Mente danzando, della sua ricchezza
>   Mi si facean stimar veloci e lente.

P. 171. Paradiso 26.115-7.

> Non il guastar del legno
> Fu per sè la cagion di tanto esilio,
> Ma solamente il trapassar del segno.

P. 172. Summa Theol. I.21.2.

Justitia igitur Dei, quae constituit ordinem in rebus conformem rationi sapientiae suae, quae est lex ejus, convenienter veritas nominatur.

P. 173. Paradiso 28.109-14.

> Quinci si può veder come si fonda
>   L' esser beato nell' atto che vede,
>   Non in quel ch' ama, che poscia seconda;
> E del vedere è misura mercede,

> Che grazia partorisce e buona voglia;
> Così di grado in grado si procede.

P. 174. Summa Theol. I.62.6.

Magister sentent. dicit quod "angeli qui natura magis subtiles, et sapientia amplius perspicaces creati sunt, hi etiam majoribus gratiae muneribus praediti sunt."

Rationabile est quod secundum gradum naturalium angelis data sint dona gratiarum, et perfectio beatitudinis. Cujus quidem ratio ex duobus accipi potest. Primo quidem ex parte ipsius Dei, qui per ordinem suae sapientiae diversos gradus in angelica natura constituit. Sicut autem natura angelica facta est a Deo ad gratiam et beatitudinem consequendam; ita etiam gradus naturae angelicae ad diversos gradus gratiae et gloriae ordinari videntur: ut puta si aedificator lapides polit ad construendam domum, ex hoc ipso quod aliquos pulchrius et decentius aptat, videtur eos ad honoratiorem partem domus ordinare. Sic igitur videtur quod Deus angelos, quos altioris naturae fecit, ad majora gratiarum dona et ampliorem beatitudinem ordinaverit. . . . Rationabile est quod angeli qui meliorem naturam habuerant, etiam fortius et efficacius ad Deum sint conversi. Hoc autem etiam in hominibus contingit; quia secundum intensionem conversionis in Deum datur major gratia et gloria. Unde videtur quod angeli qui habuerunt meliora naturalia, habuerunt plus de gratia et gloria.

P. 175. Paradiso 29.64-6.

> E non voglio che dubbi ma sie certo,
> Che ricever la grazia è meritorio,
> Secondo che l' affetto gli è aperto.

P. 176. Paradiso 29.142-5.

> Vedi l' eccelso omai, e la larghezza
> Dell' eterno valor, poscia che tanti
> Speculi fatti s' ha in che si spezza,
> Uno manendo in sè come davanti.

P. 176. Paradiso 30.122-3.

> Dove Dio senza mezzo governa,
> La legge natural nulla rileva.

P. 177.  Paradiso 32.52-66.

>Dentro all' ampiezza di questo reame
>   Casual punto non puote aver sito,
>   Se non come tristizia o sete o fame;
>Chè per eterna legge è stabilito
>   Quantunque vedi, sì che giustamente
>   Ci si risponde dall' anello al dito.
>E però questa festinata gente
>   A vera vita non è *sine causa*
>   Intra sè qui più e meno eccellente.
>Lo Rege, per cui questo regno pausa
>   In tanto amore ed in tanto diletto,
>   Che nulla volontà è di più ausa,
>Le menti tutte nel suo lieto aspetto
>   Creando, a suo piacer di grazia dota
>   Diversemente; e qui basti l' effetto.

P. 180.  Paradiso 33.144-5.

>Sì come rota ch' egualmente è mossa,
>L' amor che move il sole e l' altre stelle.

# INDEX

[Passages that occur in both the body of the work and the appendix are indexed but once.]

Achilles, 102
Adam, 114, 154; his sin explained, 170-2
Adrian, Pope, 131
Aeneas, 69
Affection, interpreted, 175
Affliction, purpose of, 112; see Punishment
Agnello, 100-1
Alberic of Monte Cassino, 88
Alchemists, 106
Ali, 104
Allegory, see Dante
Angels, orders of, 173-5
Annas, 99
Aquinas, on the counterpassion, 26-7, 76, 140; Dante disagrees with, 86; Dante follows, 155; on deliberate evil, 52, 77; on gratitude, 28-9, 54, 108; in the Paradiso, 158-9; differs from Plato, 144; on wages and desert, 153; translations and edition of, vii; on usury, 30, 93;
  works of,
    Commentary on the Ethics of Aristotle:
  mentioned by Dante, 3; on the "second" of the Ethics, Dante's reference to in Convivio, 2.15.125-7 identified, 183-4; on Ethics 1, lectio 1 known to Dante, 148; on Ethics 1, lectio 2 known to Dante, 183; on Ethics 2, lectio 11 known to Dante, 115;

Aquinas, Commentary on the Ethics of Aristotle (continued):
  on Ethics 5 known to Dante, 20; on Ethics 10 known to Dante, 20;
  1.1      148,184
  1.2      183
  2.3      63
  2.11     115
  5        v,3-66,115
  5.3      13
    Commentary on the Politics of Aristotle:
  on Politics 1, lectio 1 known to Dante, 186;
  1.1      7
  1.8      30
  3.7      10
  3.13     49
  4.1      49
  5.8      36
  7.7      25
  7.10     8
  7.11     7
    De Regimine Judaeorum:
  6        36
    De Regimine Principium:
  1.2      49
    Summa Theologica:
  edition and translation of, vii; justice in, 4; justice and charity in, 5; justice to God in, 65;
  I.21.1   146
  I.21.2   172

Aquinas, Summa Theologica (*continued*):

| | |
|---|---|
| I.23.5 | 166 |
| I.47.1 | 147 |
| I.47.2 | 148,153,155 |
| I.65.2 | 147 |
| I.96.3 | 145 |
| I.96.4 | 145 |
| II.i.46.5 | 128 |
| II.i.46.6 | 83,125 |
| II.i.46.7 | 125 |
| II.i.47.3 | 125 |
| II.i.87.3 | 63,74 |
| II.i.87.6 | 112,116 |
| II.i.87.7 | 63 |
| II.i.90.2 | 10 |
| II.i.91.4 | 42 |
| II.i.92.1 | 24 |
| II.i.93.3 | 42 |
| II.i.94.2 | 42 |
| II.i.94.3 | 42 |
| II.i.95.2 | 43 |
| II.i.100.2 | 64 |
| II.i.105.1 | 49 |
| II.i.109.7 | 153 |
| II.ii.24.1 | 6 |
| II.ii.25.1 | 5 |
| II.ii.29.3 | 6 |
| II.ii.36.2 | 123 |
| II.ii.39.1 | 104 |
| II.ii.42.1 | 104 |
| II.ii.42.2 | 104 |
| II.ii.43.1 | 103 |
| II.ii.43.7 | 63 |
| II.ii.57.1 | 65 |
| II.ii.58.1 | 6 |
| II.ii.58.4 | 7,86 |
| II.ii.58.12 | 12 |
| II.ii.59.3 | 52,89 |
| II.ii.61.4 | 27,76 |
| II.ii.66.6 | 53,63,100,101 |
| II.ii.77.2 | 106 |
| II.ii.78.1 | 93 |
| II.ii.79.i | 64 |
| II.ii.95.1 | 98 |
| II.ii.106.6 | 29 |
| II.ii.108.4 | 62 |
| II.ii.109.3 | 107 |
| II.ii.110.3 | 107 |
| II.ii.111.3 | 107 |

Aquinas, Summa Theologica (*continued*):

| | |
|---|---|
| II.ii.115.2 | 95 |
| II.ii.118.3 | 15,79 |
| II.ii.118.4 | 130 |
| II.ii.118.5 | 81,129 |
| II.ii.146.1 | 136 |
| II.ii.149.4 | 136 |
| II.ii.154.3 | 139 |
| II.ii.154.12 | 91 |
| II.ii.156.4 | 125 |
| II.ii.157.4 | 125 |
| II.ii.158 | 125 |
| II.ii.158.1 | 83 |
| II.ii.158.2 | 128 |
| II.ii.158.4 | 127 |
| II.ii.158.5 | 84 |
| II.ii.158.6 | 128 |
| II.ii.158.8 | 128 |
| II.ii.162.3 | 120 |
| II.ii.162.4 | 122 |
| II.ii.162.6 | 109,121 |
| II.ii.162.8 | 122 |
| II.ii.163.2 | 171 |
| III.86.4 | 74 |
| III supp.94.3 | 97 |
| III supp.97.1 | 115,116 |
| III.app.2,art.2 | 116 |

Argenti, Filippo, 83

Aristocracy, 21-2

Aristotle, vi; his unjust man and Adam, 171; the counterpassion in, 26-7, 76; mentioned by Dante, 3, 12, 16, 19, 36, 54, 60, 73; Dante does not follow, 88; his ideas of diversity in function, 155; on gratitude, 108; doctrine of the moral bent, 119; mentioned in the Summa Theologica, 18, 145;

works of,

The Ethics (Nicomachean):

familiar to Dante, v; Book 5, quoted in the Summa Theologica, 10; Book 5, Dante's incorrect reference to, 12; Book 5, mentioned by Dante, 16, 36, 53, 60;

# INDEX

Aristotle, The Ethics (*continued*):
Book 6, mentioned by Dante, 73;

| | |
|---|---|
| 2 | 4,31 |
| 5 | 3-66 |
| 5.3 | 53 |
| 5.5 | 13 |
| 7.7 | 83 |

The Politics:
quoted by Aquinas, 18, 145; mentioned by Dante, 19;

| | |
|---|---|
| 1.1 | 7 |
| 1.2 | 23 |
| 1.9 | 30 |
| 3 | 18 |
| 3.4 | 19 |
| 3.6 | 10 |
| 3.9 | 10 |
| 7.9 | 25 |
| 7.13 | 8 |
| 7.14 | 7 |

Art, sinners against, 92
Augustine, St., 61, 110, 116, 138, 146, 177
Avarice, deformity of, 81; in the De Monarchia, vi, 36, 37, 48, 55; the chief injustice, 9; identical with injustice, 13-18, 87; not identical with injustice, 79-80; the source of injustice, 51; a variety of injustice, 8; the enemy of justice, 162; causes breaking of law, 61; the cause of the violation of nature, 178; a cause of unjust judgment, 55; of the panders, 94; punishment of in mediaeval visions of hell, 75, 82; in Italian politics, 69-70; of rulers, 35-7; punishment of in hell, 79-82; punishment of in purgatory, 129-34; attacked in the Paradiso, 172; of the thieves, 101; causes tyranny, 35, 37; in the usurers, 92; the wolf of, 68-70

Bacon, Francis, 123-4
Barclay, Alexander, 95
Barratry, 99

Bautz, 207
Beatrice, v, 27, 177; guide of Dante, 140-75
Benedict, St., 177
Bernard, St., of Clairvaux, 115
Bertram dal Bornio, 27, 104, 105
Bestiality, 85
Bible, the

| | |
|---|---|
| Genesis 1.28 | 93 |
| Genesis 3.5 | 154 |
| Leviticus 20.14 | 137 |
| Leviticus 21.9 | 137 |
| 1 Samuel 18.9 | 124 |
| Proverbs 11.2 | 121 |
| Proverbs 21.4 | 123 |
| Ecclesiasticus 6.34 | 120 |
| Ezekiel 22.27 | 15 |
| Wisdom of Solomon 5 | 134 |
| Matthew 11.25 | 120 |
| Mark 7.22 | 124 |
| Mark 9.47-9 | 138 |
| Mark 9.49 | 139 |
| 1 Cor. 3.15 | 137 |
| 1 Cor. 3.17 | 89 |
| 1 Cor. 13 | 5 |
| James 4.6 | 110 |
| 1 Peter 4.10 | 146 |

Binding, the punishment of avarice, 130
Blasphemy, 90
Blindness, the punishment of envy, 123; in the punishment of wrath, 127
Blood, river of, 87
Boethius, 8, 110
Bonaventura, St., 158
Boniface VIII, Pope, 95
Bromiardus, 110, 115-17, 133
Brutus, 110-11
Buonconte of Montefeltro, 119
Buti, Francesco da, 82
Butler, Arthur J., 137

Cacciaguida, 160-1
Cahors, 92
Caiaphas, 99
Cain, 109
Camilla, 69
Capaneus, 90, 95
Carnal sinners, 78

# INDEX

Casella, 118
Cassius, 110-11
Centaurs, 87
Cerberus, 78, 79
Charity (or love), and justice, 5-6, 36, 51, 154, 165, 167, 169, 180; opposed to lust, 139; and schism, 104; its influence in the universe, 173
Chaucer, 82, 106, 115
Christ, 135, 164; his crucifixion just, 153-4
Church, the, allegory of, 141; nature of, 47; unity of, 103-4
Cianfa, 100-1
Cicero (Tully), 11, 86
Citizen, the good, 18-20; man happiest as a, 28, 155, *see also* Society
Community, man in the, 10
Concupiscence, 52, 77
Conquerors, 87
Constantine, 47
Contemplative, the, in heaven, 167
*Contrapassum, see* Counterpassion
Convivio, the, *see* Dante
Cornell University, vii
Counsellors, fraudulent, 103
Counterfeiters, 107
Counterpassion, in Aristotle and Aquinas, 26-7, 76; and commutative justice, 76; in the Inferno, 27, 82, 83, 87, 93, 96, 102; mentioned by Dante, 105-6; in the Purgatorio, 140; in the incarnation, 154
Crucifixion, of Christ, the justice of, 153-4; of the hypocrites, 99
Cunizza, 156
Cupidity, *see* Avarice
Curio, Caio, 104

Damien, St. Peter, 167
Daniel, 136
Dante, definition of justice, 22; dependence on Aquinas for knowledge of Aristotle, 13, 20; enemies, 160; exile, 70, 160; experience in life, 71;

Dante, (*continued*):
faith, 72; knowledge of Aquinas' commentary on the Ethics, v, 3, 20, 115, 148, 183-4; knowledge of Aquinas' commentary on the Politics, 186; edition used, vii; works of,

The Convivio:
proposed fourteenth tractate of, v, 3, 26, 66; inhuman sins of injustice in, 53, 86; Book 2.15.125-7, a new source of, 183-4; translation of, vii;

| | |
|---|---|
| 1.12.61-74 | 7 |
| 1.12.71 | 44 |
| 1.12.72-4 | 85 |
| 1.12.74-84 | 53 |
| 1.12.80 | 29,108 |
| 1.12.87 | 3 |
| 2.14.40-4 | 73 |
| 2.15.68 | 3 |
| 2.15.126 | 3 |
| 2.15.127-32 | 12 |
| 4.4.22-44 | 16 |
| 4.8.4 | 3 |
| 4.9 | 93 |
| 4.9.65-75 | 57 |
| 4.9.75-84 | 61 |
| 4.9.87 | 40 |
| 4.9.150-67 | 41 |
| 4.11.51-6 | 21 |
| 4.11.105-7 | 82 |
| 4.12 | 9,69,133 |
| 4.12.39-54 | 80 |
| 4.13 | 9,130,133 |
| 4.13.142-7 | 81 |
| 4.14 | 133 |
| 4.15.175-8 | 39 |
| 4.17.62-4 | 4 |
| 4.17.65-8 | 31 |
| 4.17.68-72 | 31 |
| 4.24.124 | 70 |
| 4.27.29 | 54 |
| 4.27.88-95 | 25 |
| 4.27.101 | 3 |

De Monarchia:
avarice in, vi, 69, 129; avarice and justice in, 15-51;

# INDEX

Dante, De Monarchia (continued):
in allegory, 141; shows hatred of injustice, 105; and just rulers in heaven, 161; proportion in, 23; the ruler in, vi, 26, 37, 87; why one ruler in, 15-18; society in, 101, 143; the theme of, 65; its theme in the Paradiso, 152; translation of, vi;

| | |
|---|---|
| 1.3.18 | 92 |
| 1.3.66-76 | 148 |
| 1.3.85-90 | 34 |
| 1.4.3 | 70 |
| 1.8.8 | 175 |
| 1.11 | 50,55,167 |
| 1.11.32-4 | 12 |
| 1.11.69-105 | 16 |
| 1.11.46-51 | 32 |
| 1.11.70-78 | 36 |
| 1.11.91-7 | 51 |
| 1.11.93-110 | 5 |
| 1.11.95-140 | 37 |
| 1.11.99 | 48 |
| 1.12.38-48 | 34 |
| 1.12.63-71 | 19 |
| 1.12.83-91 | 38 |
| 1.13.47-55 | 16 |
| 1.13.48-50 | 48 |
| 1.14.35-47 | 60 |
| 1.14.38-41 | 39 |
| 2.2.39-61 | 45 |
| 2.5 | 40 |
| 2.5.1-21 | 11 |
| 2.5.3-6 | 22 |
| 2.5.6-9 | 40 |
| 2.5.11-23 | 45 |
| 2.6.7-25 | 46 |
| 2.6.36-41 | 46 |
| 2.6.61-7 | 47 |
| 2.7.1-22 | 44 |
| 2.10.2-7 | 24 |
| 3.2.9-32 | 44 |
| 3.10.30-40 | 47 |

De Vulgari Eloquentia:
Book 1, chapter 2, a source of, 186

La Divina Commedia:
relation of man to God in, 65; allegory of, 72; autobiographical in part, 68-71;

Dante, La Divina Commedia (continued):
free will in, 50; general purpose of, 142; theme of, 150, 172;

The Inferno:
allegory of, 74-6, 86, 101-2, 104, 107, 110; avaricious and prodigal in, 133; discussed, 73-111; freedom in, 34; justice in, 140; justice of God in, 71; shows life on earth, 143; punishment not medicinal in, 63; the principle of punishment in, 84, 91, 126; sixth circle of, 85; unlike the Purgatorio in the presentation of anger, 126; habitual sinners in, 56; sufferings of, 27, vengeance in, 168;

| | |
|---|---|
| 1.1-136 | 68-70 |
| 3.4 | 73 |
| 3.125-6 | 77 |
| 4.42 | 78 |
| 7.19-21 | 80 |
| 7.77-96 | 9 |
| 7.112-4 | 82 |
| 7.121-4 | 84 |
| 8.46-8 | 83 |
| 8.60 | 83 |
| 11 | 52,89,92 |
| 11.22 | 85 |
| 11.25-6 | 54 |
| 11.110-11 | 92 |
| 12.14-15 | 84 |
| 12.104-5 | 87 |
| 12.133-4 | 87 |
| 13 | 63 |
| 13.70-2 | 88 |
| 13.105 | 88 |
| 14.5-6 | 90 |
| 14.71-2 | 90 |
| 17.34ff. | 30 |
| 17.45ff. | 92 |
| 18.95 | 94 |
| 18.114 | 95 |
| 19.2-4 | 96 |
| 19.72 | 97 |
| 19.97-8 | 96 |
| 20.28 | 97 |

Dante, The Inferno (*continued*):

| | |
|---|---|
| 20.38-9 | 98 |
| 21.53-4 | 99 |
| 24.119-20 | 100 |
| 25.13-14 | 100 |
| 25.77-8 | 101 |
| 26.89 | 103 |
| 27.74-7 | 102 |
| 27.135 | 105 |
| 27.135-6 | 103 |
| 28.35 | 103 |
| 28.36 | 105 |
| 28.48 | 71 |
| 28.139-42 | 105 |
| 28.142 | 27 |
| 29.55-6 | 106 |

The Purgatorio:
allegory of, 112-13, 114, 116-17, 127, 132, 134, 135, 136; discussed, 112-41; interpretation of, vi; justice in, 140; its penalties opposed to sins, 114-17, 135; remedial punishment in, 63;

| | |
|---|---|
| 2.94-8 | 118 |
| 3.133-5 | 118 |
| 5.106-7 | 119 |
| 6.37-9 | 119 |
| 11.7-9 | 121 |
| 11.88 | 122,131 |
| 11.125-6 | 122 |
| 12.70-2 | 122 |
| 13.86 | 124 |
| 16.10-13 | 127 |
| 16.24 | 128 |
| 16.67-78 | 51 |
| 18.115-16 | 129 |
| 18.117 | 129 |
| 19.77 | 129 |
| 19.115-17 | 131 |
| 19.118-26 | 130 |
| 20-12 | 69 |
| 21.64-6 | 134 |
| 22.49-51 | 133 |
| 23.64-75 | 135 |
| 23.125-6 | 135 |
| 23.126 | 115 |
| 24.38 | 136 |
| 24.153-4 | 136 |

Dante, The Purgatorio (*continued*):

| | |
|---|---|
| 26.81 | 138 |
| 28.91-6 | 140 |
| 30.108 | 27 |
| 31.37-9 | 140 |
| 31.40-2 | 140 |
| 32.48 | 141 |
| 33.67-72 | 141 |

The Paradiso:
allegory of, 142-6, 150, 158-9, 165, 169-70, 173, 176, 178, 179, 181; discussed, 142-81; heaven not literally represented in, 150; Aristotelian justice in, 143; interpretation of, vi; justice in distribution of rewards in, 21, 143-6; Beatrice speaks on Dante's concern with justice in, v; deals with man on earth, 142-6; society in, 180-1;

| | |
|---|---|
| 1.1-3 | 146 |
| 1.103-11 | 147 |
| 2.133-41 | 149 |
| 3.65-6 | 149 |
| 3.85 | 150 |
| 3.88-90 | 150 |
| 4.34-9 | 150 |
| 5.118-19 | 151 |
| 5.127-9 | 152 |
| 6.88 | 24,152 |
| 6.104-5 | 152 |
| 6.112-14 | 36 |
| 6.118-20 | 153 |
| 6.124-6 | 153 |
| 7.82-4 | 27 |
| 7.97-100 | 27 |
| 7.97-102 | 154 |
| 7.115-17 | 154 |
| 8.115-26 | 155 |
| 8.116ff. | 28 |
| 9.8-9 | 156 |
| 9.62 | 168 |
| 10.114 | 158 |
| 10.145-8 | 157 |
| 13.42 | 27 |
| 14.25-7 | 159 |
| 14.33 | 160 |

# INDEX

Dante, The Paradiso (continued):

| | |
|---|---|
| 14.58-60 | 160 |
| 15.1-3 | 36, 51 |
| 17.97-9 | 161 |
| 18.91-3 | 37 |
| 18.115-23 | 161 |
| 19.13-18 | 162 |
| 19.58-64 | 162 |
| 19.67-8 | 163 |
| 19.79-81 | 164 |
| 19.88 | 164 |
| 19.97-9 | 164 |
| 20.67-71 | 164 |
| 20.121 | 59 |
| 20.133-4 | 59 |
| 21.70-5 | 167 |
| 22.16-17 | 168 |
| 24.13-18 | 170 |
| 24.71 | 169 |
| 26.115-17 | 171 |
| 27.61-2 | 168 |
| 28.109-14 | 173 |
| 29.64-6 | 175 |
| 29.142-5 | 176 |
| 30.122-3 | 176 |
| 32.52-66 | 177 |
| 33.144-5 | 180 |

The Epistles:

| | |
|---|---|
| 6 | 48, 61 |
| 6.150-60 | 17 |
| 9 | v |
| 10 | 50, 142 |
| 10.172-5 | 67 |

Deceit, 53
Deformity, of avarice, 81-2, 92, 101; of the diviners, 97
Deidemia, 102
De Monarchia, see Dante
Demons, 94, 99
Derivation of words, 58-9
De Vulgari Eloquentia, see Dante
Digest, the, 39-40, 61
Dionysius the Pseudo-Areopagite, 146
Dionysius the Carthusian, 75
Disciples, the, 96-7
Discord, sowers of, 103
Diseases, as punishments in hell, 106

Divina Commedia, see Dante
Diversity, and unity, 148; see also Inequality
Diviners, 97-9
Doctors of the Church, 157
Dolcin, Fra, 104
Dominican Fathers, vii
Dominic, St., 158
Donati, Forese, 135
Dropsy, 107

Eagle, the, of the Empire, 161-4
Egotism, 109, see also Pride
Emperor, see Ruler
Empire, the, 141, 152, 161, 168-9; and living justice, 163, 169
End, the proper, 46-7; of the Church, 47; of law, 39; of man, 34, 43, 70, 73; of man, multiplicity necessary to, 148; of monarchy, 38, 47; of nature, 44; of society, 45-6
Envy, 109, 123-4, 132
Epicurus, 84
Epiichia, 58
Equality, in justice, 25, 35, 74, 93
Equity, 58-62
Euripides, 19
Euryalus, 69
Euthymius Zigabenus, 139
Eye, the, in envy, 123-4

Faith, hope, love, and divine justice, 169
Falsehood, 53, 106-8
Falsifiers, 106-8
Fame, 152-3; poetic, 161
*Fas,* 65
Fever, as a punishment in hell, 107
Filth, the, of flattery, 95
Fire, the, of charity, 138-9, see also Flames
Fiske Dante Collection, vii
Fixed Stars, the heaven of the, 168
Flames, the punishment of lust, 136-9; the punishment of the tricksters, 102-3
Flamini, Francesco, v, 68
Flattery, 95

# INDEX

Florence, 17, 70, 102, 105
Ford, John, 75
Foreknowledge of God, the, 160, *see also* Predestination
Forest, the dark, of Inferno 1, 68-71
Fornaciari, R., 117
Fortune, 8-9
Francis, St., 139, 158, 177
Fraud, 54, 70, 86; sinners by, 85-6, 105
Freedom, 34, 62, 140
Free Will, *see* Will
Fucci, Vanni, 100

Geryon, 94
Gluttony, in the Inferno, 78-9; in the Purgatorio, 134-5; punishment of in the mediaeval hell, 75, 116
Gomorrah, 137
Grades, of blessedness in heaven, 152; in blessedness, 173-7; in the universe, 166, *see also* Inequality
Grandgent, Charles H., 75, 103, 128, 130, 132, 133
Gratitude, 28-9, 54, 108
Gregory I, Pope, 74, 116, 121
Griffon, the, 141
Guido da Montefeltro, 103

Habit, 6, 56
Hail, as a punishment, 78
Happiness, the end of man, 17
Heaven, inequality in, 149; a single one for all the blessed, 150; represents a just nation, 179; *see* The Paradiso
Hell, visions of, 75, 88; *see* The Inferno
Henry, Aurelia, vi
Hesperus, 11
Hettinger, Franz, 118
Holkot, Robertus, 115
Homily, a mediaeval English, 139
Horace, 124
Hound, the, 69
Hymn, Latin, *Summæ Deus Clementiæ*, 137

Hypocrisy, 99
Hypsipyle, 94

Ice, in hell, 110
Immortality, disbelievers in, 84
Incarnation, the, 27, 154, 180
Incontinence, 52, 85
Individual, the, in the Purgatorio, 114; in society, 10; *see also* Society
Inequality, 9; among angels, 173-6; on earth, 21-2, 28, 178; in heaven, 152-3, 157, 158, 170, 173-7; and injustice, 93; *see also* Equality; in the universe, 146, 148, 166; in society, illustrations of in the Summa Theol., 144-8, 153, 155-6, 166, 174-5; *see also* Grades
Inferno, *see* Dante
Infortiatum, 39
Ingratitude, 29, 53-4
Inhuman vices, 7, 53-4, 86
Injury, the end of malicious action, 85
Injustice, 33, 48, 49-51, 55; mentioned by Dante, 21, 53, 88; deliberate, 57; not easy, 56-7; its essence, 171; in the Inferno, 85-7, 105, 107, 114; to oneself, 63, 88; and sedition, 104-5; Thomistic conception of, 9, 14, 87; cannot be suffered voluntarily, 51, 53, 55, 89, 114; weaker than justice, 72
Innocence, the state of, 144-6
Intellect, the perfection of the, 34, 43, 70, 73, 82, 148
Isidore, 39, 98
Italy, 69-70

Jackson, William W., vii
Jacomo da sant' Andrea, 89-90
Jason, 94
Jesus, 96, 99
Jews, Aquinas' work on, 36; punished for the Crucifixion, 153
Job, 72

# INDEX

Jonson, Ben, 95
Judas, 110-11
Judge, the, 24-6, 32, 36, 55, 78
Jupiter, the heaven of, 161-6
*Jus,* 65; Dante's definition of, 22; how translated, 40; *see also* Justice
Justice, too accurate, 62; and anger, 125; Aristotelian, in the Paradiso, 152-3; the balance of, 123, 124, 128, 129; and charity, 167; commutative, 27, 28, 76; Dante a preacher of, v; mentioned by Dante, v, 3, 4, 5, 7, 11, 12, 16, 17, 22, 24, 25, 32, 36, 37, 40, 44, 45, 46, 47, 48, 51, 53, 59, 67, 73, 77, 80, 87, 88, 90, 96, 100, 106, 118, 119, 129, 130, 136, 141, 152, 161, 162, 163, 164, 168, 179, 183; Dante's definition of, 22; distributive, 20-1, 35, 50, 55, 143; divine, 64-5; divine, should be rejoiced in, 83, 97; in the De Monarchia, 34, 37, *see also* Dante, De Monarchia; three aspects of in the Divina Commedia, 180; and equality, 25, 35, 74, 113, 117; and foreknowledge, 160; of God, appears unjust to men, 150-1; of God, not understood by men, 159, 162, 164-5, 167, 172; rendered to God by men, 65; in the order of the universe, 146; the good of others, 35, 37; a habit of choice, 31; the human virtue, 44, 85; legal, 10-12, 38-40, 60; living, v, 152, 163, 165, 169; and love, 119, 180, *see also* Charity; and the mean, 21-5, 30-1; natural, 38, 40, 41, 48, 55, 61-2; and old age, 25; political, 33; and proportion, 21-3; God's, called truth, 172; and truth, 108; and the will, 6, 49-50, *see also* Will; *see also* Law
Justinian, 24, 152

Lano da Siena, 89-90
Law, the directive principle of life, 60; divine, 41; the end of, 10; eternal, 41-3; human, 42-3; natural, 41-5, 61; universal and particular, 60-1; *see also* Justice
Legal justice, *see* Justice, legal
Leprosy, of the alchemists, 106
Lesbian rule, 62
Liars, 107
Liberality, 30
Liberty, *see* Freedom
Life, the perfect, 141
Limbo, 77-8
Longfellow, Henry W., vi
Love, *see* Charity
Lucifer, 11; *see also* Satan
Lukewarm, the, 77
Lust, 136-9; punishment of in mediaeval visions of hell, 75

Magicians, the, 97-9
Mahomet, 71, 104
Malebolge, 94
Malice, 30-31, 51, 85
Man, the good, 19; in the community, 10, 155; a civil animal, 54; *see also* Society
Manfred, 118, 119
Mansus, Joseph, 139
Marco Lombardo, 50, 125
Mars, the heaven of, 160-61
Marsh, of the Styx, 84
Martel, Charles, 28, 155
Mean, the, 22, 24, 30-1
Medea, 94
Mercury, the heaven of, 151-4
Milton, John, 72, 76, 110, 160, 171
Minos, 78
Minotaur, 83
Monarch, *see* Ruler
Monarchy, the best government, 49

Money, 29-30, 96; *see also* Riches
Moon, the heaven of, 149-51
Moore, Edward, 3, 12, 20
Moral philosophy, and the sciences, 183
Mosca, 104

# INDEX

Murder, the punishment of, 75, 87-8

Natural endowment of men, the, 144-6, 158-9, 175, 181; *see also* Inequality
Nature, 44, 46-8; the art of God, 90, 92; sinners against, 90; the state of, 145; *see also* Justice, natural
Nisus, 69
Norton, Charles Eliot, 126

Odersi, 122
Old age, and justice, 25

Pagans, 78
Palladium, 102
Panders, 94
Paradise, the Earthly, 139
Paradiso, the, *see* Dante, Paradiso
Peace, 6, 17, 104
Peele, George, 124
Penalties in the Purgatorio, contrary to sin, 114-17, 123, 124, 127-8, 133-4, 138-9
Perez, Paolo, 125, 130, 137
Perversion, 93, 95-6, 99, 101
Pessimism, 175
Peter, St., 96, 120
Peter of Vinea, 63, 88-9
Petrarch, 79, 82, 109, 122, 123
Philalethes, 137
Philosophy, *see* Moral Philosophy
Piccarda, 149
Pier da Medicina, 104
Pietro Lombardo, Master of the Sentences, 174
Pity, and justice, 83, 97
Plato, his theory of justice, 144, 155
Plumptre, E. H., 126, 138
Poetry, function of, 179
Potiphar's wife, 107
Predestination, 165-6, 167, 177
Pride, the, of Adam, 171; in Chaucer's Parson's tale, 115; the, of Capaneus, 90; the, of Dante, 68; in the Purgatorio, 120-3; the, of Filippo Argenti, 83; the, of Satan, 109, 174; the capital sin of, 109-10, 120, 154; the, of Vanni Fucci, 100
Primum mobile, the heaven of, 172-80
Prodigal, the, 79-82, 133
Prodigality, 30, 133
Proportion, in justice, 22-3
Punishment, medicinal, 62-3, 65, 114-17; opposed to sin, 115-17; of the wicked, pleasing to the good, 83, 97
Purgatorio, the, *see* Dante, The Purgatorio
Purgatory, the gate of, 120; general ideas of, 137
Pythagoreans, 26

Rahab, 156
Rain, as punishment, 78
Rapine, 53, 86, 87
Reade, W. H. V., 85, 86, 88, 94
Rhadamanthus, 26
Rhipeus, 59, 164
Riches, their vileness, 81-2; injustice in their distribution, 21
Right, Dante's definition of, 22; *see also* Jus
Ripheus, *see* Rhipeus
Romans, 46
Rome, 69, 168
Ruler, the (or Emperor), 16, 32, 35-8, 55, 69; in the De Monarchia, 37; good, 19, 35-8, 161; good, the reward of, 36-7; limits of his power, 41; in heaven, 161-4

Sacrilege, 100
St. Thomas Aquinas, *see* Aquinas
Sand, the burning, in the Inferno, 90-1
Satan, 108-11
Saturn, the heaven of, 162, 167-8
Scandal, 103-5
Scartazzini, G. A., 82, 97, 103, 137
Schism, 103-5
Sciences, the, and legal justice, 12-13; and moral philosophy, 183-4

# INDEX

Seducers, the, 94
Selfishness, 154, *see also* Pride
Serpents, the punishment of the thieves, 100
Shakespeare, 93
Sidrach, the Book of, 137
Simon Magus, 97
Simony, 95-7
Sin, the stain of, 113, 116
Sinon, 107
Sins, inhuman, 53, 86; the seven capital, 114
Sloth, 116, 129, *see also* Sullen, the
Small, John, 139
Smoke, in the punishment of anger, 124-7
Snow, 78; burning, 90-1
Society, undone by discord, 105; diversity needed in, 28, 153; the end of, 45; represented by heaven, 179; inequality necessary to, 155-6, *see also* Inequality; injustice in, 72; injured by injustice, 70; in the state of innocence, 145; the individual adapted to, 10, 155-6; preserved by *jus*, 22; natural to man, 42, 43-4, 54; best ordering of, 33-4; in the Paradiso, 143-4, 181; in the Purgatorio, 114, 141; reciprocity in, 28; the effects of sin on, 76, 86-7; sinners against, 89, 111; undone by theft, 53-4, 101-2; truth necessary to, 108, *see also* State, the
Sodom, 92, 137
Sodomy, 91, 137
Solomon, 160
Soothsayers, 97-9
Source, the, of Convivio 1.12.74-7, evil men love justice, 52-3; hitherto unidentified, of Convivio 2.15.125-7, moral philosophy and the sciences, 183-4; Convivio 2.15.127-32, legal justice and the sciences, 12-13; De Monarchia 1.3.66-76, multiplicity in the human race, 148; De Monarchia 1.12.67-71, the good man and the good citizen, 19-20; De Monarchia 2.5.3-6, Dante's definition of *jus*, 22-3; De Vulgari Eloquentia 1.2, language peculiar to man, 186; Purgatorio 23.125-6, the bent stick, 115
Spheres, the celestial, 173
Spiritual things, represented in allegory to human sense, 75-6
Stars, *see* Fixed Stars
State, the, 10, 23, 28, 33, *see also* Society
Statius, 133, 134, 136
Stones, rolled by the avaricious and the prodigal, 80; burden of, carried by the proud, 120-22
*Studiosum*, 52, 58
Styx, the River, 82, 118
Suicide, 63, 88-90
Sullen, the, 84
*Summa Theologica*, *see* Aquinas
Sun, the heaven of the, 157-60
*Superbia*, *see* Pride
Swift, Jonathan, 95

Talents, variation in, 142-81
Tempests, the punishment of carnal sinners, 78
Theft, 48, 53, 100-2
Thrones, the, represent "God judicant", 168
Tombs, in the Inferno, 84
Torraca, Francesco, 85, 130, 137-8
Traitors, 108-10
Trajan, 164
Treachery, 53-4
Trees, of the suicides, 88, 90
Tricksters, 102-3
Trinity, 180
Troy, 102
Truth, necessary to society, 54; the good of the intellect and man's perfection, 73; a name for God's justice, 172; part of justice, 107-8; and poetry, 161; knowledge of, hindered by pride, 120-1

Turnus, 69
Tyrant, 15, 35, 37, 87

Ulysses, 102-3
Unity, and diversity, 148
Usury, 30, 92-3; its punishment in hell, 75

Vecchio Digesto, *see* Digest
Veltro, the, 69
Vengeance, and justice, 168; in correcting evil, should be desired, 83, 97
Venus, heaven of, 155-6
Violence, sinners by, 85
Virgil, the Aeneid of, 164; as Dante's guide, 69-136
Virtues, as mean states, 31; enjoined by justice, 64
Vows, broken, 151

Will, the, actions subject to, 57; and the damned, 74; charity resides in, 6; freedom of, granted to man, 50-1; freedom of, God's greatest gift, 151; freedom of, and God's foreknowledge, 160; freedom of, for good or evil, 50-1; freedom of, sacrificed by a vow, 151; of man, in harmony with that of God, 149-50; free, in heaven, 153; free, in harmony with God, 158; man united to God by, 113; injustice cannot be suffered in accord with, 51, 53, 55, 89, 114; determines whether a man is just or unjust, 49-50; justice resides in, 6, 52, 85-6; respected by divine justice, 156; men just or unjust through, 50; and love, 167; and incontinence or concupiscence, 52, 77; indulgence to, 74; ownership depends on, 89; given up by the proud in purgatory, 121; punishment in purgatory contrary to, 134; punishment opposed to, 112-3; the rational part of man, 85; and repentance, 140; to suffer, 135; suffering against, 74
Winds, in the Inferno, 78
Wisdom, the divine, 95
Wolf, the, 69
Wrath, 82-4, 124-8

Zingarelli, Nicola, 117